ADVENTURE TRAVEL ABROAD

Other books by Pat Dickerman
(1986 editions)

Adventure Travel North America
Farm, Ranch & Country Vacations

ADVENTURE TRAVEL ABROAD

by
PAT DICKERMAN

Adventure Guides, Inc.
New York

An <u>Owl</u> Book
Henry Holt and Company
New York

COVER PHOTO CREDITS (Clockwise from upper left):

Crossing a bridge in Zanskar, India—**Piotr Kostrezewski for Cross Cultural Adventures, Virginia.**

Elephantback in Nepal—**Will Weber for Journeys International, Michigan.**

Rafting the Alas River in Indonesia—**George K. Fuller for Sobek Expeditions, California.**

Cycling in Liberia—**Bicycle Africa, Washington.**

Cruising a canal in Burgundy, France—**Floating Through Europe, New York.**

COVER AND BOOK DESIGN: Dennis Wheeler.

DESIGN IMPLEMENTATION: Doreen Maddox.

Copyright ©1986 by Adventure Guides, Inc.

All rights reserved, including the right to reproduce this book or portions thereof in any form.

Designed and produced by
Adventure Guides, Inc.
36 East 57 Street
New York, New York 10022

Published by Henry Holt and Company, Inc.,
521 Fifth Avenue, New York, New York 10175

Published simultaneously in Canada.

Library of Congress Catalog Card Number: 86-261

ISBN 0-03-008564-0 (pbk.)

First Edition

Printed in the United States of America

10 9 8 7 6 5 4 3 2 1

ISBN 0-03-008564-0

CONTENTS

7
INTRODUCTION

11
AFRICA

Algeria • Botswana • Egypt • Ivory Coast • Kenya • Liberia • Madagascar • Mali • Morocco • Rwanda • Seychelles • Tanzania • Tunisia • Zaire • Zambia • Zimbabwe •

43
ASIA

Bhutan • Borneo • Burma • China • India • Indonesia • Japan • Malaya • Malaysia • Mongolia • Nepal • Pakistan • Philippines • Thailand • Tibet • Turkey • United Arab Emirates • U.S.S.R. • Yemen •

107
EUROPE

Austria • Belgium • England • Finland • France • Greece • Greenland • Holland • Hungary • Ireland • Italy • Lapland • Norway • Portugal • Romania • Scandivania • Scotland • Spain • Switzerland • Wales • West Germany •

169
PACIFIC

Australia • Cook Islands • Fiji Island • French Polynesia • Leeward Islands • Maldives • Micronesia • New Zealand • Papua New Guinea • Pitcairn • Polynesia • Samoa • Tahiti • Tonga • South Pacific •

193
SOUTH & CENTRAL AMERICA

Antarctica • Argentina • Belize • Bolivia • Brazil • Caribbean • Chile • Costa Rica • Dominica • Ecuador • Guadeloupe • Peru • Trinidad • Tobago • Uruguay • Venezuela •

223
INDEX

A NOTE OF APPRECIATION...

The challenge of assembling reliable information on worldwide adventures, and the services offering these trips, has required more hours of research, selection, writing, and doublechecking than one can imagine.

To accomplish the task within a limited time frame, I called on a number of freelancers for assistance: Melissa Burdick, Andrea Fooner, Jason Forsythe, Joanne Greco, Deborah Joost, Cathy Lencioni, Barbara Lyons, Jean McGrail, Judith Oringer, Cathy Powell, and John Wallace. My thanks to all.

For staying with it in many capacities from start to finish, special thanks to Gay Northrup, and for much of the editing and writing, to June Rogoznica. My thanks also to Connie Smith and Betsy Baumgardner who held the office functions together, and to Doreen Maddox who contributed creativity and care to the page design and mechanicals. For helping to get the book off the ground, my appreciation to Richard O'Shea, and to Dennis Wheeler for his design concepts.

This first edition of ADVENTURE TRAVEL ABROAD reflects the combined effort of many interested individuals. We trust it will prove to be a unique and valuable source of information for its readers.

Gratefully,

Pat Dickerman

Pat Dickerman

INTRODUCTION

The adventure expedition of yesteryear required elaborate preparations on the part of private parties to gather equipment and provisions and secure the services of guides for trekking, climbing mountains, or exploring (more often, hunting) in the wild areas of the world.

About 30 years ago the first all-inclusive camping safaris for game viewing in Africa were offered to intrepid travelers who wanted adventure without having to do all the planning themselves. Soon other pre-packaged adventures for individuals wanting to join a group followed. The first were expeditions for climbers to tackle mountain peaks in many parts of the world. Later, rafting rivers—a sport gaining immense popularity in America—became possible abroad, as did walking trips, canoeing, sailing, canal barging, and other little known vacation options.

Today, the outdoorsperson—whether experienced or a complete neophyte—can choose from hundreds of adventurous journeys throughout the world complete with provisions, transportation, accommodations and/or camping equipment, and knowledgeable guides.

That is what this book is all about.

Participation is the key among the individuals who take these trips—as is exploration. On today's journeys you may explore everything from sand dunes to glaciers, from ocean depths to the highest peaks, from tribal lands and villages to cultural highlights in metropolitan areas. You may travel by camel, elephant, or dogsled, by jeep or minivan, by dugout canoe or sleek schooner, by bicycle or barge—or on your own two feet.

However remote and unique these journeys may be, the amazing thing is how many there are to choose from, and how easy they are to book.

A chapter about 100 adventures abroad appeared in our last edition of *Adventure Travel*—a book which we have published since 1972 covering trips in North America. As we expanded our research to include unusual travel on other continents, it became clear that our "adventures abroad" chapter touched only the tip of the iceberg, so to speak.

So we continued our research and found hundreds of remarkable journeys worldwide. We analyzed each according to our adventure criteria—action, challenge, remoteness, exploration, cultural exchange, or involvement with nature, mountains, rivers, deserts, archaeology, biology, photography, or unusual phenomena.

As a result, nearly 350 out-of-the-ordinary tours are reported in these pages. We could recommend hundreds more except for the page limit set for the book. Our selection provides variety for travelers wanting physical challenge as well as for those preferring easy (even luxurious) travel—and for the limited as well as the flexible pocketbook. It is a selection that encourages you to exchange routine trips for purposeful vacations on which to explore, discover, learn, observe, and share exciting, exhilarating experiences with other spirited adventurers.

SYMBOLS

As a reminder of what you can do in various parts of the world, these symbols tell the story on a map at the beginning of each chapter.

BALLOONING	CYCLING	
BIRDING	DIVING	SAILING
CAMEL TREKKING	DOG SLEDDING	SKIING
CANOEING	RAFTING	TREKKING
CRUISING	RIDING	WILDLIFE
CULTURAL	SAFARI DRIVING	

TRIP DETAILS AND RESERVATIONS:

The trip descriptions are intended to provide new ideas and considerable information about exciting vacation possibilities, but they do not pretend to give you the whole story. A telephone call or written query to the service operating each trip will bring you their brochure with full details, as well as news of other trips they operate. This also is the way to get updated details. Our reporting is accurate to the best of our ability as we go to press, but dates, rates, and itineraries are bound to change.

If you want to talk over the options, please call us at (212) 355-6334. We maintain an advisory and partial reservations service and will be glad to help with your decision on which trip best meets your requirements.

OUR SOURCEBOOKS:

For years unusual travel has been our specialty. We started several decades ago with *Farm, Ranch & Country Vacations*, a book which has sent hundreds of thousands of vacationers to the rural spots we tell about.

One thing leads to another, and that led to the book we now call *Adventure Travel North America*—which in turn has spawned *Adventure Travel Abroad*. These publications can be ordered from our office (by check or credit card) or from bookstores.

Whether you travel solo or with family or friends, whichever season and whichever continent you choose, we trust these pages will enrich your holiday travel and bring rewarding experiences into your lives.

Happy adventuring!
Pat Dickerman, *President*

Adventure Guides, Inc.
36 East 57 Street
New York, New York 10022
(212) 355-6334

AFRICA

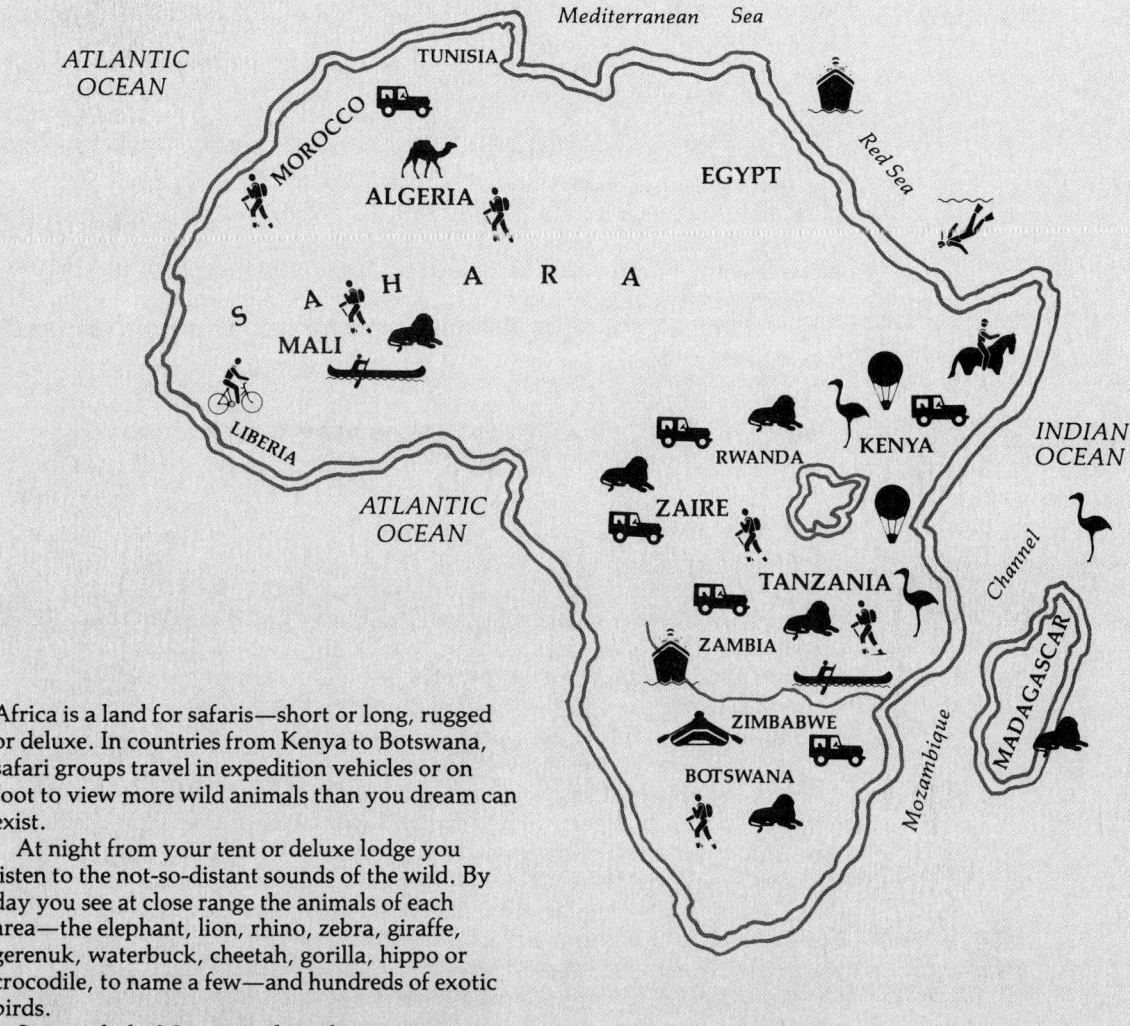

Africa is a land for safaris—short or long, rugged or deluxe. In countries from Kenya to Botswana, safari groups travel in expedition vehicles or on foot to view more wild animals than you dream can exist.

At night from your tent or deluxe lodge you listen to the not-so-distant sounds of the wild. By day you see at close range the animals of each area—the elephant, lion, rhino, zebra, giraffe, gerenuk, waterbuck, cheetah, gorilla, hippo or crocodile, to name a few—and hundreds of exotic birds.

Stay with the Masai people at their camp near the Kenya/Tanzania border. Visit the villages of pygmies in Rwanda and of bushmen in Botswana.

The Chobe River in Botswana is home for a herd of 500 elephants. At dawn the sun explodes into being, streaking the land with vivid gold, while birds chatter and hippos and elephants grunt.

In the Sahara you take a different kind of safari either by vehicle or by camel caravan to explore the undulating dunescapes, surreal volcanic landscapes, and oasis towns.

In Liberia cycle to villages of tribal people. In Mali rough it by canoe and on foot and walk through Timbuktu. In Morocco travel by vehicle and mule caravan to study the culture of the Berber tribespeople. In Kenya take a horseback safari.

Other adventurous options: Climb 19,340-foot Kilimanjaro in Kenya. Dive in the coral gardens of the Red Sea. Raft the tempestuous Zambezi below Victoria Falls. Float down the Rufiji River with its grinning crocodiles and startled hippos. Or sail up the Nile to see the glories of ancient Egypt.

Veiled Tuareg men of the Sahara—*Mountain Travel, CA.*

AFRICA

ANYWHERE ON THE CONTINENT

Do you prefer rugged tenting, camel safaris, or hot air ballooning? No matter. Born Free does everything and anything in Africa. Fill out a questionnaire with your specific needs, and they design a safari to match. "Our services stretch from East to West—North to South," director Alana Fried explains. "We provide the most deluxe safari or rugged camping holiday." The company also guarantees it will never cancel one of its tours. And it guarantees you a window seat, with never more than 20 in a group in East Africa.

Travel to all corners of Africa—throughout West Africa, Morocco, Rwanda, Zaire, South Africa. Take an off-the-beaten-track adventure—a Zambezi River rafting, gorilla tracking, a Kenya walking safari, a Mt. Kilimanjaro climb. Go it alone or with a group. Choose a low-budget tour, or be extravagant. Add a few days for Madagascar or Mauritius in the Indian Ocean. How about a stopover in Rio—yes, Rio—en route home from Cape Town? Born Free can do it all.

Year round custom trips.

Born Free Safaris, 12504-A Riverside Drive, No. Hollywood, CA 91607. (800) 372-3274 or (818) 509-8998.

ALGERIA

DESERT CAMPING

Venture into the exotic land of the Tuaregs (mysterious "blue people") on a choice of camping safaris. With a flight to Algiers and on to either Djanet or Tamanrasset, you begin six days of traveling by four-wheel-drive vehicle (sometimes on foot) and camping out, while exploring the Tassilis (Saharan plateaus) with their fascinating sand dunes, rock and stone engravings, volcanic ridge peaks, and desert oases—a world apart.

Three itineraries differ somewhat but each takes you into the heart of southern Algeria. The Atakor Mountains offer spectacular panoramas, and the rock pinnacle scenery of Aokasit is outstanding. Visit Tazrouk, with its amazing gardens, or the "red" city, capital of the Haggar area, the market and dwelling of "father" Foucauld. Travel to remote places of legendary fame like Tamrit, Sefar, Tin Zoumaitok, Assekrem (the "refugee" camp), and N'Ajjer, the world's largest "open-air museum" with its unexplained prehistoric paintings and engravings. Even Lawrence of Arabia didn't cover all this territory.

November-April, 8 days, $980-$1,250 + air. 1986 departures: Every Sunday.

(SLA) The African Experience, P.O. Box 657, Lexington, MA 02173. (617) 862-2165.

ALGERIA

SAHARA CAMEL EXPEDITION

You don't need previous camel-riding experience to traverse the little-known mountainous regions of the Sahara Desert aboard a camel, but you must be ready for adventure. Your 4-legged, sure-

AFRICA

footed desert conveyer moves like a rocking chair on the 2-week circular trek that starts at the oasis town of Tamanrasset after a transfer by plane from Paris and Algiers.

An early-morning rendezvous acquaints you with the Touareg guides and camels before setting off along the Ouan Amezegin route past the Laperrine Peak and along the plain of Tam. Dry river beds, passes, rock-ribbed plateaus, sandstone canyons, and golden washes filled with oleander, tamarisk, date palms, and acacias punctuate the route. Occasional hikes to view engravings and rock paintings, or to visit a famous rock hermitage high on the Asskrem Plateau, vary the pace and the posture. Experienced climbers may scramble up Tezouiag (9,000') or other Hoggar peaks. Sleep under the stars on this trek—no need for tents here. Return to Tamanrasset for a flight back to Algiers and Paris.

October, 18 days (from U.S.), $2,100 + air. 1986 departure: Oct. 30.

Mountain Travel, 1398 Solano Ave., Albany, CA 94706. (800) 227-2384 or (415) 527-8100.

Trekking the Sahara by camel — *Leo Le Bon for Mountain Travel*

ALGERIA

SAHARA OVERLAND

Midway in crossing the Central Sahara, former advertising executive and world traveler, Irma Turtle, decided to start Turtle Tours. This she did, with travel in the Sahara her specialty.

Fly to Paris and on to Ghardaia, a hill town in the M'Zab Valley of Algeria. Then south for hiking through the Hoggar Mountains—a spectacular volcanic landscape in a surreal and lunar setting. Then head south again to the Tassili du Hoggar to explore a very different exuberant landscape of sand and rocks at play. Hike through narrow rock fissures, over enormous dunes and across sandscapes dotted with sculptures of mushroom-shaped, wind-carved rocks. (The famous Tagrera!) Throughout the faraway journey you camp at night under the stars and bathe at wells which you may be sharing with a Tuareg caravan. The trip then continues eastward towards Essendilene and Djanet, culminating in the massive undulating sea of sand dunes, the great Admer Erg. The final treat is a day's trip up to the Tassili n Ajjer Plateau to see the world famous neolithic rock paintings.

October-April, 18 days (from U.S.), $2,350 + air NY/Paris. 1986 departures: Monthly, flexible.

Turtle Tours, Dept. AG, 251 E. 51st St., New York, NY 10022. (212) 355-1404.

ALGERIA

SAHARA TREASURES

Explore the stark and unforgettable beauty of the Sahara in this intensive 18-day trip. Fly to Tamanrasset, Algeria, via Paris, where you prepare for your 4-day camel caravan in the Hoggar Mountains. Ride or walk if you choose, through metallic colored

Around the well at Tereren, Algeria — *Turtle Tours, NY.*

lunar-type landscapes to the rhythmic pace of camel travel, camping each night where the camels can graze.

From there, fly to the tiny oasis town of Djanet, where you start your 3-day hike of the Pre-Tassili, through a variety of sand and rocks and culminating at the Admer Erg, an undulating sea of sand dunes up to 100 meters. The next four days are devoted to exploring the rock paintings on the Tassili n' Ajjer Plateau. The paintings in soft ochre, red and white tones depict boats, elephants, hunters, and dancers, and date as far back as 8,000 B.C. Camp each night in a different part of this rocky landscape covered with forests of rock needles and furrowed canyons. Ghardaia, a beautiful oasis town in the M'Zab Valley, is your last stop before returning to Paris for your flight home.

February-April, October-December, 18 days (from U.S.), $2,350 (includes air from Paris). 1986 departures: Monthly.

Turtle Tours, Dept. AG, 251 E. 51 St., New York, NY 10022. (212) 355-1404.

BOTSWANA ZIMBABWE

LIVE LIKE THE BUSHMEN

Diversity combines with discovery on this 22-day safari (Grade B) through the remote wilderness of northern Botswana. Expedition vehicles take you through dry bush country in search of elephant herds, zebra, and wildebeest. Board "mekoros"—traditional dugout canoes—in the Okavango Delta, the largest inland delta in the world, and push through the tall swamp grasses in search of hippo, crocodile, and exotic birdlife. Take foot excursions on the larger islands. Visit the Tsodilo Hills, the villages of the bushmen, and the Chobe and Moremi game reserves filled with antelope, roan, kudu, and impala.

The safari route adapts to animal migrations, so you won't miss a thing. At night, camp out in tents or reedhuts in the bushmen's villages, and let the African night speak to you. The trip begins and ends in Victoria Falls with the thunder of the magnificent cataract.

July, 22 days (from U.S.), $1,590 + air. 1986 departure: July 13.

Wilderness Travel, 1760-AT Solano Ave., Berkeley, CA 94707. (800) 247-6700 or (415) 524-5111.

BOTSWANA ZIMBABWE

RARE AND WONDERFUL WILDLIFE

"Both Botswana and Zimbabwe represent long hidden secrets of bird-and wild-life treasure, unsurpassed anywhere in the world," writes Linda Lass-Schuhmacher, President of The African Experience. See herds of elephants, zebra, tsetsebees, cheetah, lions, and leopards, not to mention crocodiles, hippos, herons, flamingoes and storks, as you explore these two countries in grand African style—on foot, by landrover, and by boat—spending nights in lodges and hotels, others in camps.

Begin your safari along the vast floodplains of the Chobe River in Botswana, then drive south through the bushveld, savanna and brush to Allans Camp on the Savuti Channel, where you'll stay for a full day of birdwatching and gameviewing. Paddle dugout canoes, walk along trails, exchange stories around the campfire and check out the hippo pools along the Khwai river, still in Botswana. After camping in the heart of the Okavango Delta it's on to Zimbabwe, for overnight in the famous Victoria Falls Hotel and a sundowner cruise on the Zambezi. Visit a croc farm and a typical

African Crafts Village before moving on to Zimbabwe's Hwange National Park, where Allen Elliot, the country's foremost ornithologist and naturalist, will supervise your safari activities. Arrive and depart via Harare, capital of Zimbabwe.

Year round, 19 days (from Victoria Falls), $3,550 + air. 1986 departures: Every Sunday.

(SLA) The African Experience, P.O. Box 657, Lexington, MA 02173. (617) 862-2165.

EGYPT

RED SEA DIVING

Diving in the Red Sea off the southern tip of the Sinai Penisula, recently a part of Israel but now Egyptian, has long been a diver's dream. The marine attractions of Sharm el Shiekh and its adjacent coast are legendary but until now unavailable to those who covet comfort and safety. From the 60'-*Colonna II* or 75'-*Colonna III*, divers explore the fish-filled reefs of Ras Muhammad, the coral gardens of the Straits of Tiran, The Temple, Jackson Reef, The Tower, the fabled wreck of the Dunraven, and the Amphora Wreck where

A diver's paradise, the Red Sea—*Carl Roessler for See & Sea Travel, Inc., CA.*

ancient amphorae and anchors litter the reef. Diving is unlimited and meals and cabins are provided aboard ship.

The trip starts with two nights in Cairo, then a flight to Ophira on the Sinai coast. Individual arrangements for a longer stay in Cairo on the return trip may be made.

Year round, 16 days, $2,700 + air. 1986 departures: Mar. 22, Apr. 19, Aug. 23, Sep. 6 & 27, Oct. 25, Dec. 20. In 1987: Jan. 17, Feb. 14, Mar. 14, Apr. 11, May 9, Aug. 22, Sep. 5 & 19, Oct. 17, Nov. 14, Dec. 19.

See & Sea Travel, Inc., 680 Beach St., /340, San Francisco, CA 94109. (800) 348-9778 or (415) 771-0077.

EGYPT

FIT FOR A PHAROAH

Discover the magic of the old world in the comfort of the new world on this 10-day journey through Egypt. From the Tomb of Tutankhamon to the famous pyramids at Giza to Greco-Roman temples, history will surround you and amaze you.

You depart from New York and spend the first two days in Cairo, the political and cultural axis of Africa. Visit the ancient bustling Khan El-Kalil bazaar, the Roman Fortress of Babylon and Sultan Hassan Mosque. The next day see the famous pyramids in Sakkara and Giza, and the fifth day, hop a flight to Abu Simbel, site of Ramses II's great temple. Then, board a luxury floating hotel—your home for the next four days and nights. Sail to Elephant Island—to Edfu and the Temple of Horus—to the riverside resort of Luxor. You cross the Nile for a close-up look of the Valley of Kings—a royal ending to a royal tour—and fly home.

Year round, 10 days (from NYC), $1,695 including air. 1986 departures: Every Friday.

Big Five Tours, 387 Park Ave. So., New York, NY 10016. (212) 686-4868 or 889-1636.

KENYA

A SATISFYING SAFARI

Join Mike Hopkins, former director of the California Living Museum, and Kini Smoot, for a close-up look at the magnificent scenery and unspoiled, untamed wildlife at its best on this Kenyan safari. Begin your adventure at the Amboseli Game Reserve, a park teeming with zebra, wildebeest, elephant, lion, leopard, and rhino, with Mt. Kilimanjaro as your backdrop. Then travel through coffee and pineapple plantations and the foothills of Mt. Kenya to Mountain Lodge, located in the Kahari Game Corridor adjacent to the traditional route used by migrating elephants. Here you view black buffalo, waterbuck, leopard, and forest hog by day or by "simulated moonlight." Head north to the Samburu Game Reserve, famous for its reticulated giraffe, Grevy's Zebra, gerenuk, and the Somali ostrich.

Next stop is the Mount Kenya Safari Club for trout fishing, horseback riding, and relaxation. Move on to Lake Nakuru in the Rift Valley, "the greatest ornithological spectacle on earth," with close to 400 species of waterbirds. Also see hippos, countless flotillas of pelicans, and thousands of flamingoes. Continue to the Masai Mara Reserve, home for lions, cheetahs, elephants, jackals, and the rare roan antelope. You have time to catch a private performance of the traditional Masai tribal dance at Mayers Ranch. Finally, hop on an overnight train to Mombasa for leisurely shopping, catch a flight to Nairobi for a gala farewell dinner, then head home.

August, 21 days (from L.A.), $3,790 including air. 1986 departure: Aug. 9.

Twende Safaris, P.O. Box 6809, Bakersfield, CA 93306. (805) 872-4113, 831-4362, or 399-2073.

KENYA

A FAMILY SAFARI

On family vacations simple pleasures are important, and adults and children learn and discover together. Sven-Olof Lindblad of Special Expeditions tested this philosophy on a safari with his 4-year-old son. "Our days were full of animal viewing, walking around camp, and playing soccer. With an Instamatic camera my son photographed everything in sight and was happy to use the same film six times." He has designed this expedition especially for families. The safari leader, author Daphne Sheldrick, shares her expert knowledge about wild animals, and the safari hands, from headman to cook, make life in the bush unusually comfortable by doing laundry, making beds, bringing hot water for showers, cooking delicious meals, and becoming your friends.

A family on safari in Kenya—*Sven-Olof Lindblad for Special Expeditions, NY.*

From Nairobi you drive to Amboseli National Park at the foot of Mt. Kilimanjaro, and in succeeding days visit Aberdare National Park, Lewa Downs, Lake Naivasha, the Masai Mara Game Reserve, and back to Nairobi. Lion, elephant, buffalo, leopard, and cheetah become familiar sights, as well as giant forest hogs, warthogs, giraffe, zebra, eland, rhino, and hippo—to name a few. Birdlife is prolific—both bush and waterbirds. You stop at a Masai village and learn about their lifestyles. As a dramatic ending to the safari—view the herds from aloft at dawn in a hot air balloon!

June-August, December, 18-23 days (from U.S.), $3,800-$4,800 + air. 1986 departures: Jun. 19 & 26, Jul. 12 & 24, Aug. 9, Dec. 18.

Special Expeditions, Dept. AG, 720 Fifth Ave., New York, NY 10019. (800) 762-0003 or (212) 765-7740.

KENYA

WILDLIFE SAFARI—FAMILIES/ADULTS

Traveling in 4-wheel-drive "go anywhere" vehicles and spending most nights at tented camps gives participants (15 maximum) a chance to get into the bush where the action is and to sleep out in the African night with all its wildlife sounds. The result is intimate connection with the wildness of Africa, yet with basic comforts. This is an easy adventure—no special expertise required. One departure the end of June is set aside for families, with special discounts for children.

From Nairobi the northward route takes you to the Meru National Park, into dry bush country and the Samburu Game Reserve, on to the lush forests of Aberdares National Park, westward through the Rift Valley and the Masai Mara Reserve, and by air back to Nairobi. Each day's highlight is wildlife viewing—from elephants, giraffes, and lions to hippos and crocodiles and dozens of other species. Other highlights: trout streams that tumble in thousand-foot waterfalls, acacia-studded plains, animals at the Ark's floodlit salt lick, encounters with the Masai, and everywhere the wild animals.

January to October, 14 days (from U.S.), $1,690 + air. 1986 departures: Jan. 5, Feb. 23, Mar. 16, Jun. 29, Aug. 2, Sep. 7, Oct. 12.

Mountain Travel, 1398 Solano Ave., Albany, CA 94706. (800) 227-2384 or (415) 527-8100.

KENYA

RED ELEPHANTS AND WHITE BEACHES

It's a land awash with color—"red" elephants, white sand beaches, and black-maned lions—a beautiful sight for the traveler with the artistic eye.

The 17-day safari starts with a visit in Nairobi then two days in the Masai Mara Game Reserve to view elephant, rhino, lion, cheetah, and other species of plains game. On to the Samburu Game Reserve where the "big five" roam—the elephant, rhino, lion, leopard, and buffalo—and the zebra, long-necked gerenuk, and others. In Nyeri stay at the Treetops Lodge for floodlit gameviewing. Cruise Lake Baringo to observe heronry, and visit

Lake Bogoria's hot springs, geysers, and millions of flamingoes. In Amboseli National Park take an early morning game drive in the shadow of Mt. Kilimanjaro. The famous "red" elephant and 60 other species are on view at Tsavo West National Park. Spend a night watching wildlife at the Salt Lick Lodge waterhole. Wind up with three days at Mombasa's white sand beaches and rinse off the safari dust.

Year round, 17 days (from Seattle), $2,960 including air. 1986 departures: Every Tuesday. In 1987: Every Tuesday.

Folkways International Trekking, Inc., 14903 S.E. Linden Lane-AT, Oak Grove, OR 97267. (503) 653-5882.

KENYA — ON HORSEBACK IN MASAILAND

Mount your Somali pony. Gallop after zebra. Breathe the dust. Bathe in warm-water springs. Share camp with the Masai people. It's a 300-mile horseback safari through Africa's Masailand, and it's not for rank beginners. But for the experienced cross-country rider, it's the perfect way to discover the charm of Africa "much the way Teddy Roosevelt did in 1909," says Bayard Fox, a Wyoming rancher who winters in Kenya and leads the rides with his Kenya-born wife.

You ride 15 to 35 miles a day around the Masai Mara Game Reserve just north of the Serengeti in Tanzania at an altitude of about 6,000 feet. Trucks carrying camping gear and food circle around to set up each night's camp before the riders arrive. Gameviewing by landrover alternates with horseback riding. During most of the two-week trip, you sleep in tents with the benefit of a shower tent nearby; other nights at lodges. Campfires take the chill off cool nights, and camp cooks display expertise at open-fire cooking.

January, February, August, 15 days (from U.S.), $2,000 + air. 1986 departure: Aug. 10. In 1987: Jan. 15, Feb. 7, Aug. 10.

Equitour/Bitteroot, 27 East Fork, Dubois, WY 82513. (800) 545-0019 or (309) 455-2778.

KENYA — SAFARI IN COMFORT

Here's a 15-day, first-class safari that combines luxurious accommodations with dramatic wildlife encounters. Your party of two to four departs from the U.S. for two nights in Nairobi, before driving to the Athi Plains and Amboseli National Park to see gazelle and zebra. Take to the treetops next at the Ark, a hotel built in the trees. North across the Equator, drive to Lewa Downs and stay in a private residence. Continue to the world famous Mt. Kenya Safari Club and then by plane to the deluxe tent lodge at Governor's Camp in the Masai Mara Game Reserve. Return to Nairobi for a final night.

The chief safari goal is sighting the "big five"—elephant, buffalo, lion, leopard, and rhino. The treetop hotel affords great views of animals at the waterhole and salt lick. But for all the wild animal

AFRICA

Mt. Kilimanjaro, a favorite for trekking and climbing—*Ted Cordingley for Overseas Adventure Travel, MA.*

watching, comfort is never sacrificed. Safaris are flexible. In the foothills of Mt. Kilimanjaro, you may tour by foot, horseback, or overland vehicle. Porters carry your gear and supplies. In the Masai Mara Reserve, view the wildlife from aloft in a hot-air balloon.

Year round, 15 days (from U.S.), $2,200 + air. 1986 departures: Open.

Big Five Tours, Ltd., 387 Park Ave., So., 8th Fl., New York, NY 10016. (800) 245-3434 or (212) 686-4868.

KENYA

CLIMBING KILIMANJARO

"Perhaps no other mountain on earth has the mystique and appeal of Kilimanjaro," comments this mountain travel specialist. "It rises in isolation from game-covered plains to 19,340 feet." No technical climbing, but the hiking at high altitudes is strenuous, with long days on the trail. Participants should be strong, experienced hikers in peak condition.

After arrival in Nairobi, groups up to 15 travel into Tanzania by landrover for several days of fantastic gameviewing in Lake Manyara National Park and the Ngorongoro Crater. Spectacular close-ups of waterbirds, impala, elephant, and more. The trek itself is planned for six days, with nights at Mandera Hut (9,000'), Horombo Hut (12,500'), and Kibo Hut (15,500'), before making it to the top—with the reward of a sunrise from "the roof of Africa."

Year round, 15 days (from U.S.), $2,090 + air. 1986 departures: Jan. 11, Mar. 8, Jun. 14, Aug. 2, Oct. 4, Dec. 6.

Mountain Travel, 1398 Solano Ave., Albany, CA 94706. (800) 227-2384 or (415) 527-8100.

KENYA

A SAFARI WITH STYLE

Discover unspoiled Kenya on this 15-day deluxe safari tour—you'll be completely spoiled. Stay at the best hotels—the luxurious Nairobi Hilton, the Mountain Lodge Tree Hotel built on eucalyptus tree trunks, the Mount Kenya Safari Club set in the shadow of Mt. Kenya.

Travel in a minibus equipped with pop-up roof and guaranteed window seats for each person. Your driver/guide takes you through the Athi Plains to the Salt Lick Lodge and Water Hole—it's roofed in typical African thatch and perched atop concrete stilts with interconnecting bridge-like walkways. See thirsty game, big and small. On to the Kilaguni Safari Lodge in Tsavo West, one of the best game lodges. There's more to come—Shetani Lava Flow, the aftermath of a volcanic eruption; snowcapped Mt. Kilimanjaro; picturesque Chania Falls; Lake Naivasha, home of varied birds; and as excitement builds day by day the journey culminates in the Masai Mara Game Reserve home of the "big five"—elephant, lion, leopard, buffalo, and rhino.

Year round, 15 days (from NYC), from $2,099 including air. 1986 departures: Every Thursday, Jul. & Aug.; alternate Thursdays other months.

Safariworld, 1500 Wilson Blvd., Arlington, VA 22209. 800) 336-5500 or (703) 525-3605.

KENYA

FOLLOWING GAME IN GRAND FASHION

Your head will, quite literally, be in the clouds during this 15-day safari to Nairobi and beyond as you soar over the Great Rift Valley, grassy plains and wildgame sanctuaries from Nairobi to Northern Serengeti. It's a deluxe journey all the way, topped off by a three-day stay at the world-famous Governors Camp in the Masai Mara Game Reserve. You'll live in tented luxury, experiencing the excitement of camping in the wild with the old-English traditions. Also, spend a night at the Treetops Hotel built on cape chestnut trees and overlooking a large salt lick and waterhole that attracts game day and night.

Among the other highlights: flying from Amboseli National Park to the Mt. Kenya Safari Club...flying from Nairobi to Governor's Camp, and back...enjoying the deluxe suites at Nairobi's new Lilian Towers. Your spectacular trip ends with a farewell dinner at the Nairobi Hilton International.

Year round, 15 days (from NYC), $3,199 including air. 1986 departures: Jan 9, Feb. 13, Mar. 13, Jun. 12 & 26, Jul. 10 & 24, Aug. 7 & 21, Sep. 11, Oct. 16, Nov. 20.

Safariworld, 1500 Wilson Blvd., Arlington, VA 22209. (800) 336-5500 or (703) 525-3605.

KENYA

NOMADS' LAND

Visit not only known areas of Kenya but also some of the special and overlooked spots in this itinerary which Sven-Olof Lindblad has developed from six years of living in Kenya. He carefully

AFRICA

Camping and trekking in nomad's land—*Sven-Olof Lindblad for Special Expeditions, NY.*

chooses trip leaders for their understanding of the wildlife and their knowledge and appreciation of the nomadic peoples. His luxurious safari takes you by charter aircraft from one point to another. Lodges, tented camps, and meals are first class—from breakfast tea to formal dinners.

Fly from Nairobi to snowcapped Mt. Kenya and the elegant Safari Club. From this lush lodge on the equator, view the rare black rhino, leopard, and the elusive bongo. Drive through Meru National Park—home of waterbuck, zebra, elephant, and the gerenuk. Then north to remote Lake Turkana where desert nomads roam. Cross the Great Rift Valley and Lake Baringo, and arrive at the Ark in the Aberdares Mountains—a hotel built over a floodlit waterhole and salt lick and outstanding for gameviewing. On to the Masai Mara Game Reserve, known for large prides of lions, cheetah, buffalo, and exotic birds. An optional hot-air balloon flight makes a dramatic end to the safari before your return to Nairobi.

December-March, July-October, 18 days (from U.S.), $4,350 + air. 1986 departures: Jan. 11, Feb. 1 & 22, Mar. 8, Jul. 12, Aug. 9, Sept. 6, Oct. 4, Dec. 20.

Special Expeditions, Inc., 720 Fifth Ave., Dept. AG New York, NY 10019. (800) 762-0003 or (212) 765-7741.

KENYA

MEET THE PEOPLE OF KENYA

On this 16-day East African tour, you meet not only the wildlife, but the rich and diverse tribes of this land. Fly via London to Nairobi, where your overland adventure begins. Driving northwest into the Rift Valley, you stop overnight at Lake Nakuru, en route to Lake Baringo, the Kerio Valley, and the Kakamega

Forest—the easternmost remnant of an ancient rainforest that once covered most of East Africa. Spend several days on Lake Victoria and two days at the world-renowned Masai Mara Game Reserve, then return to Nairobi, London, and home.

At Lake Nakuru, glimpse such birdlife as the night heron, little bittern, and flamingoes. From a boat on Lake Baringo, view the hippos, giraffe, topi, and impala. At informal meetings you have a chance to visit with local school teachers, sugar and tea plantation managers, and others when you attend a display of Kenya traditional dancing, visit the Njemps Manyatta (tribal dwellings), and pause at the local markets to buy pottery and Kiisi soapstone carvings.

>   **Year round, 16 days (from U.S. or Canada), $1,300 + air.** 1986 departures: First Sunday of each month.
>
>   **East African Travel Consultants, Inc., 574 Parliament St., Toronto, Ont., Canada M4X 1P8. (416) 967-0067.**

KENYA & MORE — CLASSIC SAFARI

Roughing it is not your style? Choose this 15-day deluxe tenting safari in Kenya with an optional extension in Tanzania, the Kenya coast, Egypt, South Africa, or Botswana. The itinerary is the one offered discriminating travelers by renowned zoological societies. The camping amenities include large tents with beds, linens, and hot showers, with laundry done daily, and food freshly prepared. A far cry from scout camp of yesteryear. Pack your binoculars and get ready to view the best of the beasts—wildebeest, zebra, lion, giraffe, rhino, elephant, and more.

On your game plan are the Masai Mara Game Reserve with huge migratory herds; Lake Nakuru National Park, famous for birdlife; the Samburu Game Reserve (among others, see the long-necked gerenuk); the luxurious Mount Kenya Safari Club (gourmet meals and a beautiful swimming pool); the Tree Hotel above an illuminated waterhole; and the Amboseli Game Reserve at the base of Mt. Kilimanjaro. Return to Nairobi to fly home—or to continue your African adventure.

>   **Year round, 16 days (from U.S.), $1,996 + air.** 1986 departures: Jan. 19, Feb. 9, Mar. 2 & 23, Apr. 13, Jun. 15, Jul. 6 & 27, Aug. 17, Sep. 7 & 28, Oct. 19, Nov. 9, Dec. 21.
>
>   **Born Free Safaris, 12504-A Riverside Dr., No. Hollywood, CA 91607. (800) 372-3274 or (818) 509-8998.**

KENYA / TANZANIA — A PARADE OF PRIMATES

From the baboons of the Serengeti and Lake Manyara to the chimps at Gombe to the gorillas of Rwanda, this safari is packed with primates and with excitement. Don't miss it. Overseas Adventure Travel claims it's the first in the U.S. to offer this exclusive tour. Track gorilla, rhino, lion, zebra, and elephant. Catch a rare glimpse of village life in rural Tanzania, Rwanda, and Burundi. The scenery is breathtaking—from the lush montane

AFRICA

forests to the magnificent Ngorongoro highlands.

Your 26-day adventure begins in Parc des Volcans, Rwanda. Some of your stops: Gombe Stream National Park, Mwanza, Serengeti, Ngorongoro Crater, Lake Manyara National Park, and Arusha. Travel by expedition vehicle. Spend most overnights camping with several hotel stays along the route. Enjoy several days of shopping at the end of your journey.

Meet the Masai—
Richard Bangs for Overseas Adventure Travel, MA.

June-October, 26 days (from U.S.), $3,060 + air. 1986 departure: Oct. 3. In 1987: Jun. 8, Oct. 2.

Overseas Adventure Travel, 6 Bigelow St. /102, Cambridge, MA 02139. (800) 221-0814 or (617) 876-0533.

KENYA
TANZANIA

HIKE THE HIGHLANDS

Tackle two mountains in one trip—climb both Mt. Kenya and Mt. Kilimanjaro during this 20-day expedition. It commences at Naro Moru River Lodge near Mt. Kenya. Depart by landrover to the 10,000-ft. base camp for orientation and leisurely nature walks. Trek up Mackinder's Valley to begin circumambulation of Mt. Kenya. Continue to Lenana Peak (16,355') with its outstanding views of Batian and Nelion, Mt. Kenya's jagged summits. Glaciers gleam and shimmer in the morning sun. Descend to starting point. Two days of big game tracking in Samburu Game Reserve break up the climbing.

Mystical Kilimanjaro is next. Fly to Arusha and begin the Tanzania climb through lush forests to Uniport Hut. Cross the

Shira Plateau's eland-populated moorland. The path continues up to Barranco Hut (13,500'). Follow on beneath the south face of Kilimanjaro to Barafu Hut (15,000'), set high on a ridge overlooking Mawenzi Peak, Mt. Meru, and Moshi. The final and most difficult part of the climb is still to come—to 19,340' Uhuru Peak—but the breathtaking views are well worth the physical effort. Descend with overnights at Kibo Hut and then Kibo Hotel.

Year round, 21 days (from U.S.), $1,860 + air. 1986 departures: Feb. 7, Jun. 6, Sep. 5, Dec. 12.

Folkways International Trekking, Inc., 14903 S.E. Linden Lane-AT, Oak Grove, OR 97267. (800) 547-7400 or (503) 653-5882.

KENYA TANZANIA

THE ULTIMATE COMBINATION

Experience the luxury of Kenya with the spectacular game reserves of Tanzania on this 15-day expedition. Meet the environment—the red plains of Amboseli, the snows of Mt. Kilimanjaro, the rolling plains of the Serengeti. Meet the wildlife in the best national parks—Tsavo, Amboseli, Lake Manyara, Serengeti, Ngorongoro Crater. Visit Olduvai Gorge, the excavation site of Dr. Richard and Mary Leakey. Enjoy a buffet lunch and afternoon at Gibbs Farm, shrouded in vivid flora and coffee fields. Shop for Masai handiwork and Makonde carvings in the Mto Wea Mbu market. Your journey begins and ends in Nairobi.

You travel via safari minivans all equipped with photographic roof hatches with a guaranteed window seat for each person. Experienced English-speaking driver-guides escort you. The overnight accommodations are the best available including the Mt. Kenya Safari Club, Seronera Lodge in the Serengeti and the Ngorongoro Wildlife Lodge at the rim of the crater, to name just a few of your homes away from home.

Year round, 15 days (from NYC), $2,999 including air. 1986 departures: Jan. 9, Feb. 13, Mar. 13, Apr. 10, May 29, Jun. 12, Jul. 10 & 24, Aug. 7 & 21, Sep. 11, Oct. 16, Nov. 20, Dec. 18.

Safariworld, 1500 Wilson Blvd., Arlington, VA 22209. (800) 336-5500 or (703) 525-3605.

KENYA TANZANIA

PLANNING YOUR OWN SAFARI

Explore East Africa the way you want to. Catering to flexible, individual departures, Journeys International combines basic hiking and camping trips out of Nairobi that involve animals, people, and the natural environment. Start with a Mt. Kenya trek, then link up with a Lake Turkana exploration, a Masai Mara hiking trip, a week of wildlife viewing or a Tsavo-Amboseli adventure. These itineraries are not for the idle onlooker; all emphasize active exploration. But the basic safaris also combine with your choice of luxury hotels or game resorts for add-ons of two days to six.

For big gameviewing, choose the "Wildlife Bus"—a converted four-wheel-drive Mercedes flatbed truck redesigned with comfortable seats for 18 passengers and gear—which takes you to

AFRICA

the Samburu camp, Thompson's Falls, and the Masai Mara. For a demanding hike, choose the Mt. Kenya Trek. Each group is accompanied by skilled guides, and is made up of English-speaking adventurers from around the world.

Year round, 10-24 days (from U.S.), $795-$1,195 + air. 1986 departures: Every Friday.

Journeys International, Box 7545-AG, Ann Arbor, MI 48107. (313) 665-4407.

Flamingoes on Lake Manyara, Tanzania—*Will Weber for Journeys International, MI.*

KENYA
TANZANIA
RWANDA

EAST AFRICA WILDLIFE SAFARI

Would you like to snap a picture of a gorilla close up or observe cheetah in their natural habitat? Your backdrop—endless savannas, volcanic calderas, acacia woodlands, snow-peaked mountains—is a photographer's dream come true. This 25-day East African safari is designed for the wildlife photographer and the naturalist.

View game in Lake Manyara, Olduvai Gorge, Ngorongoro Crater, and the Serengeti. Explore volcanic rain forests on foot for the rare mountain gorilla in Rwanda. Observe some of the 400 species of birdlife in the Rift Valley. Visit sites of early man and various tribal cultures. Also encounter zebra, giraffe, wildebeest, and leopard. Your accommodations are set in the wilderness in lodges or camp sites. Your guide, an expert in natural history and wildlife, provides insight along the way. The trip begins in Arusha and ends in Nairobi.

January-September, 25 days (from U.S.), $3,190 + air. 1986 departures: Jan. 9, Feb. 6, Jun. 19, Jul. 17, Sep. 4. In 1987: Jan. 8, Feb.5, Jun. 18, Jul. 16, Sep. 10.

Nature Expeditions International, 474 Willamette, P.O. Box 11496, Dept. AG, Eugene, OR 97440. (503) 484-6529

KENYA
TANZANIA
RWANDA

EXPLORING EAST AFRICA

Nothing compares to the firsthand experience of viewing the lowing herds of wildebeest on Kenya's infinite savanna, the snow-mantled grandeur of Tanzania's Mt. Kilimanjaro, and the magnificence of a mountain gorilla in Rwanda. You see it all on this natural history expedition through East Africa.

Your safari begins in Kenya, where the awesome escarpments and flamingo-covered soda lakes of the Great Rift Valley, and the majestic peaks of Mt. Kenya represent just a few of the wondrous spectacles. Here you observe 50 species of mammals, strange and exciting birdlife (ostriches, crown cranes, hornbills), and the Masai and Samburu tribes. Tanzania, crowned by the continent's highest mountain, offers incredible concentrations of wildlife within world-renowned game reserves. You have time to explore Ngorongoro Crater, a collapsed volcano, and the endless Serengeti, scattered with rocky outcrops, acacia trees, and a stronghold for more than two million animals. The mountainous, evergreen country of Rwanda in the heart of Africa boasts Akagera National Park and Volcanoes National Park—the sanctuary of the mountain gorilla. Live the dream of your childhood, and experience East Africa. Separate departures for Kenya and Tanzania are available.

January-March, 20 days (from NYC), $3,295 including air. 1986 departures: Jan. 3, 17 & 31, Feb. 14, Mar. 7.

International Expeditions, Inc., 1776 Independence Crt., /104, Birmingham, AL 35216. (800) 633-4734, or (205) 870-5550.

KENYA
TANZANIA
ZAMBIA
BOTSWANA

A WILDLIFE ADVENTURE

The wilderness is your home. Wildlife are your companions. Your form of transportation—a minibus, landrover, or your feet. Your adventure begins in Nairobi. Take the 13-day trip through Kenya and Tanzania, or continue on through Zambia, Victoria Falls, and Botswana for another 11 days.

The first two weeks, you search for animal life through the foothills of Mt. Kilimanjaro, through the home of the Masai tribe, in several national parks, and the Ngorongoro Crater (the site of archaeological findings). You scout for elephant, buffalo, cheetah, antelopes, zebra, flamingoes. If you choose to continue on, a flight takes you to the 6,000-square-mile Luangwa Valley National Park in Zambia. Another short flight away is Victoria Falls and a night of African tribal dancing. Your last few nights are spent along the banks of the mighty Chobe River in Botswana—home for a herd of 500 elephants. Evenings, you rest your weary limbs in a hotel or lodge. Mornings, the sun explodes into being, streaking the land with vivid gold, while birds chatter and hippos and elephants grunt. This is Africa!

June-October, 24 days (from U.S.), $3,789 + air. 1986 departures: Jun. 4 & 18, Jul. 2, 16, 30, Aug. 13 & 27, Sep. 10 & 24, Oct. 8 & 22.

Born Free Safaris, 12405-A Riverside Dr., No. Hollywood, CA 91607. (800) 372-3274 or (818) 509-8998.

LIBERIA

BICYCLE THE BACKROADS

You're a two-wheel traveler on this 26-day, 700-mile journey through the oldest independent sub-Saharan nation. Your bicycle gives you access to virgin tropical forests, diamond mines, small

Cycling through a Liberian village—*Mozer for Bicycle Africa, WA.*

farms, and villages of the Bassa and Loma tribal people, and lets you experience Liberia on a distinctly personal level.

Travel under 50 miles a day. Taste exotic fruit, traditional rice, and sauce dishes along the way. A sagwagon carries baggage, food, and sometimes cyclists. You don't need to be a serious cyclist, but you should be fit for long rides. The emphasis is on fun and education—acquainting riders with local music, art, customs, and history. David Mozer—an accomplished bicyclist, educator, and collector of African art—is your tour leader.

January & December, 26 days (from U.S.) $1,050 + air. 1986 departure: Dec. 18. In 1987: Jan. 8.

Bicycle Africa, 4247-CB 135th Place S.E., Bellevue, WA 98006-1319. (206) 746-1028.

MADAGASCAR PRIMATES TO ORCHIDS

You seem to be on another planet. There are 2-foot-long multi-colored chameleons, carnivorous plants, 1,000 species of orchids, and strangely beautiful beasts with lithe bodies, tails of monkeys, and delicate, foxlike heads. You walk through tropical rainforests and over high plateaus. You are in Madagascar, a Texas-sized piece of land in the Indian Ocean off the southeast coast of Africa, but you might as well be on Mars.

You reach Tananarive (Tana, the capital) by air from Nairobi for the start of an overland exploration with a driver/guide, and sometimes with local flights. Your trip can center on lemurs (the island's evolutionary sideshow), incredible plant life, the natural and anthropological diversity, the wildlife, the natural history, the ethnology, or whatever combination you want. Whatever the itinerary, count on out-of-this-world foods, smiling people with ancestry from Indonesia, Polynesia, and Africa, and accommodations from hotels to village huts. Forum offers itineraries with two or more days on the island—or custom arrangements to fit your schedule.

Year round departures. Average rates from $85/day + air.

Forum Travel International, 91 Gregory Lane,/21, Pleasant Hill, CA 94523. (415) 671-2900 or (415) 946-1500.

MALI OFF THE BEATEN TRACK

Get ready to rough it once you land in Niger and head for Mali. Leave the cities and roads behind you. You're off to find the true Africa—the remote reaches—by river canoe and on foot (Grade C). Head up the Niger River for eight days by "pirogues" (motor-powered canoes). Pass huge sand dunes, rice paddies, a bird sanctuary, and the straw huts of fishing villages accessible only by water. Meet Peul, Bozo, Maur, and Tuareg people. Walk through the remains of the once glorious Timbuktu. Set out on foot for the cliff-top villages of the Dogon tribespeople, hiking almost five hours a day through hilly terrain with donkeys carrying your gear. Once there, view the ancient cave paintings. Witness the unique animistic rituals, and perhaps, a colorful mask dance.

That's only part of your trip. Discover more along the way in Ayorou, Gao, Mopti, Sangha, and end with a farewell dinner at Bamako. At night, you stay close to the land and the people, camping in the dunes or sleeping in the villages.

January, 23 days (from Paris), $1,890 + air. 1987 departure: Jan. 19.

Wilderness Travel, 1760-AT Solano Ave., Berkeley, CA 94707. (800) 247-6700 or (415) 524-5111.

MALI ROAD TO TIMBUKTU

No, it's not the name of a Hope-Crosby film! The Road to Timbuktu is a 15-day exploration of the vestiges of a legendary

AFRICA

Celebration by Zaiane tribe in the Middle Atlas—*Piotr Kostrzewski for Cross Cultural Adventures, Inc., VA.*

kingdom at the crossroads of great sub-Saharan cultures. Emphasis is on the magnificent past and on today's handicrafts: brass amulets and massive silver from the desert-roaming Tuaregs; wooden carvings, animistic head-dresses, ceremonial statues from the Senufu and Bambara; brass figures and masks from the Dogon. Appropriately, the trip's host is head of the Mali Cultural Center.

The itinerary covers cliff-hanging villages that shelter complex ancient customs and traditions, the Sudanese-style domed adobe architecture of West Africa's oldest city, and traders from a dozen ethnic groups at the Sahel's largest market town. You start in Bamako, Mali's capital, a city big on handicrafts—in the museum, the workshops, and a nearby Monday market. On to Mali's best wildlife refuge for a nice change of pace. The journey ends with a train ride through Africa's hinterland to stylish Dakar, capital of Senegal and a gourmet's delight. (Limited to 10 people.)

January, 15 days (from U.S.). Rate to be announced. 1987 departure: Jan. 17.

Cross Cultural Adventures, Inc., P.O. Box 3285, Arlington, VA 22203. (703) 532-1547.

MOROCCO | **THE HIGH ATLAS TREK**

Cross Cultural Adventures offers a really great one—a journey to the last strongholds of true Berber culture in the High Atlas Mountains. The venture begins and ends in Marrakech—famous for its crafts and souks.

Then start your 7-day trek in the valley of the Ait Bou Guemez with a mule caravan. You pass tiny remote villages girdled by walnut groves and meet colorful native tribesmen. Snow-line permitting, climb the peak (13,560') of Mgoun (Morocco's second highest mountain) and descend following the Mgoun River through a spectacular narrow gorge. A minibus meets up with the group for the second segment of the trip: a ride to Ouarzazate passing dozens of adobe castles, and continuing through the southern highlands to the 11th century walled city of Taroudant. Then back to Marrakech for a flight home or an optional 3-day extension to North Africa's highest summit, Mt. Toubkal (13,876'). (Limited to 10 people.)

May, 15 days (from U.S.), $975 + air. 1986 departure: May 31. In 1987: May 30.

Cross Cultural Adventures, Inc., P.O. Box 3285, Arlington, VA 22203. (703) 532-1547.

MOROCCO

IMILCHIL BETROTHAL FAIR

On a trip that begins and ends in Marrakech, with its legendary covered bazaars, splendid palaces, labyrinths of alleyways, and the Jemaa-el-Fna square teeming with snake charmers, storytellers,

Young girls at the Imilchil Betrothal Fair in Morocco— *Piotr Kostrzewski for Cross Cultural.*

acrobats, and dancers, participants travel by minibus into the High Atlas Mountains in time for the annual Imilchil Betrothal Fair. Here members of the Ait Hadiddou Berber tribe hope to find spouses during a great 3-day bazaar. Lodged in enormous black-wool tents—the khaima—specially set up for visitors, you examine the wares for sale and watch the handsome Berber men meet women bedecked in jewelry, their eyes outlined in dark kohl, cheeks rouged with carmine and honey, mouths covered by black cloth. The clasping of hands signals betrothal.

You crisscross the Atlas chain to and from the fair, follow spectacular valleys to the Sahara, stop in verdant oases guarded by fortified villages, observe pasturing camel herds, spy monkeys in forests of giant cedars, and all the while learn the mysterious ways of the mountain and desert dwellers. (Limited to eight people.)

September, 15 days (from U.S.), $1,900 + air. 1986 and 1987 departure: Late September.

Cross Cultural Adventures, Inc., P.O. Box 3285, Arlington, VA 22203. (703) 243-7194.

MOROCCO

DISCOVERING CULTURE IN CRAFT

A wooden sculpture made from the roots of the Thuya tree, a tribal carpet, nomadic silver ornaments; all elements of Morocco's folkcraft from yesterday and today. On this 16-day tour you get an "insider's look" at the people and their art, including the wood crafts in the fishing town of Essaouira, the silver capital of Tiznit, the carpet-weaving center of Khenifra, and the leather-tanning quarters in Fez. This unique tour is exclusive with Cross Cultural Adventures (as are all of their tours). Director Piotr Kostrzewski—who speaks Arabic, is an expert on travel in Morocco, and a collector of Moroccan tribal carpets and jewelry—will escort the group.

Along the way, you meet Berber craftsmen, stay in a former palace, tour folkcraft museums, travel through the Sahara Desert, spectacular river valleys, and the High Atlas chain, and, of course, bargain for treasures. Enjoy a farewell dinner with traditional music and dances at a sumptuous restaurant. The itinerary starts in Casablanca and ends with two days in "Africa's most enchanting city"—Marrakech. (Limited to eight people.)

October, 15 days (from U.S.), $1,645 + air. 1986 departure: Feb. 21. In 1987: Feb. 27.

Cross Cultural Adventures, Inc., P.O. Box 3285, Arlington, VA 22203. (703) 243-7194.

MOROCCO TO KENYA

TRANS AFRICA SLOWLY

If you're a high-speed traveler who prefers to cover a lot of ground in little time, this trip is not for you. However, if you want to truly absorb the mystery and magic of Africa, this slow-paced 21-week overland camping adventure is probably just your cup of tea. In a semi-open expedition vehicle, cover about 8,000 miles in North, East, West, and Central Africa, traveling through vast deserts, teeming forests, majestic mountains, to open savannas. Starting in London, then through France and Spain, the incredible journey continues to Morocco, Algeria, Mali, Burkina Faso, Togo,

Benin, Nigeria, Cameroon, Central African Republic, Zaire, Burundi, Tanzania, and Kenya.

Some highlights along the route—the Grand Erg Occidental, a sea of pink and yellow sand dunes in the Sahara, the stark Tademait plateau…legendary Timbuktu…Mopti, a city built on three islands…the green highlands of Cameroon. Your activities—crossing the Zaire River by ferry, climbing the active Nyiragongo volcano, trekking for gorillas, bantering for handmade spears and ornaments in remote jungle villages—total adventure for the young in heart.

February & October, 21 weeks (from London to Nairobi), $3,730-$3,850 + air. 1986 departures: Feb. 28, Oct. 25.

Adventure Center AG, 5540 College Avenue, Oakland, CA 94618. (800) 227-8747 or (415) 654-1879.

Black-maned lion with lioness—*East African Travel Consultants, Inc., Ont., Canada.*

RWANDA ZAIRE

MOUNTAINS OF THE MOON

Looking for some adventure—on a grand scale? Then, this one's for you. Search on foot for gorillas, take a lesson on poison-arrow making from pygmies, and hike up glaciers.

Your 24-day expedition begins in Kigali, capital of Rwanda, where you meet your leaders and your equipment. A four-wheel-drive vehicle transports you into Zaire (the Congo) to Bukavu on Lake Kivu. Team up with expert trackers at nearby Mt. Kahuzi, the famed jungle habitat of the silver-back mountain gorilla. You'll see these gentle, vegetarian giants at altitudes between 9,000 and 12,000 feet. On to Goma, for a quick trip to the active Nyiragongo

Volcano and a visit to a village of pygmies in the Ituri Forest. Finally, a 5-day strenuous hike (with guides and porters) up the Ruwenzori Mountains (known as "Mountains of the Moon"), with overnight stays in mountain huts. (Nonhikers may opt to stay at the Mutwanga base camp.) Then back to Kigali.

Year round, 24 days, $590-$690 + air. 1986 departures: Jan. 20, Feb. 10, Jun. 9 & 30, Jul. 21, Aug. 11, Sep. 1 & 22, Nov. 24, Dec. 15. In 1987: Jan. 12, Feb. 2.

Adventure Center AG, 5540 College Ave., Oakland, CA 94618. (800) 227-8747 or (415) 654-1879.

TANZANIA

A WALK IN THE WILD

"Rugged but rewarding"—that's Overseas Adventure's label for this 19-day walking safari through Tanzania. It's appropriate, to be sure. You spend nearly two weeks traveling by foot and cover about 75 miles. It's a great way to combine physical exercise with animal viewing. You're accompanied by an experienced Masai guide and sure-footed donkeys to carry your water and supplies. You travel through Masailand, from the rim of Ngorongoro Crater, down on to the Rift Valley floor. Along the way, meet and trade with the Masai, camp, view the exotic birdlife and spectacular wildlife. Then, breathe deeply, stretch your hamstrings, get your porters geared up, and you're off on a six-day climb up Mt. Kilimanjaro (19,340 feet).

All meals are included except lunches and dinners in hotels. Bring your own backpack, sleeping bag, mess kit and tent.

January & February, 19 days (from U.S.), $2,300 + air. 1986 departures: Jan. 31, Feb. 21. In 1987: Jan. 30, Feb. 20.

Overseas Adventure Travel, 6 Bigelow St. /102, Cambridge, MA 02139. (800) 221-0814 or (617) 876-0533.

TANZANIA

CAMPING IN THE SERENGETI

Penetrate Africa's wildest bush on this 19-day camping expedition starting in Arusha. In landrovers you cross Tanzania's mountains, forests, valleys, savanna, and volcanic zones. In a land where tourists are few and the Masai still follow traditional ways, you view cheetah, rhino, ostrich, hippo, leopard, and other wild animals at close range.

Your first encounter with wildlife and scenery is in Masailand. Here you camp in the Rift Valley, hike along the Ngare Sero River, and view amazing birdlife at Lake Natron. Then, move into the "wilds" of the Serengeti Park where giraffe, ostrich, cheetah, and zebra greet you. On to one of your most intriguing stops, Olduvai Gorge, where the Leakeys unearthed the jawbone of Zinjanthropus man. The same day, descend to the floor of Ngorongoro Crater, and camp for two nights. Before heading back to Arusha, swim and relax at Gibb's Farm, located in the Ngorongoro highlands, and make your last camp at Manyara National Park, known for its large elephant and lion populations.

TUNISIA TO IVORY COAST

THE SAHARA SENSATION

This adventure through the world's largest desert (8-million square miles) is a fantasy come to life—from 700-feet high sand dunes, to the stone forest, to 8,000-year-old, prehistoric rock drawings. It's for the resilient traveler and expedition enthusiast, starting with a flight from Frankfurt to Tunis, and returning to Munich from Niamey.

Forum Travel offers six trip variations, ranging from 16 to 25 days. Concentrate on Tunisia and Algeria, from the Atlas Mountains to the oasis In Salah. If you wish, take a boatride on the Niger River, catching a glimpse of exotic birds. Or choose the challenging 2,500-mile trek which begins in Niamey and explores the Air Mountain Range. Still another route detours into Erg Occidental and its red oases of Timimoun and Adrar, then follows the Niger River down across the Ivory Coast. All trips are rough-it style. Camp out and travel by expedition vehicle.

Sarari Trail in Kafue National Park, Zambia—*East African Travel Consultants, Inc., Ont., Canada*

September-December, March-May, 16-25 days (from Frankfurt), from $2,026 including air. 1986: 14 departures.

Forum Travel International, 91 Gregory Lane, /21, Pleasant Hill, CA 94523. (415) 946-1500 or (415) 671-2900.

ZAMBIA

WILDLIFE WALKING SAFARI

In a party of six you walk in the cool of early morning and late afternoon, observing a vast variety of elusive animals and birds—

elephants, antelope, zebras, lions, carmine bee-eaters, lilac-breasted rollers, eagles, and others. The wild-game walking safari in Zambia's Luangwa Valley is escorted by a knowledgeable guide and an askari (armed guard).

Fly to Lusaka, capital city of Zambia, via London, then to Mfuwe for transfer to the base camp for six nights. Each day you set off on a new route. (Driving in an open landrover may be arranged.) Next, a flight to Livingstone to view the mighty Victoria Falls, known for centuries as Mosi-oa-Tunya (the smoke that thunders). A visit to the Livingstone Museum, a Sundowner Cruise aboard the *MV Makumbi* on the Zambezi River, and time to watch Zambian dancing and singing before returning to Lusaka, and back to London.

May-November, 14 days (from U.S.), $1,550 + air. 1986 departures: First Friday of each month.

East African Travel Consultants, Inc., 574 Parliament St., Toronto, Ont., Canada M4X 1P8. (416) 967-0067.

ZAMBIA
ZIMBABWE

CUSTOM WILDLIFE SAFARIS

Ever see a black rhino? This practically endangered species is yet abundant in Zambia's Luangwa Valley, along with impala, waterbuck, kudu, zebra, giraffe, wildebeest, lion, leopard, monkey, and hippo. These 21-day custom tours guided by naturalist experts are arranged for zoological societies and other groups, from six to 16 participants, traveling by open landrover and on foot.

Arriving in Lusaka after a quick tour of Rome, start your forays into the bush at the Chinzombo Camp, a beautiful wildlife sanctuary. Then on to Kariba and Mana Pools, where you visit an island by boat to watch animal herds or to catch Tiger Fish. Spend several days in the Hwange National Park in Zimbabwe at the Safari Lodge or at a tree house camp to view the wildlife, including huge numbers of elephants. A highlight is seeing Victoria Falls, the greatest waterfall in the world. Here you have time to pick up batiks and unique carvings, stroll through the rainforest, take a sunset cruise on the Zambezi, and watch a special performance of tribal dancing by the Shangaan and Mkishi tribes. Safari lodges, chalets, camps, hotels, and tree houses provide a variety of accommodations on these special tours.

April-October, 21 days (from NYC), $3,475-$3,600 depending on group size, including air. 1986-87 departures: Custom arranged.

Fun Safaris Inc., P.O. Box 178, Bloomingdale, IL 60108. (800) 323-8020 or (312) 893-2545.

ZAMBIA

RAFTING THE ZAMBEZI

For an unforgettable, adventurous week in South Central Africa, raft the Zambezi River from the base of Victoria Falls to the headwaters of Lake Kariba—a 100-kilometer expedition for wild river connoisseurs.

The roaring falls—a two-kilometer-wide curtain of falling water—is an awesome starting point for a weeklong navigation of the river and the great gorges which David Livingstone wisely detoured on his 1855 exploratory canoe expedition. In 1981, SOBEK negotiated the first descent of the wild river corridor. "The rapids

Rafting the Zambezi below Victoria Falls—*Bart Henderson for SOBEK Expeditions, Inc., MI.*

were Bio-Bio big," they report, "the scenery stunning, the wildlife wondrous. This is incontestably one of the world's finest whitewater and wildlife adventures." Trip starts and ends in Livingstone.

August-December, 7 days, $1,195 + air. 1986 departures: Every Sun. from Aug. 24 to Dec. 7.

SOBEK Expeditions, Inc., Box AG, Angels Camp, CA 95222. (209) 736-4524.

ZAMBIA
ZIMBABWE

THE ZAMBEZI WILDLIFE SAFARI

A whitewater roller-coaster ride down the Zambezi rapids below spectacular Victoria Falls highlights this exciting 12-day safari. You fly to Bumi Hills Safari Lodge via Harare and Karami. Comfortable chalets overlook Lake Kariba and the sweeping purple panorama where buffalo, elephant, and waterbuck roam the grassy slopes. Experienced rangers take you on foot, in boats, or in 4-wheel vehicles to see the game. The next day you fly to the vast Hwange National Park. The uncommon white rhino can be watched here from treehouse-like platforms. You stay in an exclusive tented camp and are treated to night game drives.

From there, fly to historic Victoria Falls Hotel from where you can cross the bridge over the Zambezi which separates Zimbabwe from Zambia. Optional activities: an overflight of the falls and a sundowner cruise on the Zambezi. For a climactic ending to the safari, spend a day rafting the river's tumultous rapids. Like David Livingstone, SOBEK keeps its groups small—4-16 people.

Year round, 12 days (from U.S.), $2,249-$2,499 + air. 1986 departures: Feb. 14, Mar. 7, Apr. 4, May 16 & 20, Jun. 13 & 27, Jul. 11 & 25, Aug. 1, 15, & 29, Sep. 12 & 26, Oct. 17 & 31, Nov. 21, Dec. 12, 19, & 26.

SOBEK Expeditions Inc., Box AG, Angels Camp, CA 95222. (209) 736-4524.

ZAMBIA
ZIMBABWE
BOTSWANA

A SAFARI FOR THE NATURALIST

Take advantage of Africa's best kept secrets—Zambia, Zimbabwe, and Botswana—far from the maddening crowd, where you can truly become a part of the landscape of old Africa. The American Museum has designed a special itinerary so you can photograph with ease from an open landrover, cruise among the wading birds in dugout canoes, and learn the noctural ways of the bush.

Fly through London, Lusaka, and on to Mfuwe for the start of your safari, led by two extraordinary naturalists: Dr. John Cooke, a former curator at the American Museum, and Phil Berry, Zambia-born and the former head of the anti-poaching unit that protects the endangered rhino. With these experts you see in close proximity a vast number of wild animals and birds. You are taken to Victoria Falls for the "smoke that thunders;" to Luangwa, home of the black rhino; to Hwange National Park, famous for its vast elephant herds; to Xaxaba Safari Camp, deep in the Okavango Delta, with magnificent birdlife—over 300 species; and to Tsoldilo Hills, home of the last true Bushman and 2,000-year-old rock paintings. Travelers should be in good physical health and capable of walking over rough terrain. And photographers should make certain their shutter fingers are strong.

September-October, 18 days (from U.S.), $4,300 + air. 1986 departure: Sep. 26.

Discovery Tours, American Museum of Natural History, Central Park West at 79th St., New York, NY 10024. (800) 462-8687; (212) 873-1400 or 799-7157.

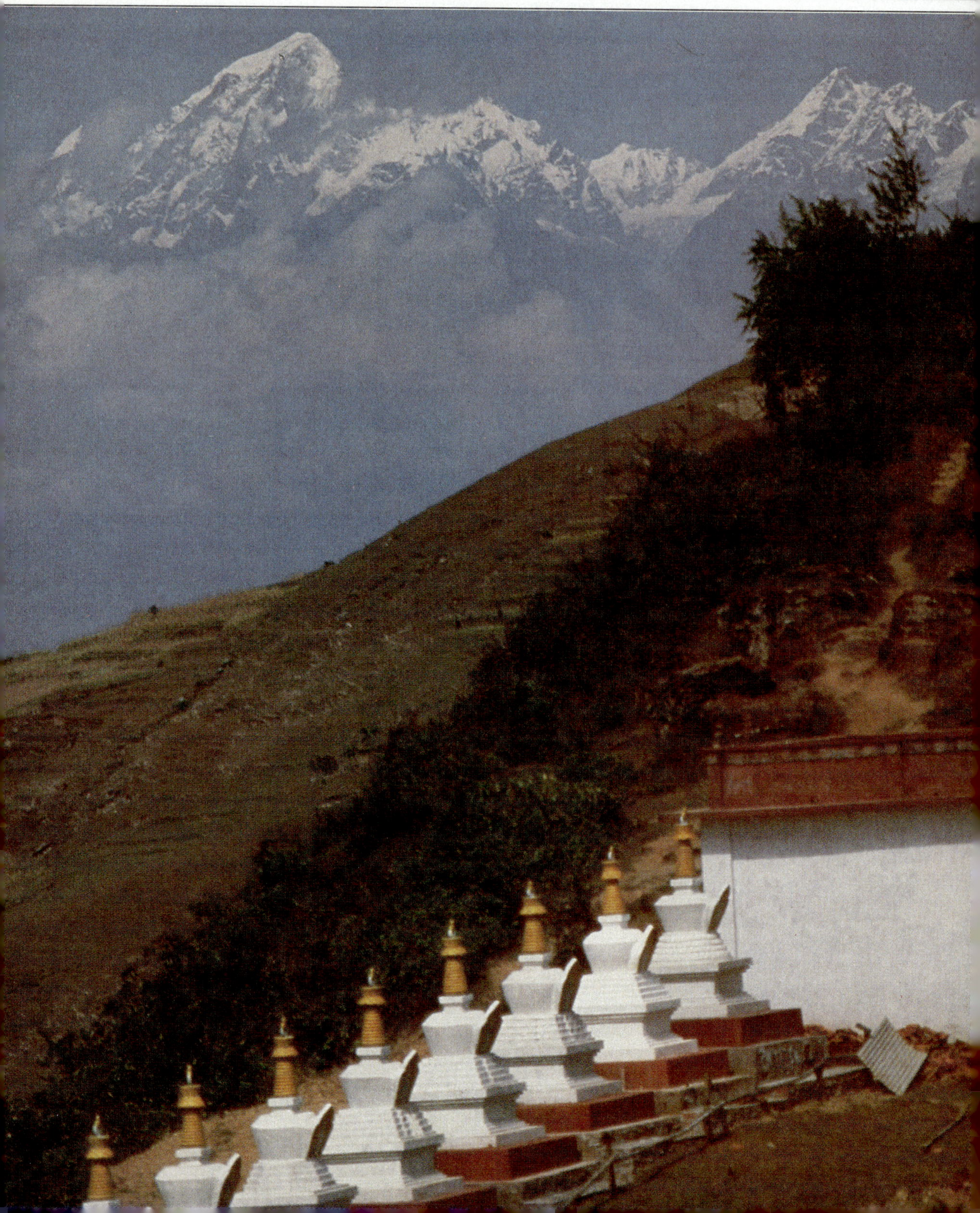

ASIA

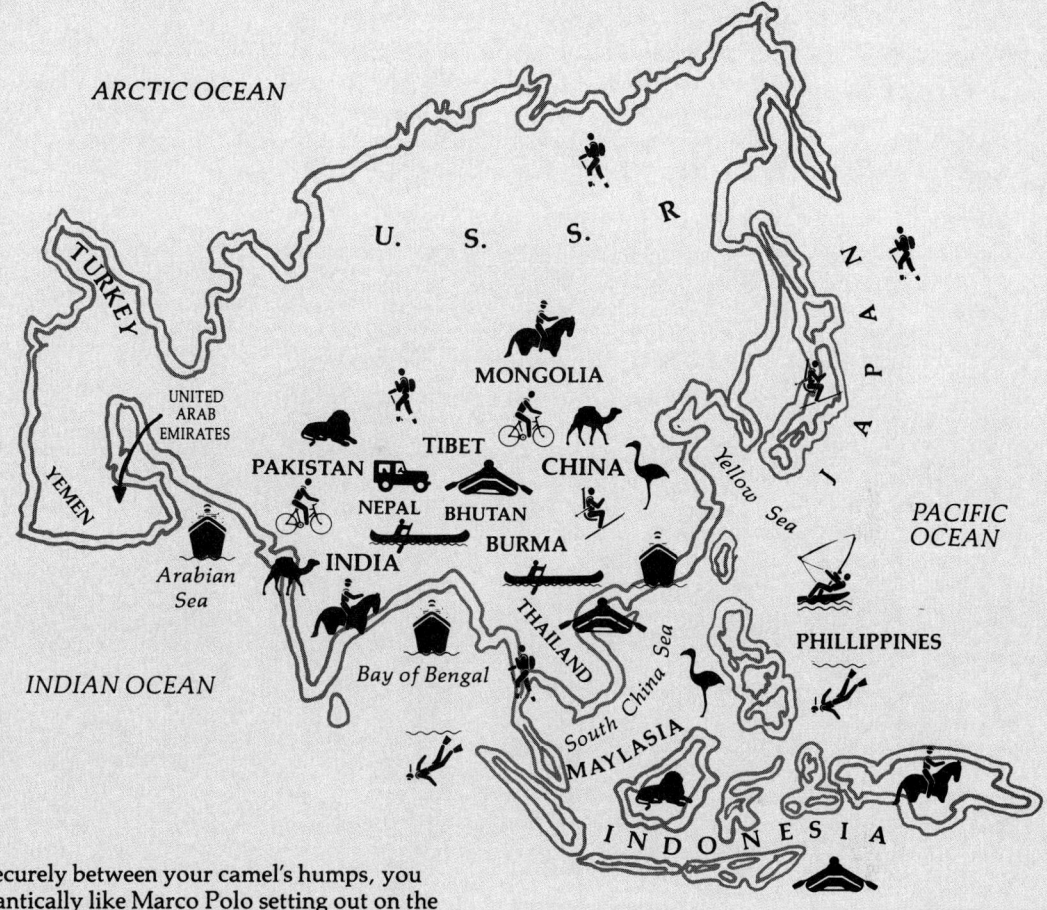

Seated securely between your camel's humps, you feel romantically like Marco Polo setting out on the Silk Route in Inner Mongolia. You *are* on the Silk Route, but Marco Polo you're not. You're a traveler, off on a grand guided adventure which you arranged back home with a single phone call.

There's so much to discover in this vast continent. Choose a cultural exploration—easy travel which takes you to temples, castles, monasteries, bazaars, pavilions, pagodas, tranquil gardens, scenic landscapes, and a wealth of art, crafts, jewels, silver, murals, mosaics, museums—and, if you are in China, to the life-sized terra cotta army in Xi'an.

In the Himalayas, treks graded from A (easy) to D (strenuous) lead you to spectacular views and friendly people. On some you can take the whole family. You'll feel pampered when your Sherpa guide brings steaming milk-tea to your tent at dawn.

For less pampering, cycle your way over mountain roads in Tibet, ride camelback across India's Thar desert or horseback in Inner Mongolia. In Thailand travel by train, bus, elephant, bamboo raft, ferry, express boat, and plane on a single journey through tribal hill country, jungle, and a tropical island.

On other trips—raft rivers, paddle a dugout canoe, relax Raj-style in an elegant houseboat, stop at a Bedouin camp, climb a high peak, or dive into the sublime beauty of a reef.

Whatever your choice, Asia presents a veritable kaleidoscope of adventure.

Shrines of Tibetan Buddhists in Nepal—*Steve Conlon for Above the Clouds, MA.*

BHUTAN

A WEEK IN DRUK YUL

Only 12 years ago the kingdom of Bhutan opened its doors to travelers. Today tourists can arrange journeys which center on the culture and beauty of Bhutan—known as "Druk Yul, the Dragon Kingdom." Its 18,000 square miles are tucked between Tibet, India, and Nepal. Flights depart Calcutta every Wednesday for Paro, a western valley, once the center of Tibetan trade routes. Dividing your stay between Paro and Thimphu, the capital, you visit dzongs (fortified monasteries), museums, handicraft centers, shops, temples, and dance performances.

Taktsang Monastery, known as the "Tiger's Den"—
Marie Brown for Bhutan Travel Service, NY.

Near Paro a cluster of monastery buildings known as the "Tiger's Den" cling at 10,000 feet to a sheer rock face. Getting there is unforgettable—by pony and footpath. In Thimphu the "Fortress of the Glorious Religion" is a memorable stop. It was originally built in 1641 and rebuilt 300 years later following the ancient tradition using no blueprints or nails. Its 100 rooms house the King's throne, government departments, and the nation's largest monastery. At the Handicraft Emporium you find Thankhas (Buddhist religious paintings), masks, baskets, and hand woven fabrics. Extraordinary in every way are the Royal Dance troupe's mask and folk dances—with music of conch shells, long horns, drums, cymbals, trumpets, and bells. It's a fascinating land—remote, beautiful, and amazingly easy to reach.

Year round, 8 days, $968-$1,150 + air. 1986 departures: Every Wednesday.

Bhutan Travel Service, 120 E. 56 St., Dept. AG, New York, NY 10022. (212) 838-6382.

BHUTAN
INDIA

BUMTHANG CULTURAL TREK

Wedged between India and Tibet, Bhutan, "The Land of the Peaceful Dragon," is the last of the tiny hidden kingdoms in the Himalayas to open its borders for visitors. Few westerners have been here. It's like entering another century from the moment you arrive in the small city of Paro.

Drive and hike to Tiger's Den, a monastery clinging tenaciously to the side of a cliff at 9,840 feet. Then continue to Thimphu (present capital), Punakha (old capital), and Jakar. Trek for eight days through the Bumthang region at a leisurely pace along the Chamkarchu River, past temples, soaring peaks, verdant valleys, cliff-hanging monasteries, yak herds, rhododendron forests. You meet natives in brilliant costumes, and cross Phephela Pass at 11,000' to see a 14th-century palace (Ugyenchoeling). Visit a temple where the mystic keys to the future are hidden! The tour includes overnights in India before and after Bhutan.

March-May, October-November, 23 days (from U.S.), $2,380 + air. 1986 departures: Mar. 8, Apr. 5, May 3, Oct. 4, Nov. 1.

Folkways International Trekking, Inc., 14903 S.E. Linden Lane-AT, Oak Grove, OR 97267. (800) 547-7400 or (503) 653-5882.

CHINA

FROLIC AT THE WATER FESTIVAL

Bring along your festive spirit and plenty of film on the 23-day tour covering China's more unusual paths and waters. First, meet in Hong Kong and tour Victoria Peak, Aberdee, and Tiger Balm Gardens. Then fly to Guangzhou, China's southern gateway, and on to Kunming, "City of Eternal Spring." In Xishuangbanna, take a boat ride on the Lanchang River and join in the Dai people's celebration of the New Year.

Return to Kunming for exploration of the legendary Stone Forest and a train ride through magnificent southern landscapes to the sacred Buddhist peak of Mt. Emei and to Leshan, home of the world's largest Buddha statue. Complete your tour with stops in Chongqing, famous for its spicy Szechuan cuisine, and in Xi'an, the former capital of imperial dynasties. Back to Beijing for visits to the Great Wall, Ming Tombs, the Summer Palace, then home.

April, 23 days (from San Francisco), $2,908 including air. 1986 departure: April 9.

Kuo Feng Tours, 15 Mercer St., New York, NY 10013. (800) 233-8087 or (212) 219-8383.

CHINA

EXPEDITION FOR BIRDERS

Nine species of pheasants, five partridges, 11 laughingthrushes, 10 parrotbills, 12 *Phylloscopus* warblers, several fulvettas, the Silver Oriole, Purple Cochoa, Gray-cheeked Liocichla, and Red-billed Leiothrix—a heady list of possible species for the alert birder to spot. Yet these and dozens of other exotic species may be seen in West China on this expedition on the eastern slopes of the Tibetan plateau.

Participants spend three weeks at the Dafengding and Wolong Panda Reserves in Szechuan, led by ornithologist/explorer Ben King who has spotted 1,860 species of birds during eight years in Asia. The trip involves camping and trekking as well as extensive tape recording. "We try to find all the species present rather than just skimming for the easy ones," King reports."Our trip list should be around 200 species. If exploration in magnificent surroundings is your idea of fun, here it is," he promises. The tour starts and ends in Hong Kong, with flights to and from Chengdu, the capital of Szechuan.

April-May, 30 days (from U.S.), $4,319 (including air from Hong Kong) + air from U.S. 1986 departure: Apr. 18. In 1987: Apr. 17.

King Bird Tours, P.O. Box 196, Planetarium Station, New York, NY 10024. (212) 866-7923.

CHINA

CYCLING THE LAND OF ETERNAL SPRING

Cycle a remote region positioned between Tibet and the rainforests of Burma, with a moderate climate earning Yunnan province the name "land of eternal spring." The route, filled with rock forests and tiny towns dotting the shores of small lakes, was researched and developed by China Passage with the help of Dr. John Israel, professor of Chinese History at the University of Virginia, and Tovya Wager of *Ms. Magazine*. Enter the long-isolated rural region of Dali, home to the Bai nationality. Pedal through its valley, once part of the Burma Road, nestled between snow-capped mountains and the deep blue waters of Erhai Lake.

Your Guilin/Yunnan cycling adventure begins in Beijing with time to visit the monuments of China's fascinating imperial past. From there, fly to Guilin, arguably one of the most beautiful spots on earth, memorialized by poets and artists. A 6-hour excursion down the Li River past sugar-loaf mountains, rice paddies, villages, and bamboo rafts. Riders of all ages take this trip, with a sagwagon to carry gear to evening retreats in guest houses and rustic shelters. Rent a bike or bring your own.

February & March, May, August, October, 23 days (from U.S.), $2,350 + air. 1986 departures: Feb. 6, March 20, May 1, Aug. 7, Oct. 2.

China Passage, 168 State St., Teaneck, NJ 07666-3516, (201) 837-1400.

CHINA

YANGTSE VALLEY BY BICYCLE, BOAT, TRAIN

See the favored Yangtse Valley tourist destinations a bit differently—via bicycle, boat, and train. Your 24-day journey (21 days in China) takes you through the "rice bowl" and the chain of ancient cities that first introduced silk, porcelain, and jade to the outside world.

Begin in Beijing. Pedal in heavy Chinese bicycle traffic through this city where early emperors allowed no building to be taller than the Temple of Heaven. Fly to Xi'an for a 3-day excursion where you see the 6,500 terra cotta soldiers of China's first emperor. Fly to the university city of Nanjing. See the vast Yangtse Bridge (western engineers said it couldn't be done!) before beginning your serious bike tour on rented Chinese-made "Forever" 10-speeds. Bike along the mighty river and through the countryside as far as the southern city of Suzhou, "the Venice of the East," with winding canals and beautiful gardens. Train to Shanghai, for a 3-day visit. See Western-style architecture for the first time in almost a month and cruise for an afternoon on one of the busiest harbors in the world.

Year round, 24 days (from U.S.), $2,150-$2,350 + air. 1986 departures: Mar. 26, Apr. 16, Apr. 30, May 19, May 26, Jun. 4, 18, & 26, Jul. 3, 10, 18, & 23., Aug. 1, 10, & 25., Sep. 3, 10, 17 & 24., Oct. 8, 22, & 29, Nov. 12.

China Passage, 168 State St., Teaneck, NJ 07666-3516, (201) 837-1400.

CHINA

BIRDWATCHING IN THE ORIENT

Pull out your binoculars, brush up on rare tropical south China birds, and get ready to feast your eyes on bulbuls, barbets, drongos, fulvettas, prinias, and many more. And birds aren't the

Grey Heron in Yunnan Province, China—*World Nature Tours, Inc.*, MD.

only creatures you encounter—you meet wildlife, plantlife, and interesting peoplelife as well.

Start with a short stay in Hong Kong, then hop a train to Guangzhou to sample the city's food. From here, fly to Hainan Island to visit nature reserves for three days. Fly back through Guangzhou to Guilin, where you view steep mountains from your Li River cruise boat. The best is yet to come—fly to Kunming to spend more than a week in Yunnan Province, the best birding area and perhaps one of the most beautiful. It's located near a large lake with lush, green mountains surrounding the entire plain. On to the borderland of little known Xishuangbanna for a look at some of the rare birds and to meet the minority peoples of modern China, then up to Beijing to view some rare manmade sights—Ming Tombs, Temple of Heaven, and the Great Wall—for three days. Bob Fleming Jr., an expert in Himalayan birds, leads your adventure.

May, 24 days, (from U.S.), $2,820 + air. 1986 departure: May 12.

World Nature Tours, Inc., P.O. Box 693-G, Silver Spring, MD 20901. (301) 593-2522.

CHINA

CYCLING TO THE GREAT WALL

See China the way the Chinese do—on a bike! Join thousands of locals as you pedal your way through Beijing. Both here and in countryside towns, two-wheel locomotion lets you explore twisting back lanes, stop for a quick lunch in a tiny tea and noodle shop, hunt for antiques at bargain prices, or pick up a juicy Chinese pear apple from the local fruit market. It's a personalized way to see China—and to make friends with English-speaking locals along the way.

After three days of sightseeing in Beijing—the sprawling Forbidden City, the magnificent Temple of Heaven, the Emperor's lakeside Summer Palace—travel 80 miles by bus for a 5-day cycling journey through the windswept countryside. You'll criss-cross the Great Wall en route to Beidaihe, a resort on the Bohai Sea where you share the surf with workers from Beijing. In the walled city of Shanhaiguan, see the end of the Great Wall as it dramatically disappears into the sea. Return by train to Beijing. Bilingual guides accompany riders and assist with repairs. A motorcoach carries the luggage and gives tired riders a lift. Bring your own bike or rent a Chinese "Forever" 10-speed.

May-October, 15 days (from U.S.), $1,650 + air. 1986 departures: May 1, Jun. 5, Jun. 19, Jul. 3, Aug. 21, Sep. 4, Sep. 25, Oct. 16.

China Passage, 168 State St., Teaneck, NJ 07666-3516, (201) 837-1400.

CHINA

AN ASIAN NATURE TOUR

Travel the great caravan route—the Silk Road—once China's main link to ancient India, Persia, and Rome, and discover a great assortment of eye-opening, mind-boggling wonders for nature and history lovers. Your 27-day journey, which begins in Beijing and ends in Shanghai, takes you to agricultural communes, market towns, rock quarries, the Nanshan grasslands, Northern Beijing Botanical Garden, the Imperial Gardens, the Turpan Oasis and its 2000-year-old irrigation system, and the Temple of Heaven set in a 667-acre park of pines and cypress. Take assorted field trips into the mountains and the desert, traveling by private motorcoach, minibus, four-wheel-drive vehicle, or rail. The cities along your route include Urumqi, Kashi, Jiayuguan, and Xi'an.

This exploratory tour may have some "rough spots," so be prepared to be flexible and to "rough it." Questers is noted for its special nature tours.

April, 27 days (from U.S.), $3,745 + air. 1986 departure: April 14.

Questers Tours and Travel, Inc., Dept. AG, 257 Park Ave. South, New York, NY 10010. (212) 673-3120.

CHINA

EASY CYCLING IN GUANGDONG PROVINCE

China's most popular mode of transport—*Tovya Wager for China Passage, NY.*

Board an overnight steamer in Hong Kong to sail for the South China port of Huangpu and the start of a biking excursion of northern Guangdong Province, a geographic and historic microcosm of the People's Republic. A leisurely pace allows for individual exploration. A sag wagon carries the gear. After cycling around the bustling city of Guangzhou (2 million population), set out for the countryside.

A figure-eight route on this "South China Supersaver" takes you from unspoiled highlands to rice paddies, canals, and hill country. Visit Foshan, a folk center known worldwide for its ceramics, and Xiqiao, a Daoist retreat from the Ming Dynasty, now incredibly updated with air conditioning and a disco. Pedal past the scenic Seven Star Crags and through the canal-laced Pearl River Delta where villages retain the flavor of ancient China. Back to Guangzhou for a loop past terraced hills to the fabled hot springs spa of Conghua (huge tubs fed by underground springs in each room) and on through lichee groves before the journey ends with a farewell banquet and a kaleidoscope of memories. "That freewheeling fling around Guangzhou was one of my most memorable rides," recalls one cyclist. "Like an exotic Five-Boro (New York) tour in a foreign world, with all the spectators riding along with us!"

Year round, 18 days (from U.S.), $1,325 + air; 5-day Beijing extension, $675. 1986 departures: Jan. 13, Feb. 17, Mar. 17, Apr. 7, Aug. 25, Sep. 22, Nov. 17, Dec. 8 & 22, Jan. 5 & 19.

China Passage, 168 State St., Teaneck, NJ 07666-3516, (201) 837-1400.

CHINA

RUN THE GREAT WALL

Runners take note! The China Sports Association and Kuo Feng Tours invite you for a run to the Great Wall—just for fun. And if racing satifies your competitive spirit, join runners from around the world—2,000 participated last year—on 3-mile and 6-mile runs on a boulevard in Jinan. Runners are feted at special pre- and post-race activities "which include a marvelous banquet and disco party," Kuo Feng explains, "and prizes are presented to winners in various age categories." Besides, everyone receives a specially designed Great Wall Run medal, a T-shirt, and a certificate. Bill Whiston and his excellent crew of running coaches will conduct running clinics.

For 14 days you wander through China—Shanghai, Suzhou, Hangzhou, Jinan, and Beijing. See ancient temples and palaces, explore world-famous gardens, cruise on West Lake, visit museums, homes, schools, work places, meet friendly people, enjoy acrobatic and musical performances, feast on meals that seem to go on forever, and go shopping. But the big highlight is the Great Wall—winding, undulating, in some places sloping at a 45-degree angle.

April, 14 days (from U.S.), $2,395 from San Francisco, $2,695 from NYC, including air. 1986 departure: Apr. 3.

Kuo Feng Corp., 15 Mercer St., New York, NY 10013. (800) 233-8687 or (212) 219-8383.

CHINA
JAPAN

SKI THE SLOPES OF TWO COUNTRIES

Enjoy challenging downhill skiing in two diverse countries with this winter sports program offered by China Passage. You have opportunities to cross-country ski, skate, and sled in the winter playgrounds of Asia, as well as visit the major cities and their cultural sites along the way.

Your first stop is Beijing where you may have a chance to ice skate on the Imperial Palace moat. Next, fly to Harpin, the capital of Heilongjiang Province, and partake in some of the city's winter sports—skating on the Songhua River, ice boating, and sledding. You may get the chance to participate in Harbin's Winter Festival, famous for its ice sculptures. Then, board a train for a scenic ride through the mountains to Yabuli, where you transfer to Qing Yun Ski Area. Though limited by U.S. standards (only one ski lift and one rope tow), Qing Yun offers spectacular challenges—runs with vertical drops as much as 884 meters and a peak elevation of 1,170 meters. There's a cross-country track and a set track as well. Return to Harbin and Beijing for short stops en route to Tokyo. Next morning, fly to Sapporo and shuttle to your ski site in the Tienne Highlands. Enjoy three days of fine skiing (by day or night) and plenty of night life. It would be wise to bring your own skis since rentals are available in Japan but not in China.

January & February, 16 days (from U.S.), $1,950 + air. Departures: Jan. & Feb.
China Passage, 168 State St., Teaneck, NJ 07666-3516, (201) 837-1400.

Join in a run to the Great Wall—*Mountain Travel, CA.*

CHINA
MONGOLIA

FOLLOW MARCO POLO

Camels are your means of transportation, yurts—traditional Mongolian felt tents—your abode, as you wend your way into the Gobi Desert, part of a 24-day trip that traces the path of Marco Polo. It's an adventurous, yet comfortably condensed, journey that starts out in Beijing. By train, plane, and jeep, venture into Inner Mongolia and the city of Hohhot. From there, embark on camelback for a desert oasis. On by train to Baotou, Datong, Taiyuan, and other exotic cities, before another camel trek and back to Beijing and home.

In a thorough visit to Beijing, tour the Imperial Palace, travel to the Great Wall, and see the Summer Palace, among other sights. In Mongolia, you encounter cultural and historical monuments of an otherworldly and mystical nature—temples and pagodas that house some of the world's largest lama communities, and Yunggang Buddhist caves—entire cities underground. You have a full day at the important Qin Dynasty Imperial Tomb excavations. On the camel caravan trips, you experience the austere majesty of the Gobi desert as you strike out for Hongge'er Oasis and Silk Road Oasis. All in all, it's a unique vantage point for a unique culture.

May, 24 days (from U.S.), $2,750 + air. 1986 departure: May 17.

Wind Over Mountain, Box 7190-AG, Boulder, CO 80306. (303) 444-8028; or (212) 219-2527 (New York Open Center).

CHINA
MONGOLIA

CARAVAN ON HORSEBACK

Experienced riders with a sense of adventure follow the caravan routes of Marco Polo on this journey through the wild and dramatic landscape of Inner Mongolia—across sandy steppes and past nomads still herding their livestock on horseback. Visit small settlment towns on the grasslands and stay in rustic accommodations, sometimes in yurts—the traditional tent-like homes of the region. The locals pamper you and let you experience the potent powers of fermented mare's milk.

Begin in Beijing, with visits to all the historic high spots. Then board a train (which may be headed all the way across Siberia) to the northern Chinese city of Datong, a Communist modern version of an ancient trading town, famous for the Yungang Caves and their 5th-century Buddist carvings. On to Hohhot, capital of Inner Mongolia, where your 8-day loop on horseback begins, visiting the well-known communities of E'erdun'aobao, Hongge'er, and Siziwangqui. A truck follows your caravan with baggage and supplies. From Hohhot, return by air to Beijing for one day of sightseeing, then home.

June, 21 days, (from U.S.), $2,800 + air. 1986 departure: Jun. 15.

Boojum Expeditions, Dept. A, Box 2236, Leucadia, CA 92024. (619) 436-3927.

ASIA

CHINA
TIBET

ART AND CULTURE

"The sights, the sounds, and even some of the smells keep returning like a whirling musical ball of color," recalls a traveler on this cultural visit in China and Tibet. Hank Baum, art gallery director and faculty member of the University of California-Berkeley/Extension, leads art enthusiasts on the tour which he calls "educational, exciting, and fun!"

Master ivory carver in Shanghai—*Hank Baum for Art Explorer's Tours, CA.*

In Shanghai, watch master craftsmen teach skills that used to be passed down from father to son—such as ivory and bamboo carving, doll and silk-flower making, and hand-knotting rugs. Then discover why Guilin, one of China's most beautiful places, has been a destination for artists and poets for more than 2,000 years. Cruise for five hours down the Li River past villages, lush farmlands, and scenic peaks. Explore Yangshuo at the end of the cruise, then drive back to Guilin and fly to Lhasa. Only 600 visas are issued each year by Tibet, making your week here very special. In Lhasa, visit the 1,000-room Potala Palace, last home of the Dalai Lama (now a museum), as well as temples, monasteries, and marketplaces cluttered with unusual "treasures". In bazaars you find heirlooms, silver, gemstones, turquoise, beaded ornaments. Take a yak-skin boat ride before leaving for Gyangze at 18,000 feet to see its famed White Pagoda. On a nine-day optional extension fly to Xi'an and Beijing.

> May, 16 days (San Francisco and return), $4,300 including air; extension, $1,095. (9 days.)
>
> Art Explorer's Tours, P.O. Box 26689-AT, San Francisco, CA 94126. (415) 921-7677.

CHINA
TIBET

TIBET AND THE YANGTZE RIVER

Cap off this cultural tour of China and Tibet with a cruise on the magnificent Yangtze River. In Beijing visit the Great Wall, Ming Tombs, and Summer Palace. Then on to Xi'an, the capital of China,

Sugar-loaf mountains on the lovely Li River, China—*Kuo Feng Tours, NY.*

and its archaeological rarities. Proceed to Chengdu, the gateway to Tibet. Among other sights, visit the Embroidery Factory, the cottage of the great Tang poet Du Fu, and the Dujiang Yan Irrigation Project.

Then on to Lhasa, capital of Tibet, known as "The Sunlight City." Here you have time to visit Potala Palace bordering Dragon King Lake, the 1,300-year-old Jokhang Temple, and the Drepong Monastery. There's also a side trip to Xigaze, seat of the Panchen Lama. Stop in Chongqing for some spicy Szechuan cuisine. In Wuhan, the site of the 1911 Revolution, you board your luxury liner *Emei*, and for five days glide along the river toward glorious Shanghai. Spend several days in this bustling city for shopping and sightseeing, then depart for home.

September, 26 days (from San Francisco), $4,670 including air. 1986 departure: Sep. 21.

Kuo Feng Tours, 15 Mercer St., New York, NY 10013. (800) 233-8687 or (212) 219-8383.

CHINA
TIBET

THE ART OF ASIA

Using art and archaeology as your focal points, delve into the cultures of China and Tibet. Under the leadership of Dr. Ronald M. Bernier, Professor of Art History at the University of Colorado, Boulder, this spirited 27-day tour introduces you to six major cities of China with four days devoted to Beijing, the cultural center and capital of The People's Republic of China.

Six days are spent in Tibet, first opened to travel in March, 1985. Absorb the images, sounds, and scents in the subtropical city of Guilin; travel down the Li River through the limestone-pinnacled landscape (described by poet Han Yu as "blue jade hairpins"); wander down Shanghai's crowded lanes and view the impressive art collection in its Museum of Art and History. Discover the life-sized terra cotta army of Xi'an, first uncovered by farmers in 1974. Learn how the silks and brocades of Chengdu were first used as tribute to emperors. Then on to Lhasa, your home base for the next week. One day a bus excursion takes you through rugged and mountainous country up to altitudes of 17,000 feet. Pass by Tibetan towns and hamlets, glaciers and waterfalls on your way to Shigatse, the historically famous and second largest city in Tibet. See the Great Wall and explore the Forbidden City on return to Beijing.

August, 27 days (from U.S.), $6,396 + air. 1986 departure: Aug. 16.

Discovery Tours, American Museum of Natural History, Central Park West at 79th Street, New York, NY 10024. (212) 873-1440.

CHINA
TIBET

WALKING ODYSSEY

From sublime monasteries to spectacular Stone Forests, this 25-day walking odyssey through Szechuan Province, southwestern China, and Tibet leaves you with an amazing first-hand acquaintance with faraway places. After visiting Hong Kong, fly to historic Chengdu, capital of the Szechuan Province. Bus to Leshan for a 3-day trek up the sacred Buddhist mountain of Omei (10,000'), then on to Lhasa, Tibet's fascinating capital for eight days. Continue to Kunming, in the Yunna Province (just above North Vietnam) and visit Canton before returning to Hong Kong for your flight home. All meals and overnight lodging are included.

Trek along trails and stone steps with Buddhist pilgrims as you climb the majestic mountainside headed toward sacred shrines. Visit a jade factory and shop in bustling bazaars for silks, rugs, and jewelry. Go biking in Chengdu, passing pavilions, pagodas, and colorful gardens. See the beautiful lakes and valleys as you hike through the Tibetan countryside on your way to temples atop mountain cliffs. An extraordinary glimpse of this exotic part of the Orient.

October, 25 days (from U.S.), $3,750 + air. 1986 departure: Oct. 15.

Boojum Expeditions, Dept. A, P.O. Box 2236, Leucadia, CA 92024. (619) 436-3927.

INDIA

RAJASTHAN—CARAVANS, CAVES AND PALACES

Explore India off the beaten trail in Rajasthan and the Thar Desert, where cities and towns remain unchanged since the days of the great camel caravans. Sleep in a palace on the edge of the desert (it's still occupied by members of the royal family!), explore the most fascinating bazaar in all India, and watch people at work on ghats floating on Lake Pichola—all part of this remarkable journey, a natural choice for return visitors to India.

Begin in Delhi—then it's "all aboard" the Taj Express Railway to Agra where you pay a sunset visit to the Taj Mahal. Other destinations: the pink city of Jaipur; the 34 Ellora Caves, with remarkable sculpture encompassing the three great religions of India; the Ajanta Caves with Buddhist paintings dating from 200 B.C., and the famous rock-cut temples (450-750 A.D.) of the Elephanta Caves. Also visit the fortress-city of Jodhpur and Udaipur, a cool oasis in the heart of this hot, arid region. Sightsee in Bombay before returning home. Inner Asia is committed to providing not just a holiday, but a total travel experience!

November-February, 15 days (from U.S.), $1,705 + international & domestic air. 1986 departures: Jan. 25, Feb. 8, Nov. 22. In 1987: Jan. 24, Feb. 7, Nov. 21.

Inner Asia, 2627 Lombard St.-AB, San Francisco, CA 94123. (800) 551-1769 or (415) 922-0448.

INDIA

A RAJ-STYLE SOJOURN

From New Delhi to the Vale of Kashmir to Ladakh to the Taj Mahal—this 22-day odyssey planned by Lute Jerstad, a foremost expert on the Himalayas, combines the great travel experiences of the entire region. Start with a New Delhi-to-Srinagar flight and relax Raj-style in an elegant houseboat. Paddle the canals in gondola-like shikaras to see the floating vegetable market and hear Kashmiri shouting. The following segment is an 8-day trek through gypsy villages, pine forests, and open meadows to the upper reaches of Dachigam Wildlife Sanctuary (about 12,000') before making the descent. Ponies carry heavy gear, and trekkers camp out each night before returning to Srinagar and the houseboat. The journey continues with an adventure-packed drive across the

Trekking in Ladakh in northern India—*Belinda Fuchs for Lute Jerstad Adventures International, OR.*

Himalayan Range to Ladakh and its capital city of Leh—an area opened to tourists only 12 years ago. Several days to explore the palace-museum, bazaars, monasteries. Fly back to Delhi for the climax—the Taj Express to Agra and the incomparable Taj Mahal.

June, 22 days (from U.S.), $1,995 + air. 1986 departure: Jun. 19.

Lute Jerstad Adventures International, P.O. Box 19537, Dept. A, Portland, OR 97219. (503) 244-6075.

INDIA

KASHMIR AND LADAKH BY JEEP

Stop jogging around the block! There's no real need to get in shape for this nontrekking introduction to the Himalayas. The 15-day (Grade A) tour begins in Delhi with a flight to Srinagar—Kashmir's mile-high capital—where you stay overnight on a deluxe Victorian houseboat. Travel by jeep over high passes to the Indus Valley for an 8-day venture into Ladakh.

Visit Lamayuru, a major Buddhist monastery, and Alchi, the art center of Ladakh. Finally, cross the dry, craggy landscapes to Leh—your home for several days. Explore and photograph the exotic local markets and monasteries at Hemis, Shey, and Stok before flying back to Srinagar. You can visit the Mogul Gardens and old mosques and bazaars, take an optional day trip to Gulmarg, or enjoy a water trek—then return to Delhi for your flight home.

June-August, 15 days (from U.S.), $1,350 + air. 1986 departures: Jun. 5, Jul. 3, Aug. 7. In 1987: Jun. 4, Jul. 2, Aug. 6.

Himalaya, Inc., 1802-E Cedar St., Berkeley, CA 94703. (415) 540-8031.

INDIA

BY AIR, ELEPHANT, COACH, CAMEL, TRAIN

In Rajasthan, fleet camels race in fierce competition across the sands at Pushkar. It happens every November at the Annual Camel Fair. Thousands of people from remote villages feverishly buy, trade, and sell their camels and cattle. Top off the day as the natives do—with a midnight dip in Pushkar Lake under a glistening full moon.

This is only one of the highlights of your stay in Rajasthan. From Delhi fly to Jaipur, and ride by elephant to view a lovely complex of forts and palaces. A camel transports you on a four-day safari through remote villages and across the Thar Desert. Meet ethnic groups, and see a plethora of wildlife and birds of prey. Time for more traditional sightseeing, too—to the Gajner Wildlife Sancturary, a camel breeding farm, the ornate havelis of Jain merchants in the 12th century, and colorful bazaars and splendid palaces in Jodhpur.

February & November, 21 days (from U.S.), $1,690 + air. 1986 departures: Feb. 15, Nov. 8.

Mountain Travel, 1398 Solano Ave., Albany, CA 94706. (800) 227-2384 or (415) 527-8100.

INDIA

THE FESTIVAL TREK

Join a stream of villagers at Hemis Gompa, richest of Kashmir's great monasteries, for the exotic, clamorous Hemis festival of the Tibetan Lamas—the highlight of this marvelous cultural and wilderness trek into the Himalayas (Grade C). It's a colorful, phantasmic affair—featuring bright masks, fantastic costumes, and dances accompanied by the music of clarinet-like shanai and 14-ft. trumpets.

Begin at Srinagar, capital of Kashmir, where you stay on a luxurious Victorian houseboat. Ride through arid mountainous landscape to Leh, captial of Ladakh, and explore local markets and monasteries. After the festival, trek for eight days to the base of the Stok-La, a 16,000'-pass, cross the rocky mountains of the Kunda-la Pass and down into the greener regions and the plains of Nimaling. All along the way, admire the panorama, meet the local people, and catch glimpses of the elusive Himalayan birds. Lucky trekkers may even spot the unusual blue sheep. The tour begins and ends in Delhi.

June, 25 days (from U.S.), $1,850 + air. 1986 departure: June 19. In 1987: Jun. 18.

Himalaya Inc., 1802-E Cedar St., Berkeley, CA 94703. (415) 540-8031.

INDIA AWAKENING AN ANCIENT MOUNTAIN KINGDOM

Zanskar—it feels like the magical kingdom of Camelot, with deep snows making the parched canyons impassable for all but a few months of the year. This Buddhist enclave is actually an ancient "kingdom" with its medieval architecture intact, its handsome people colorfully dressed, and two ceremonial monarchs still in

The remote Chenab Canyon in Kistwar, northern India—*Leo LeBon for the Mountain Travel, CA.*

residence. Your party (a maximum of 15) and its leader, camp manager, and pack animals, penetrate the region. Camp and hike for 18 days, mostly at heights over 10,000 feet.

You start out in Delhi, then fly to the Kulu Valley hill town of Manali (6,000'), and then drive to Darcha (11,000') for the start of the Grade C-3 trek. Hike up to Shingo La (16,700'), then begin a 2-week traverse across Zanskar. Follow twisting river gorges and rocky passes, and walk through high mountain villages to scenic campsites. Meet the Zanskari people along the way. Continuing through the arid landscape to Wanla and its apricot orchards, you wind up at the Lamayuru Monastery. Sightsee at the major monasteries at Leh, then fly to Srinagar and the luxury of a houseboat stay on Dal Lake before you return to Delhi and home.

June, 30 days (from U.S.), $2,090 + air. 1986 departure: Jun. 27.

Mountain Travel, 1398 Solano Ave., Albany, CA 94706. (800) 227-2384 or (415) 527-8100.

INDIA

KASHMIR FAMILY TREK

Hiking through scenic Kashmir on this 16-day adventure may claim top spot on your list of favorite family memories. Connect in Europe or Bangkok, then fly to Kashmir via Delhi. Start and end the itinerary with two days in colorful Srinagar. In between explore the beautiful Sind Valley on an easily-paced, 7-day (Grade 4) trek, where youngsters may take pony rides to rest—or just for fun.

The entire trip is filled with excitement and adventure. Walk to the edge of a glacier and traipse through meadows carpeted with wildflowers. Visit ancient villages and lavish temples. Learn local customs from the gypsies and nomadic shepherds you meet while crossing the Nichinai Pass (13,387'). Travel through the floating gardens and marketplaces in Karniri gondolas. There's ample time for swimming, waterskiing, and trout fishing. Nights, relax in deluxe houseboats or tent camps nestled near lakes and beneath the snow-capped Himalayan peaks. Enjoy a farewell Wazwan feast before returning to Delhi for your U.S. flight. Your family album will later confirm that it really happened.

June & July, 16 days (from U.S.), $1,090 + air. 1986 departures: Jun. 7, Jul. 1.

Wilderness Travel, 1760-AT Solano Ave., Berkeley, CA 94707. (800) 247-6700. (415) 524-5111.

INDIA

CITYLIFE AND WILDLIFE SAFARI

Only a few people in the world have seen the proud Bengal tiger. During four days at Tiger Haven, a wilderness resort, search for the tiger and view other animals native to northern India. Spot wildlife in Kanha National Park outside of Nagpur while staying at a Forest Lodge for two days. Later, focus your binoculars on brightly colored native birds at Baratpur's bird sanctuary. Relax that night at another Forest Lodge.

This wildlife-centered safari allows time also to experience the architecture and history of this crowded, colorful subcontinent. In Delhi, visit Parliament House and the cremation sites of Mahtma Gandhi, Nehru, and Indira Gandhi and in Agra the Taj Mahal. Excite your tastebuds with hot and hearty Indian cuisine and shop in the noisy, lively bazaars. Transportation is by minibus and by air, and comfortable accommodations are at hotels and lodges.

October-May, 14 days (from Seattle), $2,760 including air. 1986 departures: Every Monday.

Folkways International Trekking, Inc., 14903 S.E. Linden Lane-AT, Oak Grove, OR 97267. (800) 547-7400 or (503) 653-5882.

ASIA

INDIA

WESTERN HIMALAYA—IN DEPTH

Scholars, trekkers, and adventure lovers with a month to spare trace the mysteries of Lamaist Buddhism firsthand, visiting the rugged region of the Western Himalaya which has sheltered this faith for centuries. The journey begins with a special program of orientation to Tibetan arts, medicine, religion, and thought in Dharamsala. While there, you may be one of the few westerners to meet with Dalai Lama, head of the faith. Move on to Manali and

A Zanskari woman and child, India—
Piotr Kostrzewski for Cross Cultural Adventures, Inc., VA.

the valley of Lahoul, where you camp for the first night. Next day, begin your 12-day trek up to the 16,700' Shingo La pass and down into the hidden valley of Zanskar, the world's highest inhabited land, stopping at Phuctal Gompa, a honeycomb monastery, and Karsha, this Kingdom's largest monastic city. At Padum, an overland vehicle takes you into Ladakh and its ancient Buddhist sites, including majestic Rangdum and 1,000-year-old Lamayuru, and on to cultural and religious centers of the upper Indus Valley. Then, hop a plane for Srinagar where you transfer to houseboats on Kashmir's Lake Dal to soak up the sun and shop in the bazaars. Back to Delhi for flight home. (Limited to 10 people.)

August, 31 days (from U.S.), $2,200 + air. 1986 departure: Aug. 1. In 1987: July 31.

Cross Cultural Adventures, Inc., P.O. Box 3285, Arlington, VA 22203. (703) 532-1547.

INDIA

THE LAND OF RAJAS

"India—a land of incredible contrasts in culture, religion, art, landscape, and ideas—is heady stuff," Sven Lindblad of Special Expeditions observes. For this journey he chooses Rajasthan, the "Land of the Rajas" in northwestern India. It's a mixture of the unyielding Thar Desert, the bleached countryside, a fantasyland of palaces and forts, of pink and white turbans, of special lodgings which only India could hide from the world. The 21-day sojourn is an exhilarating exploration of an enchanting region, with many nights spent in former palaces, and excellent leaders to bring balance and insight to each day's travel.

Start in beautiful Delhi, then fly to Udaipur, "the Vale of Serenity," and Jodhpur, gateway to the desert. The Maharaja's private train transports you to the magical walled city of Jaisalmer. Other highlights: Mandawa in the Shekhavati region—a profusion of fresco paintings; Jaipur, the pink city, capital of Rajasthan; Ronthambhor Game Sanctuary; Agra and its glorious Taj Mahal; and temples, palaces, castles, wind pavilions, mansions, latticework facades, winding streets, a wealth of art, color, jewels, silver, murals, mosaics, museums, miniatures, marble—a kaleidoscope of beauty.

February-March, October-December; 21 days (from U.S.), $3,240 + air. 1986 departures: Feb. 3, Feb. 28, Sep. 12 & 26, Oct. 9 & 31, Nov. 28., Dec. 12.

Special Expeditions, Dept. AG, 720 Fifth Ave., New York, NY 10019. (800) 762-0003 or (212) 765-7740.

INDIA
NEPAL

INDIA'S WOMEN

This in-depth, 20-day tour offers an intimate look at the status of women on the Indian subcontinent. Meet a broad spectrum of women—midwives, weavers, social workers, artists, students, legal and medical professionals. Perhaps enjoy a visit with Mother Teresa in Calcutta. Indian women from several professions join you for dinner and lively discussions. See the classic sights as well: Taj Mahal, Rajasthan's palaces and the Himalayas. Delhi, Agra, Jaipur, and Bombay are among the cities you visit. Travel by boat, bus, train, plane, and even elephant. Spend overnights in deluxe and first class hotels.

Gretel Goldsmith, the founder of Odyssey Tours, is your guide. American by birth, she lived in an extended Indian family, later spent 10 years in the U.S. women's movement, and offers unique insight into the country.

February-March, September-December, 21 days (from U.S.), $3,240 + air. 1986 departures: Feb. 3, Feb. 28, Sep. 12 & 26, Oct. 9 & 31, Nov. 28, Dec. 12.

Odyssey Tours, 1821 Wilshire Blvd., Santa Monica, CA 90403. (800) 654-7975 or (213) 453-1042.

INDIA
NEPAL

BIRDING IN ASIA

In the company of Ben King, renowned author of *A Field Guide to the Birds of Southeast Asia* (and currently working on an Indian bird guide), you explore some of the world's richest birding regions. The tour in north India is three weeks, with a 10-day extension in Nepal. Accommodations are in comfortable sanctuary-side lodges and hotels. The tour starts in Delhi and moves on to Keoladeo National Park (Bharatpur), Kanha, Kaziranga, and other famous sanctuaries, with 11 days in deciduous and thorn forests, plains, and high deserts, and 10 days in tropical rainforests and river regions. Expect to sight Siberian Cranes, Great Indian Bustards, Bengal Floricans, three species of sandgrouse, and hundreds more.

The Nepal excursion ranges from the Himalayan foothills around Kathmandu to the subtropical forests of the terai at Tigertops. Count on seeing the Kalij Pheasant, Red-naped Ibis, Great Thick-knee, and many others. "Your total bird list should be over 500 species on this excursion," says King. "You should also see tiger, elephant, and Indian rhinoceros."

January-February, 21 or 31 days, about $140/day. 1987 departure: North India, Jan. 2; Nepal, Jan. 25.

King Bird Tours, P.O. Box 196, Planetarium Station, New York, NY 10024. (212) 866-7923.

INDIA
THAILAND

Rajasthan camel safari, India— Mountain Travel, CA.

TREKKERS IN KASHMIR

Easy trekking (Grade B-2) in Kashmir combines with other Asian highlights on this 16-day sojourn. Start in Bangkok with boating on the klongs and a day to visit the Grand Palace and the Golden, Reclining, and Emerald Buddhas in their respective temples. Then a stopover in Old Delhi before flying to Srinagar and the Vale of Kashmir—a delightful life, Raj-style, in a Victorian houseboat on

Dal Lake. An easy 5-day camping trek takes you through flowery meadows, alpine hills populated by nomadic herders, over a 10,000'-pass, and back through Kashmiri villages for another night of houseboat luxury. Boat people serenade you that evening with folk songs.

During four more days you see the sights of Delhi; drive to Agra to view the Taj Mahal by day—and perhaps by moonlight; visit the abandoned 15th century capital, Fatephur Sikri; and in Jaipur ascend to Amber Palace, a 12th century fortress, on elephantback! Additional stops in Delhi and Bangkok, then home.

May-September, 16 days (from U.S.), $2,690 including air from Seattle; from Dallas, $2,920. 1986 departures: May 10, Jun. 5, Jul. 7, Aug. 2 & 30, Sep. 27.

Mountain Travel, 1398 Solano Ave., Albany, CA 94706. (800) 227-2384 or (415) 527-8100.

INDONESIA

A JAUNT IN JAVA

You're the center of attention on this 22-day tour that takes *you* to remote Indonesian villages (four islands all told) where U.S. citizens create a stir. The tribes and treasures you meet along the way will stir you as well.

First, fly through Taipei to Jakarta, Java, where you pack your mountain clothes for a pony trek through shifting sands to the summit of Mt. Bromo. Then fly to the walled town of Tenganan in Bali for a visit with the aborigines. See the earthy robust dancing that Bali is famous for, hear its exquisite music, and visit Denpasar, its capital. On to Wamena in the highlands of Irian Jaya (the Indonesian side of west New Guinea), where tribes still live a stone-age existence. On Sulawesi (the former Celebes), where people's houses look like the front of ships, you take trips to curious, unique villages way off anyone's idea of the "beaten track." You also take a 3-hour hike to meet the Soka tribe and the famed smoked mummy. Later, greet Kurulu, chief of the Jiwika confederation. Still to come: the cliff tombs at Lemo, the burial caves at Londa, and stays in tribal homes. Fly to Yogyakarta for visits to famous temples and royal graves. Finally, back to Jakarta to swim, shop, relax, and pack for the flight home.

June, 23 days (from U.S.), $4,200 + air. 1986 departure: Jun. 15. In 1987: Jun. 14.

Capers Club 400, P.O. Box 5489, Beverly Hills, CA 90210. (213) 657-0916.

INDONESIA

RIVER OF THE RED APE

Meet the "man of the forest"—the rare wild orangutan—one of mankind's closest relatives. He's just one of the hairy highlights on this two-week adventure that takes you down the magnificent Alas River on the island of Sumatra. The trip begins in Medan, ventures into the interior highlands of Sumatra and Gunung Leuser National Park. Also known as the "East Africa of Asia," Gunung Leuser harbors elephant, tiger, rhino, leopard, and of course, the great orangutan. You also spend five days on inflatable rafts

The Alas, "River of the Red Ape"—*Bart Henderson for SOBEK Expeditions, Inc., CA.*

floating through Fantastique Gorge with its limestone canyons, cascading crystal waterfalls, and safe but exciting rapids. Camp in the gorge and on beaches, and bathe in the waterfalls.

All this, and there's still time to explore the arts, crafts, and architecture of Samosir Island. Your last day, return to Medan for a farewell dinner. If you'd like to continue your travels, Sobek offers Alas extensions to Bali, Komodo Island, or a combination of the two.

June, August, October, 14 days, $1,570 + air. 1986 departues: Jun. 6, Aug. 14, Oct. 3.

SOBEK Expeditions, Inc., Box AG, Angels Camp, CA 95222. (209) 736-4524.

JAPAN

A TRICKY TREK IN THE KITA ALPS

Don't let the elevation fool you! "Though we never go above 10,000 feet, this trek in the Kita Alps is more difficult and strenuous than trekking in Nepal," warns Smoke Blanchard, your leader with 20 years travel and study experience in Japan. The trek (Grade C) is longer and more remote than standard routes (be prepared to put up with occasional cold, wind and rain), but the rewards are great: magnificent vistas, green alpine meadows, and deep gorges.

Arrive in Tokyo and travel by rail and bus to Murodo, where you trek to your first yamagoya or mountain inn. Sleep the way the locals do, on futons, then start your climb to the summit of the sacred peak Tateyama. You spend 13 days trekking, eating Japanese cuisine, staying in mountain inns. Optional climbs are arranged on such non-technical but challenging peaks as Yari, or "Spear Peak in the Clouds," and Tsurugi. Reward yourself for a job well done with some sightseeing at the end of the trail, visiting historic Kyoto and the sacred deer park of Nara. Return to Tokyo for some shopping, before departing for home.

August-September, 21 days, (from U.S.), $1,975 + air. 1986 departure: Aug. 9. In 1987: Aug. 8.

Above the Clouds Trekking, P.O. Box 398-V, Worcester, MA 01602. (800) 233-4499 or (617) 799-4499.

JAPAN

A RAMBLE THROUGH THE ALPS

This 16-day (Grade 3) ramble is a non-traditional tour of a very traditional country. (Don't expect to see any other westerners along

Mountain hut in the Japan Alps—*Jim Wills for Guides for All Seasons, CA.*

the way!). You stay in local inns, eat Japanese-style, treat yourself to a nightly ofuro—the native bath—and sleep ever so peacefully on your futon covered with a cozy pile of quilts. Travel at your own pace, choosing winding paths or more arduous peaks that may require mountain climber's crampons and ice axes. Shelter for resting and eating is always nearby.

The journey through the culture and life of Japan begins with two days in ultra-modern and ultra-safe Tokyo. Also spend two days in the scenic Fuji Five Lakes region, where you can climb Mt. Fuji—actually an easy walk done by thousands each year—if weather permits. After the Alps trek, depart for ancient Kyoto where you can visit temples, palaces, and gardens. Or plan day excursions to other cities such as Osaka, Nara, and Kobe.

May-October, 16 days (from U.S.), $1,395 + air. 1986 departures: May 10 & 24, Jul. 19, Sep. 20, Oct. 4. In 1987: May 9 & 23, Jul. 25, Sep. 19, Oct. 3.

Guides For All Seasons, P.O. Box 97-AG, Carnelian Bay, CA 95711. (800) 457-4574, (916) 583-8475 or (916) 583-7797.

JAPAN

A POWDERED PARADISE

Ski the Alps with stark white mountains, bright blue skies, and snow-capped volcanoes just over your shoulder. It's a magnificent sight, one that makes skiing in this country particularly exhilarating. Two different 11-day packages are offered. Choose from Happo-one in the Chubu-Sangaku National Park with 28 lifts. Or take a "ski safari" at Zao Onsen in Zao Quasi National Park, a resort with seven peaks served by 31 ski lifts and cable cars. Both start off with two days of sightseeing in Tokyo, five days (and nights) of skiing, and end with two days for relaxation in Tokyo. Daily lift passes are included.

After a long day on the slopes, return to your Minshuku, the traditional inn. Shed your skis and slip into house sandals and a yukata robe, shuffle down the hall and soak in a steaming hot tub. Evenings, dine on local delicacies. Finally, plunge onto your futon mattress smothered in down quilts.

February, 11 days, $1,095-$1,125 + air. 1986 departures: Feb. 1 & 22. In 1987: Jan. & Feb. Every Week.

Off the Deep End Travels, P.O. Box 7511-F, Jackson, WY 83001. (800) 223-6833 or (307) 733-8707.

JAPAN

MOUNTAINS, HAMLETS, AND TEMPLES

From the magical, forested trails of the Kita Alps to the rich cultural heritage of Kyoto, Japan is a rare cultural and natural history experience. With fellow Japanese walkers, hike in the North Alps to majestic views of Japan's major peaks. In the Takayama countryside, see local craftsmen at work—carvers, sakemakers, and potters. In Kyoto, explore the temples, gardens, and shogun palaces.

Travel as the Japanese do, staying in traditional ryokans (guest houses) which feature futons, sweet-smelling tatami mats, soaks in traditional hot tubs, tea service, and a delectable Japanese cuisine. In October, the landscape is a rich palate of maples and birches. Include visits to Mt. Fuji and Tokyo. No hiking experience required. Optional rigorous day hikes for avid hikers.

June & September, 16 days (from U.S.), $2,520 including air. 1986 departures: May 31, Sep. 27.

Wilderness Journeys, Box 807-AG, Bolinas, CA 94924. (415) 868-1836.

JAPAN

CAPTURING CULTURE AS YOU CYCLE

The history and magic of the orient unfolds as you pedal along the backroads of this Asian wonderland. This 15-day bicycle tour takes you to feudal towns of ancient Japan with their castles and temples of olden days, to tranquil gardens of rock and water, past farmhouses set in rice paddies, to steaming hot streams where you sit and soak. With arrival and departure in the teeming metropolis Tokyo, the cycling tour begins in Takayama and ends in Nikko. Other highlights: a visit to historic Takayama and the spa towns of Bessho Onsen and Kusatsu, the Crow Castle in Matsumoto, a roll down the shores of scenic Lake Chuzenji, a thrilling ride down the hairpin turns into Nikko.

Stay in a Minshuku, the traditional inn, complete with rice paper walls, tranquil gardens, and Japanese-style baths. All trips are designed to coincide with local festivals—Takayama Float Festival (April), Lake Chuzenji Floating Lantern Festival (July), and Toshugu Shrine Grand Festival (October).

April, July, October, 15 days, $1,425 + air. 1986 departures: Apr. 12, Jul. 19, Oct. 4.

Off the Deep End Travels, P.O. Box 7511-F, Jackson, WY 83001. (800) 223-6833 or (307) 733-8707.

Cyclists in Kyoto—
Off the Deep End Travels, WY.

JAPAN

OF CLIMBS AND KIMONOS

Combine culture with exercise on this 19-day hiking adventure. Spend three days in Tokyo, four days in Sapporo, two days in Kyoto and Nara, and seven to nine days hiking in the northern island of Hokkaido and climbing Mt. Fuji. It's less strenuous than a trek in Nepal, but you still need to be active-minded and physically fit.

Along the way, you learn about the people, culture, and landscape of the country. Some of the trip's highlights: hiking in the volcanically active Japanese Alps and climbing the volcano of Mt. Fuji with thousands of local climbers and pilgrims. With luck, you witness the inspiring dawn ceremony at the 12,338' summit. The accommodations are part of your cultural education—you stay in a "ryokan" or Japanese guest house. Slip out of your shoes, into a kimono, and experience the overwhelming hospitality of this Asian land.

July, 19 days (from U.S.) $2,694 including air + some meals. 1986 departures: Sep. 15, Jul. 15.

World Adventure Travel/Tenzing Treks U.S.A., 2836-78th S.E., Mercer Island, WA 98040. (206) 232-2700.

MALAYA BORNEO

BIRDING IN SOUTHEAST ASIA

For a first birding trip in Asia, renowned ornithologist, Ben King, (author of *A Field Guide to the Birds of Southeast Asia*) considers Malaysia the ideal place. "The birding is superb, the accommodations and food good to excellent, facilities modern, and roads and transportation very good," he says. "The people are friendly and helpful, and the distances from hotels to birding areas are short." The tour begins and ends in Singapore.

In the rainforests birders will see over 350 species of birds, many new to their life lists. Among the exotic and colorful birds are pheasants, hornbills, trogons, pittas, barbets, green pigeons, fruit-doves, hanging parrots, drongos, bee-eaters, minivets, and flowerpeckers, to name a few. On the trip in Borneo you may see orangutans as well as beautiful butterflies (the exquisite Rajah Brook's Birdwing is one), flying lizards, pitcher plants. Be prepared for strange and wonderful noises from birds, mammals, frogs, insects, and lizards.

July-August, 17 or 31 days (from U.S.), $4,420 + air. 1986 departures: Malaya, Jul. 18; Sabah (Borneo), Aug. 4.

King Bird Tours, P.O. Box 196, Planetarium Station, New York, NY 10024. (212) 866-7923.

MALAYSIA

SAILING FROM SINGAPORE

The long, narrow Malay Peninsula, jutting southeasterly from Thailand, separates the Andaman Sea from the South China Sea. From Singapore, at its tip, one can cruise up the seldom-visited east coast of Malaysia, dotted with beaches, bays, rivers and timeless villages. Or explore the west coast through the Strait of Malacca, putting in at Penang, beautiful Phuket Island, an old Portuguese settlement on the Spice Islands route.

This spectacular cruising may be arranged any time of year on a fully-crewed charter basis. Vessels accommodate from four to eight participants. They are scuba equipped (at an extra charge), and skippers are experts in knowing where to sail for the best dive sites.

Year round, any number of days, $125-$175 per day per person.

Ocean Voyages, Inc., 1709 Bridgeway, Sausalito, CA 94965. (415) 332-4681.

MONGOLIA

CYCLING THE ANCIENT "WINDING ROAD"

Launched in 1983 as the world's first cycling excursion into Mongolia, the route circles the Ordos region, homeland of the pre-Mongol Huns and was the base for Genghis Khan's 13th century conquest of China. You follow a segment of the ancient caravan route known as the "Winding Road," charted by the British explorer Owen Lattimore in 1926.

Begin the journey in Beijing and the trading town of Datong, where you visit the Yungang caves, a monumental depository of 5th-century Buddhist carvings. Then go by train to Hohhot, capital of today's Inner Mongolia Autonomous Region, to start the 12-day cycling trip. Pedal across a pristine natural wilderness and grasslands where nomads still wander. Spend nights in yurts (felt tents), live among local tribes and pastoral communities, and sample Mongolian hot pot and mare's milk. On the unique excursion, you cycle about 310 miles on 15-speed, all-terrain mountain bikes (or you may bring your own), before returning to Beijing.

May-September, 24 days (from U.S.), $2,350 + air. 1986 departures: May 22, Jun. 26, Aug. 14, Sep. 4.

China Passage, 168 State St., Teaneck, NJ 07666-3516, (201) 837-1400.

NEPAL

A HIMALAYAN SAFARI

This 20-day journey offers a delightful kaleidoscope of activities—trekking along seldom-explored Himalayan trails, rafting to remote villages, and exploring the jungles and plains of Royal Chitwan National Park in the hope of spotting a rare Bengal tiger or one-horned rhino.

Begin with sightseeing in Kathmandu where you dodge buffalo, bicycles, and cattle on streets that still reflect much of ancient Asia. Then travel by minibus to Gorkha, Nepal's ancient capital, and the trailhead for your 9-day trek. Once in the wilderness, you rise early, greeted by the morning sunrise. Cover four to eight miles per day. Trek into a river valley and push higher into the mountains (reaching altitudes up to 13,000 feet), watch for barking deer, owls, and rare mush deer. At the end of the second week, take a short raft trip down the Trisuli River—warm even in winter. Then on to the jungle lodge in Chitwan, where gamespotting is done on elephantback and in dugout canoe, and where local Tharu boys often stop to perform their formidable stick dance. Your last day in Kathmandu is free, so you can spend your last "rupees" in the Old Bazaar.

September-March, 20 days (from U.S.), $1,245 + air. 1986 departures: Feb. 2, Mar. 7, Sep. 27, Nov. 15, Dec. 4. In 1987: Feb. 1, Mar. 6, Sep. 26, Nov. 14, Dec. 3.

Journeys International, Box 7545-AG, Ann Arbor, MI 48107. (313) 665-4407.

Nepalese market—
Will Weber for Journeys International, Inc., MI.

NEPAL

A HIMALAYAN PILGRIMAGE

Experience the Buddhist cultures of Nepal as you visit remote monasteries and sacred sites on this 16-day (Grade 3) trek in the Mt. Everest area of the Himalayas. You learn about the Sherpa culture through the vision of Buddhist monks and lamas, particularly through your trek leader Topkhay, a Buddhist monk for 24 years. Join chanting sessions with monks or nuns, or meditate on your own in natural environments.

Fly from Delhi or Bangkok to Kathmandu, where you explore the town of Tatopani along the way. Continue down to the floor of the Kalindaki Valley enveloped in rhododendrons and terraced hillside fields. Return to Kathmandu and home.

April & October, 31 days (from U.S.), $1,650 + air. 1986 departures: Apr. 3, Oct. 25. In 1987: Apr. 2, Oct. 24.

Himalaya Inc., 1802-E Cedar St., Berkeley, CA 94703. (415) 540-8031.

NEPAL

A JOURNEY 'ROUND ANNAPURNA

Each place is unique in its landscape and people, and David Christopher of Folkways urges travelers to look for that special "spirit of place" wherever they go. On his Annapurna journey you become vividly aware of tumbling glaciers, sky-high summits, gleaming ice walls, and the Sherpas who live amid this beauty. The 30-day itinerary includes flying to Kathmandu via Bangkok or Delhi, then driving to Gorkha to start the trek, Grade C-3.

Walk up the lush valley of the Marsyandi river and through a gorge walled by peaks rising to over 20,000 feet. In the Manang Valley you meet traders of Tibetan origin whose villages are clusters of medieval stone dwellings. Cross over the Annapurnas and descend past terraced hillsides and rhododendron groves to end the trek in Pokhara. Then back to Kathmandu and home.

March-May, October & November, 30 days (from U.S.), $1,590 + air. 1986 departures: Mar. 29, May 3, Oct. 4, Nov. 1.

Folkways International Trekking, Inc., 14903 S.E. Linden Lane-AT, Oak Grove, OR 97267. (800) 547-7400 or (503) 653-5882.

NEPAL

AROUND ANNAPURNA

Never retrace a step on this 3-week trek (Grade 4) around Annapurna, where diverse topography and a variety of local cultures greet you at every turn in the road. Led by Sherpas and accompanied by a team of porters, travel past subtropical Dumre through several climate zones to the Thorong Pass at 17,700 feet and back down to the holy Kali Gandaki River.

Days begin early here—with steaming milk-tea delivered to your tent in the crystal-clear dawn. Each day's walk holds surprises as you hike along narrow winding paths, established as trade routes centuries ago, and climb endless trails of stone steps, passing landscapes decorated with prayer flags and dripping rainforests. Interact with local children and sometimes fall into step with donkey traffic along the wider roads. Your journey begins and ends in Kathmandu, where you select luxury or economy hotels.

April, October, 32 days (from U.S.), $997 + hotel/meals Kathmandu + air. 1986 departures: Apr. 3, Oct. 25. In 1987: Mar. 7.

Guides For All Seasons, P.O. Box 97-AG, Carnelian Bay, CA 95711. (800) 457-4574, (916) 583-8475 or (916) 583-7797.

NEPAL

CIRCLING THE ANNAPURNA

Cross five life zones—from high desert and snow forests to

sunny subtropics—on this trek around the Annapurnas. By landrover you leave the candle-lit backstreets and medieval architecture of Kathmandu and travel through hill country and terraced farmland to the village where your trek begins. It's a magnificent walk around this incredible mountain range. Your trail

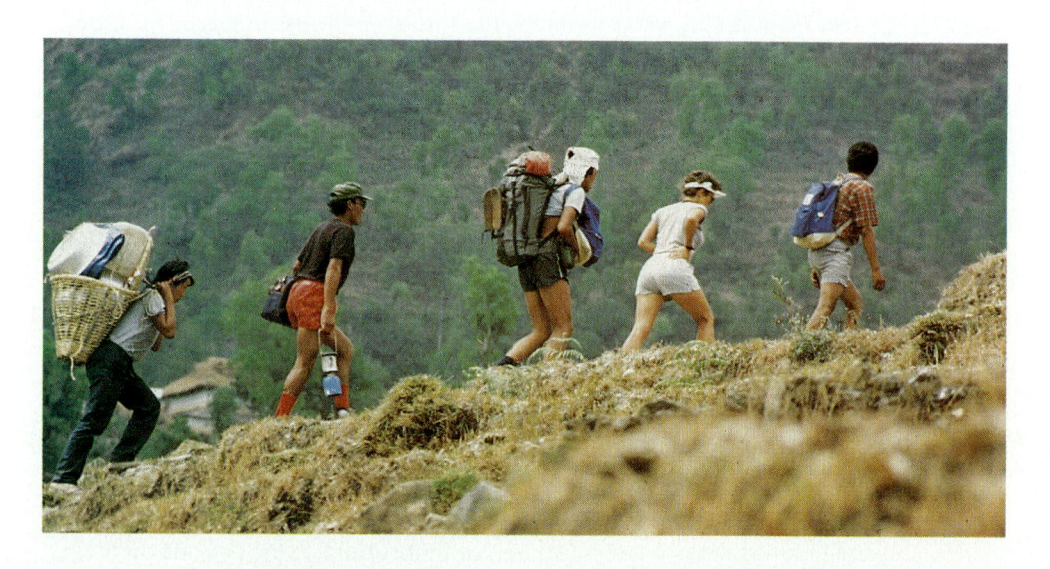

Trekkers in the Annapurna region of Nepal—Fran Sherpa for Himalayan Excursions, TX.

crosses the Thorung La Pass at 17,771 feet and leads to the village of Muktinath, a holy site for both Hindus and Buddhists. Peer into the Kali Gandaki Gorge, deepest in the world—a breathtaking experience—and continue down to subtropical rhododendron forests and hot springs. Ang Kaji Sherpa (a head guide for 10 years, and before that with Mountain Rescue in Austria) and his American wife Fran operate both scheduled and custom treks, September through May, and lead many themselves. "Our goals are a fun trek and meaningful cultural exchange," Fran reports, "and we specialize in quality food and equipment. We personally know and hire each member of our staff." Comments a trekker from San Francisco, "Well organized from the top down…The Sherpa disposition of warmth, caring and spontaneity were everpresent…Ang Kaji is a recipient of a Hilary Scholarship for excellence."

October & May, 29 days, $1825 + air. 1986 departures: Oct. 7 & Mar. 4.

Himalayan Excursions, P.O. Box 11204, Midland, TX 79702. (915) 682-9565.

NEPAL

FAMILIES WHO TREK TOGETHER

Even a 2-year-old can come along on this trek, (Grade B-2), carried by a friendly porter. The close-knit Sherpas and their children are fascinated to meet "foreign" youngsters. Itineraries vary depending on how adaptable the children (or their parents) prove to be. Although the schedule is relaxed, the trek requires hikers who can function in altitudes above 10,000 feet. Porters (two for each trekker) make it easy by carrying the camping and personal gear and preparing the meals.

Starting with a day or so in Kathmandu, you fly to Lukla at 9,300 feet and from there circle into the Khumbu region (near Everest) for nine days. Meet the people in Sherpa villages, visit a Sherpa market town and monasteries, descend into the Dudh Kosi gorge, and have rest days as needed. Even here civilization intrudes. One village boasts a UNESCO-sponsored hydroelectric plant and two 40-watt bulbs in each house! April is springtime in Nepal, with crisp morning air, snow-dappled forests, and rhododendron in full bloom. Back in Lukla, with luck you'll catch a flight to Kathmandu—or wait a day or so for the unpredictable plane to arrive.

April, 19 days (from U.S.), $1,570/adult, $695-$785/child. 1986 departure: Apr. 2.

Mountain Travel, 1398 Solano Ave., Albany, CA 94706. (800) 227-2384 or (415) 527-8100.

NEPAL

CYCLING ON TOP OF THE WORLD

This 18-day cycling journey (Grade B) through the foothills of the Himalaya offers world-class leadership and some of the finest scenery on the planet. Led by Olympic bronze medalist Ron Kiefel and his cyclist wife, you have the choice of getting instruction in speed and distance techniques, or just rolling along at your own speed. During the seven days on the bikes, you cover up to 40 miles a day, pedaling past terraced rice fields and quaint villages backdropped by the soaring Himalaya.

The terrain is relatively gentle, following river roads and varying from flat to rolling, with only an occasional 'monster hill.' In between cycling stints you make two short treks, have a day of whitewater rafting on the Sun Kosi River, and sightsee in the historic Kathmandu Valley. You also may do some swimming and boating in Pokhara's Phewa Lake, in the shadow of Annapurna. A sagwagon accompanies the cyclists. Nights are spent at tented camps, hotels, and mountain lodges.

December, January, 18 days (from U.S.), $1,775 + air. 1986 departure: Jan. 2, Dec. 18. In 1987: Jan. 1.

Above the Clouds Trekking, P.O. Box 398-V, Worcester, MA 01602. (800) 233-4499 or (617) 799-4499.

NEPAL

FOR TREKKERS AND CLIMBERS

This challenging trek (Grade D) into the Langtang National Park, with an optional ascent of 18,044' Yala Peak, is scheduled in springtime with the rhododendrons in riotous bloom. The area is rich in wildlife and flora. Your guide is the experienced Lopsang Sherpa, a native of the Solu Khumbu District of Nepal and a 19-year trekking veteran whose five languages include excellent English.

After several days in Kathmandu, begin the 19-day trek in the Trisuli River lowlands, moving along the river and eastward into pristine, dense forests. Climbers establish two camps above Kanjin

Gompa in preparation for the summit day. Nonclimbers take side trips while the climb is in progress. The return route via the Gosainkund Lakes follows ridge tops back to Sundarijal. Another visit in Kathmandu before returning home.

April-May, 27 days (from U.S.), $945 + hotel/meals Kathmandu, + $135 for climb, + air. 1986 departure: May 3. In 1987: Apr. 4.

Guides For All Seasons, P.O. Box 97-AG, Carnelian Bay, CA 95711. (800) 457-4574, (916) 583-8475 or (916) 583-7797.

NEPAL

CLIMBING THE ANNAPURNAS

The Annapurnas constitute one of the most varied of all the regions within the immense Himalaya Range. On this program you trek up the beautiful Marsyandi River Valley, visit villages of different cultural groups, view several of the highest mountain groups in the world—Manaslu (26,760'), Annapurna (26,545'), and Dhaulagiri (26,795')—and make two major ascents.

Walking through rice fields in the Marsyandi Valley—Mark Houston for American Alpine Institute, WA.

The trek into the mountains is gradual, giving time to adjust to the altitude. The first climb from a base camp (15,600') leads to Chulu West at 21,060 feet. Establish three camps before the ascent to the summit over several short sections of 40 to 45 degrees. The second climb is an easy ascent of 20,096'-Thorong Peak, or a more challenging route on 21,021'-Muktinah Peak. In addition to tremendous views of the entire Lamjung and Annapurna Himal, you will see yaks, perhaps the rare blue sheep, monasteries, and the donkey trains of traders heading into Tibet, before returning to Kathmandu.

March & October, 30 days, $2,280 + air. 1986 departures: Mar. 1, Oct. 11.

American Alpine Institute, 1212 24th D, Bellingham, WA 98225. (206) 671-1505.

NEPAL

FAMILY TREK

Take the children trekking in Nepal? Why not? The younger ones will soon be playing okhar kuti, gatthi, and kamakuti with their Nepalese counterparts—variations of hopscotch, jacks, and jump rope. The extremely family-oriented Nepalese welcome westerners with unprecedented warmth and hospitality. This 17-day trip is led by bilingual families (often by Above the Clouds founder Steve

Children play on their ferris wheel swing—*Above the Clouds Trekking, MA.*

Conlon, his Nepali wife, and bilingual four-year-old son). Menus are planned with children in mind and porters carry not only your gear but small children as well. (Infants ride in safe, comfortable baby backpacks.)

The trip begins and ends in Kathmandu. From Hindu temples and Buddhist stupas to performances by native dancers, from medieval towns to the spectacular palace of Nepal's founder, experience the country's culture, charm, and history. The trek itself lasts eight days in elevations from 2,000 to 4,500 feet. Most trekking is easy, and strenuous trips are limited to half days. There is ample time for rest and visiting with Nepalese. A truly fascinating exchange with friendly, hardy people amid the towering Himalayas.

December & July, 17 days (from U.S.), $1,150/adult, $200-$500/child, + air. 1986 departures: Jun. 27, Dec.19. In 1987: June 26.

Above the Clouds Trekking, P.O. Box 398-V, Worcester, MA 01602. (800) 233-4499 or (617) 799-4499.

NEPAL

EXPLORING GLACIERS AND WHITE WATERS

Enjoy some of the most exciting whitewater rafting anywhere as you float down the Arun River bordered by subtropical vegetation and colorful village life. After a day in endlessly fascinating Kathmandu and its surrounding villages, a thrilling mountain flight east brings you to Tumlingtar and the beginning of the 16-day hike. Climb through bamboo and rhododendron forests to Khandbari, Bhotebas, and Sekidim—treating yourself to fabulous views of Mt. Everest's east face along the way.

Continue to the yak pastures of Sherkha (12,000'), and up to the Makalu Base Camp (14,500'), surrounded by high peaks and glaciers. Slowly retrace your steps to Tumlingtar where a whitewater rafting crew awaits you. An exhilarating 4-day trip takes you down the Arun, past enchanting countryside to Chatra. Drive back to Kathmandu for an overnight, then home.

April & October, 30 days (from U.S.), $1,550 + air. 1986 departures: Apr. 3, Oct. 25. In 1987: Apr. 9, Oct. 24.

Himalaya Inc., 1802-E Cedar St., Berkeley, CA 94703. (415) 540-8031.

NEPAL

EVEREST ESCAPADE

Experience the quiet beauty of the Buddhist culture on this 7-day trek through the southern flanks of Nepal's Himalayas. Visit the major Sherpa villages of Khumba and Thyangboche Monastery for amazing views of Everest, Kangtega, Thamserku, and the obelisk of Ama Dablam. The villages lie between 11,000 and 13,000 feet, and are connected by well-trodden paths. Though you needn't be an expert trekker, you should be physically fit and should have done some recent hiking. Day hikes can vary from an easy three hours to a more rigorous seven hours. Air transportation is provided to Lukla, where the trek starts. Porters carry your camping equipment.

The 16-day trip begins and ends with overnights in Bangkok. All meals on treks, breakfasts in Kathmandu, and air are included.

January-March, October-December; 16 days; including air—$2,690 from Seattle, $2,990 from Dallas. 1986 departures: Feb. 15, Mar. 1, 15 & 29, Apr. 12 & 26, Oct. 25, Nov. 8 & 22, Dec. 6 & 20. In 1987: Jan. 10 & 24, Feb. 7 & 21, Mar. 7.

Mountain Travel, 1398 Solano Ave., Albany, CA 94706. (800) 227-2384 or (415) 527-8100.

NEPAL   **EXPLORING SHERPA VILLAGES**

You make many friends among the warm-hearted Nepalese. Begin your visit with a stroll through the winding lanes and ancient courtyards of Kathmandu, and tour the history-rich Durbar Square, Temple of the Living Goddess, and Royal Palace. Then fly to Lukla—a remote landing strip on a mountainside at 9,400 feet—and greet the friendly Sherpa guides and porters who accompany your trek.

Hike into villages and through magnificent forests, rhododendron, magnolias, and giant firs. Visit Namche Bazaar, a busy trading center (virtually unchanged) since the days when grain from the south was exchanged here for salt from Tibet. Then it's a short climb to the foot of Mt. Everest, towering at 29,029 feet. Talk with the Lamas at the Thyangboche monastery and nunneries, and (perhaps) visit your Sherpa's family in Khumjung, a town of symmetrically-laid out stone houses. The five or so hours of daily walking leave time to explore on your own. The trek includes 13 nights of camping and 3 nights in hotels.

April, October-January, 17 days (from U.S.), $1,705 + air. 1986 departures: Apr. 10, Oct. 30, Dec. 18. In 1987: Jan. 4, Apr. 9, Oct. 29, Dec. 17.

Inner Asia, 2627 Lombard St.-AB, San Francisco, CA 94123. (800) 551-1769 or (415) 922-0448.

NEPAL   **INSTANT EVEREST**

This 8-day trek through the remote Solu Khumbu region of Nepal is specially designed for the hearty trekker with a tight schedule. A 45-minute flight to the Lukla airstrip bypasses a 2-week walk from Kathmandu, so you can enjoy a visit to ancient monasteries, view the highest mountain in the world, and meet Sherpa locals within a 2-week vacation period.

This 12-day trip (Grade C-2) takes you to an elevation of 12,600 feet—giving spectacular Everest views without the altitude adjustment involved in Everest Base Camp treks. Hike through the Dudh Kosi Valley, then up to Namche Bazaar where Tibetans and Sherpas from the higher, more remote villages trade their woolens for rice and green vegetables grown in the lower, warmer hills. Return via Thyangboche Monastery and through tiny Sherpa villages. Explore historic Kathmandu before your return flight.

October-May, 12 days, $745 + air. 1986 departures: Every Tuesday.

Himalayan Travel, Inc., P.O. Box 481-AB, Greenwich, CT 06836. (800) 225-2380 or (203) 622-0068.

NEPAL   **GATEWAY TO NEPAL**

Whether you're a shopper, walker, tourist, or trekker, you'll find on this 12-day trip a veritable feast of sights and activities. View the majesty of the high Himalaya, Kathmandu's temple-strewn maze of streets, and the wildlife in the jungles of Chitwan National Park. There's plenty more to do—take an elephant ride to see the rare one-horned rhino, float across Phewa Lake in a dugout canoe, or cross rice fields at the foot of the Annapurnas.

This tour, which begins and ends in Bangkok, is designed for the traveler with no previous mountaineering or trekking experience. Porters and animals carry your personal and camping gear. Sherpas pitch the tents and serve as cooks. Stay in comfortable

Small village among the peaks—*SOBEK Expeditions, Inc., CA.*

hotels and lodges, except when camping. For those who prefer not to trek, Sobek offers a nontrekking option with more time to explore the cultural wonders of Kathmandu, and you can add a visit to India and Thailand or a Mt. Everest trek to the itinerary.

Year round, 12 days (from Seattle), $2,149-$2,590 + air. 1986 departures: 1 or 2 Saturdays monthly.

SOBEK Expeditions, Inc., Box AG, Angels Camp, CA 95222. (209) 736-4524.

NEPAL

HIMALAYAN ADVENTURE

If you're short on time, but eager for a trip loaded with exotic appeal and adventure, try this 12-day (Grade-4) trek through breathtaking Nepal. From Seattle, connect in Bangkok for Kathmandu, where your exploration of this intriguing culture begins. Drive to the Annapurna region in central Nepal for a 6-day trek on trails few have traveled. This package includes comfortable hotel and tent camp accommodations, most meals, and porters to carry gear to each day's destination.

Hike past banana, mango, and banyan groves, rice paddies, and tea houses. Marvel at the magnificent views of Annapurna II (22,599'), Annapurna IV (24,682'), Lamjung Himal (22,914'), and the beautiful Machapuchare (23,942'). Meet the friendly Gurung people of Siklis, with its tiered dwellings and grain drying on the flat slate roofs. Shop and sightsee in Kathmandu before your farewell feast. Exhilarated by the mountain air and magical memories, head for home via Bangkok.

September-April, 12 days (from Seattle), $1,990 including air. 1986 departures: Feb. 8, Apr. 12, Sep. 27., Oct. 25, Dec. 6. In 1987: Feb. 7.

Wilderness Travel, 1760-AT Solano Ave., Berkeley, CA 94707. (800) 247-6700 or (415) 524-5111.

NEPAL

HIGH ALTITUDE HIKES

Rated Grade D, this 21-day trek is for the experienced and physically fit hiker. It focuses on the culture of the Sherpa people and the world's tallest peaks. After a day of sightseeing in Kathmandu and a flight to Lukla, follow a steep switchback trail to Namche Bazaar at 11,300 feet, a Sherpa center of travel and commerce for the Khumbu region. Continue on a beautiful walk to the monastery at Thame.

This is only the start of the ultra-scenic route. At Dudh Kosi you leave the main trail and climb high above the river valleys, then drop steeply to Phortse, with spectacular views of 22,000' peaks. At Gokyo (15,580'), climb the ridge above camp for views of four of the 10 highest mountains in the world—Everest, Lhotse, Cho Oyu, and Makalus—all over 25,000 feet. Climb over rock, snow, and perhaps ice at Chhuguima pass (17,780'). Hike up Kala Patar for sunset viewing of Everest, or venture toward the Everest Base Camp. On a route toward the Pumori summit, the black diamond of Mt. Everest's South Face appears. Days to rest and explore punctuate the trek, on which you finally return to Lukla and Kathmandu.

October, 30 days (from U.S.), $1,650 + air. 1986 departure: Oct. 17.

Himalaya Inc., 1802-E Cedar St., Berkeley, CA 94703. (415) 540-8031.

NEPAL

IN THE FOOTSTEPS OF HILLARY

Discover both old and new Nepal as you sightsee in the city and trek in the Himalayans. Begin your journey with several days' exploring Kathmandu's ancient temples and candle-lit backstreets. Then go out by landrover through terraced farmlands to the Kirantichap village, the starting point for your trek.

You follow the classic route of Sir Edmund Hillary, from Kirantichap to the Everest Base Camp. Hike at your own pace through the lush green hills of the Solu region, then turn north into the Dudh Kosi River Valley leading into the heights of the more barren Khumbu area. Here, isolated yak pastures are surrounded by five of the world's highest mountain peaks, and here you meet the friendly Sherpa people. Within four trekking days, you reach

The stupa in Namche Bazaar near Mt. Everest—Fran Sherpa for Himalayan Excursions, TX.

the Thyangboche, a monastery set snugly below Ama Dablam. Further along, view Mt. Everest at its most dramatic. Himalayan Excursions also offers custom-designed and private treks.

November, 30 days (from U.S.), $1,990 + air. 1986 departure: Nov. 10.

Himalayan Excursions, P.O. Box 11204, Midland, TX 79702. (915) 682-9565.

NEPAL

POKHARA—SLOWLY

For first-time trekkers this easy 20-day journey combines 11 days of trekking (Grade B), river rafting, and gameviewing, and five days in Kathmandu. Fly to the lakeside city of Pokhara, with time to paddle a dugout canoe on Phewa Tal or to investigate the Bagar

Bazaar. Next morning start off on a 5-day trek. The views of the soaring, jagged peaks of the Annapurna Himal are just as magnificent as those on the more arduous routes. English-speaking Sherpas guide you through the scenic area.

Back to Pokhara to board a raft for floating down the lower Trisuli River for two days, camping overnight. Then overland to Chitwan Jungle Lodge—rustic, comfortable, and designed to harmonize with its jungle surroundings. For three days, view wildlife of the jungle by vehicle, dugout canoe, and from the back of an elephant. With visions of rhino, deer, wild boar, and possibly the seldom-seen Bengal tiger, return to Kathmandu and home.

November, December, February; 19 days (from U.S.); $690 + hotel/meals Kathmandu, + air. 1986 departures: Nov. 22, Dec. 6. In 1987: Feb. 7, Nov. 21.

Guides For All Seasons, P.O. Box 97-AG, Carnelian Bay, CA 95711. (800) 457-4574, (916) 583-8475 or (916) 583-7797.

Riding elephantback in the terai—*Jim Traverso for Overseas Adventure Travel, MA.*

NEPAL

JOURNEY BY RAFT, ELEPHANT, AND FOOT

Even the most well-traveled adventurer will find excitement on this Nepal trip (Grade C), which combines trekking, rafting, and gameviewing. Begin by exploring Kathmandu, visiting the ancient Durbar Square with its many temples, shrines, and markets, and simply walking through the winding city streets. Then travel overland to Gorkha, Nepal's ancient capital and the starting point for your trek.

Follow a route seldom explored by westerners, enjoying good views of Manaslu and Annapurna as you hike to your destination in Trisuli. From there you begin a 5-day rafting adventure (maybe with time to swim, sun, and fish) as you float down the Trisuli River to southern Nepal and the third leg of your journey, in the Chitwan National Park. Here you stay at a rustic but charming jungle lodge and ride out on elephantback in search of the rhino, wild boar, deer, and magnificent birdlife which populate the region.

>December, January, 22 days (from U.S.), $890 + air. 1986 departure: Dec. 17. In 1987: Jan. 7.
>
>Guides For All Seasons, P.O. Box 97-AG, Carnelian Bay, CA 95711. (800) 457-4574, (916) 583-8475 or (916) 583-7797.

NEPAL

TREK, RIVER RAFT, WILDLIFE SAFARI

One of the most fascinating aspects of a journey through this small Asian kingdom is the extreme diversity of climate and culture it embraces. Not only do you enjoy the thrill of a mountain and jungle adventure (Grade B), but also the exposure to a kaleidoscope of ethnic and religious heritage that begins in exotic Kathmandu.

From the markettown of Pokhara, walk through villages of varied cultures on a moderate 8-day trek into the Annapurna foothills, with magnificent views of Annapurna, Machapuchare, Dhaulagiri, and the deep chasm of the Kali Gandaki. Following the trek, jeep to Dumre for an exciting 3-day raft trip on the Trisuli. Run rapids and float peacefully past friendly villages where the mountains become a backdrop to the subtropical Terai. In the Royal Chitwan National Park, travel by elephant and dugout canoe, searching out the one-horned Indian rhinoceros and elusive Bengal tiger. The jungle, grasslands, and waterways are also home to spotted deer, monkeys, several crocodile species, and the rare freshwater dolphin.

>January-April, September-December, 22 days (from U.S.), $1,050 + air. 1986 departures: Jan. 4, Feb. 1, Mar. 8, Apr. 5, Sep. 6, Oct. 4, Nov. 1, Dec. 6. In 1987: Jan. 3, Feb. 7, Mar. 7, Apr. 4, Sep. 5, Oct. 3, Nov. 7, Dec. 5.
>
>Himalaya Inc., 1802-E Cedar St., Berkeley, CA 94703. (415) 540-8031.

NEPAL

MOUNTAINS AND RIVERS

The rugged itinerary of this 4-week adventure combines extensive high altitude trekking and whitewater rafting, covering some of the richly varied geography of this tiny kingdom at the top of the world. Approach the windswept heights of Everest, ride the rapids of the Sun Kosi River, and observe traditional village life. Make camp with Sherpas and Nepalese guides.

Explore Kathmandu by bicycle, then take a twin-engine plane 9,000 feet up into the Himalayas to begin 12 days of trekking through the Khumbu region, where hill people harvest and weave with hand-forged tools. On the two days of the full moon, the group joins a Sherpa celebration as the Buddhist dance-drama,

Mani Rimdu, is performed in the courtyard of Thengboche Monastery. Contemplate Everest from Kala Pattar, 18,450 feet. Then pack river gear for eight days on the Sun Kosi, paddling past the vastly different terrain of the middle hills, riding Class II and III rapids (some IV's), and relaxing on sandy beaches for picnics and swims. Or, if you prefer, take an all-river trip. Spend four weeks traveling on the Trisuli, Mersyandi, and Sun Kosi rivers by kayak and raft.

October & November, 30 days (from U.S.), $1,975-$2,300 + air. 1986 departure: Oct. 16 (all river), Nov. 19 (trek and river).

Nantahala Outdoor Center, U.S. 19W Box 41, Bryson City, NC 28713. (704) 488-2175.

NEPAL

RAFTING THE "RIVER OF GOLD"

The Sun Kosi "River of Gold," rising in Tibet, drains the rivers of the southern slopes of the Great Himalayan Range as it flows through Nepal. Still largely undiscovered as a rafting river, its

Rapids on the Sun Kosi in Nepal—*Himalayan Travel, Inc., CT.*

waters require no previous whitewater experience (Grade B-2), but you must know how to swim and be prepared to work hard. Drive east from Kathmandu to Dolaghat and take to the river for sights few have seen in a sturdy long-oared seven-person raft commanded by an experienced boatman.

For two days the river is relatively quiet. Then suddenly you're battling through rushing white water, swirling eddies, deep holes, and huge boulders, and navigating tortuous gorges surrounded by dense jungle. There's time to swim, talk to villagers, and watch birdlife. (Consider adding another 10 days for Annapurna or Everest trekking.)

October-April, 10 days, $652 + air. 1986 departures: Jan. 7 & 21, Feb. 25, Mar. 11, Apr. 1.

Himalayan Travel, Inc., P.O. Box 481-AB, Greenwich, CT 06836. (800) 225-2380 or (203) 622-0068.

NEPAL — TO LANGTANG, GOSAINKUND, AND HELAMBU

Your blue jeans and Swiss Army knife are certain to attract attention on this trek into one of Nepal's most culturally isolated areas. The villagers here follow a centuries-old lifestyle and have rarely seen western dress and tools. The excursion begins and ends in Kathmandu.

Langtang's dramatic landscapes recall pictures from your childhood fairytale books. Walk past rushing rivers, ancient forests, on up to fields and high desert. Finally you stand face-to-face with the massive mountain range marking Tibet's border. Cross the Gosainkund Pass where Hindu holy lakes are set in stark grandeur, and descend to the lush Helambu region leading back to Kathmandu Valley. This is a Sherpa-owned and operated company, which means native experience all the way. You visit Sherpa homes and enjoy laughter-filled evenings of spontaneous dancing and celebration. One trekker tells what it's like to interact and become a part of Sherpa family life: "I'll never forget the special attention given by uncles and cousins when I was nursing a blister—genuine concern, gentle teasing, and companionship."

November, March-April, 26 days, $1,590 + air. 1986 departures: Oct. 27, Mar. 17.

Himalayan Excursions, P.O. Box 11204, Midland, TX 79702. (915) 682-9565.

NEPAL — TREKKING AND CLIMBING NEAR EVEREST

Explore three of the four largest mountain valley systems in the Khumbu Himal and ascend two high-altitude peaks after orientation in Kathmandu. Fly into Lukla (9,000') and hike through pine forests along the Dudh Kosi (river). Gain altitude gradually as you move into the heart of Sherpa country. A steep climb to Namche Bazaar (11,300') opens your first views of Everest.

Rest days are scheduled at Gykyo Lakes (15,585') where both trekkers and climbers scramble up an 18,000' peak with stunning views of surrounding peaks. Trekkers visit the Everest Base Camp while climbers take on the 20,076' Lobuche Peak. "The climb is airy, scenic every step of the way, and strikingly photogenic," say these experts. A second climb is to Island Peak in the midst of the great Lhotse Basin, "a beautiful glacier climb which includes an ascent of 800-ft., 40- to 45-degree snow and ice slope." Trekkers and climbers converge on the walk back to Lukla, through beautiful villages—"a fitting cultural high point on a magnificent mountain journey."

November & April, 28 days, $2,190 + air. 1986 departures: Apr. 5, Nov. 15.

American Alpine Institute, 1212 24th D, Bellingham, WA 98225. (206) 671-1505.

NEPAL

THREE TREKS TO ANNAPURNA

Three distinct treks of varying length, altitude, and difficulty allow trekkers of all skill levels to experience the Annapurna Range of central Nepal—one of the most dramatic and scenic span of peaks in the world. The least difficult journey, Annapurna Panorama, lasts nine days and approaches Annapurna from Pokhara, taking you through ridge-top trails and passes of the

A challenging foot bridge in Nepal— Will Weber for Journeys International, MI.

Himalayas middle hills and past picturesque villages up to 10,000 feet. Annapurna Sanctuary, a slightly more difficult 15-day trek, passes through rhododendron forests and Himalayan villages to the sanctuary valley surrounded by the Annapurna massif, Machhapuchhare, and Lamjung Himal. For those in peak physical condition, the 21-day rigorous trek over a 17,000'-pass is a true challenge. You climb among spectacular peaks, view exotic flora and fauna, and meet Tibetan migrants.

All three treks begin in Kathmandu and end at Pokhara, where you may extend your trip to the Royal Chitwan National Park for elephant safaris or for a bit of gamewatching. None of the treks requires technical climbing experience. A special family trek to the Annapurna region is also offered.

May, October-December, 18, 21 & 29 days (from U.S.), $895-$1,325 + air. 1986 departures: May 3, Oct. 2, Nov. 10, Dec. 20 & 27.

Journeys International, P.O. Box 7545-AG, Ann Arbor, MI 48107. (313) 665-4407.

NEPAL

TREKKING NORTH OF GORKHA

The area just north of Gorkha, between Kathmandu and Pokhara, has been somewhat overlooked in this magical land known as a trekker's paradise. Besides premier trekking, it offers a remote cultural experience more authentic than on the heavily-trekked routes. Villagers here rarely see trekkers.

From Kathmandu, travel to Gorkha where all routes start from the royal palace. With nine days of easy trekking (Grade B) on the Manakamana route, you pass through lush forests and villages which reflect cultural changes from Aryan to Mongolian in faces and houses. The trek ends at the Hindu temple of Manakamana, a goddess revered for her powers to grant wishes. Another route, the Singla (Grade C), requires 16 days of challenging trekking—three of them particularly stiff as you cross the mighty Buri Gandaki River and make your way through some of the wildest country in all the Himalaya. Among the rewards—being close enough to touch Ganesh Himal, and visiting remote tribal villages of primeval Nepal.

October-April, 9-23 trekking days, $60-$65 per day.

Above the Clouds Trekking, P.O. Box 398-V, Worcester, MA 01602. (800) 233-4499 or (617) 799-4499.

NEPAL

SHORT WALK IN THE ANNAPURNAS

"To see the great Himalayan peaks at close distance, go to the Annapurna foothills," advises an experienced trekker. "There's no other place in the world where you can view them so easily." On this new 4-day trek (Grade B-2) from Pokhara, you follow a special route virtually unused by other trekkers. You get marvelous views of Annapurna and other mountains in the range, including the incredible "fishtail" peak of Machapuchare. The route takes you over ridges with intricately-terraced mustard fields, groves of citrus and banana, rhododendron and oak forests.

Short though it is, the trek touches on the country's ethnic diversity. You visit the villages of Brahmin and Chetri hill people as well as Gurungs and Magars, and sightsee in the subtropical city of Pokhara. Bangkok and Kathmandu are stopovers both en route to Pokhara and on the return home, with time to see the highlights of both cities.

October-March, 12 days (from U.S.), $1,990 from Seattle, $2,220 from Dallas, including air. 1986 departures: Jan. 11 & 25, Feb. 8 & 22, Mar. 8 & 22, Oct. 18, Nov. 1, 15, & 29, Dec. 13 & 27. In 1987: Jan. 10 & 24, Feb. 7 & 21, Mar. 7.

Mountain Travel, 1398 Solano Ave., Albany, CA 94706. (800) 227-2384 or (415) 527-8100.

NEPAL

THE CLASSIC TRAIL TO EVEREST

Dedicated trekkers in excellent condition find challenge in this difficult (Grade E-2) 23-day trek to Everest, following the classic trail taken by Edmund Hillary and Tenzing Sherpa. It's part of a 31-

On the trail to Everest—*Himalayan Travel, Inc., CT.*

day journey. Begin with exploration time in Kathmandu, then ride (via jeep or bus) 45 miles to the trailhead at Kirantichap.

Walk through idyllic forests, pastures, and villages, then climb along terraced farming areas. The steadily rising terrain takes you to the market town of Namche Bazaar (11,300')—then higher to the Thyangboche Monastery, located on a spur surrounded by mountain peaks. Finally, it's the Everest Base Camp (17,500')—a magnificent reward for a hard climb! Truly hardy trekkers can take the optional climb of Kala Pattar, a rubble-covered ridge at 18,250 feet. Your additional effort pays off with spectacular views of Everest, its surrounding peaks, and the vast Khumbu Glacier.

February-March, October-December; 31 days, $1,490 + air. 1986 departures: Mar. 5, Oct. 1 & 15 , Nov. 5, Dec. 12. In 1987: Feb. 18.

Himalayan Travel, Inc., P.O. Box 481-AB, Greenwich, CT 06836. (800) 225-2380 or (203) 622-0068.

NEPAL / INDIA

FROM POKHARA TO GHORAPANI

Combine sightseeing with a less demanding 8-day (Grade 2) trek on this 21-day sojourn through Nepal and India. Led by your Sherpa guide, you find history and culture in the cities and wildlife and physical exercise on the walk from Pokhara to Ghorapani and back.

Spend the trekking days amidst the spectacular Annapurna and Dhaulagiri mountain ranges—breathtaking scenery from the lush irrigated valley to the high arid country in the north. Look high for splendid views of Annapurna South, Machapuchare, and the Hiunchuti peaks. Your path joins the fertile Yangdi River valley and ends in the heavily farmed vale of Pokhara. Stay in wilderness accommodations, including Fishtail Lodge, and Tiger Tops Jungle Lodge and Tented Camp. Then explore Nepal, the mysterious forbidden kingdom, with its mix of old and modern worlds. Finally make your way to India for a visit to the Taj Mahal and other romantic and rich wonders. Return home via Bangkok.

February, November, 21 days (from U.S.), $1,925 + air. 1986 departures: Feb. 15, Nov. 15.

Lute Jerstad Adventures International, P.O. Box 19537, Dept A, Portland, OR 97219. (503) 244-6075.

NEPAL / TIBET

FOR THE HALE AND HARDY

Calling all travelers strong of mind and body! Lute Jerstad's new-routed tour from Nepal to Tibet is designed for you. Travel in Tibet is tough. The land is large, barren, and remote, with the possibility of vehicle breakdown. Accommodations there range from tent camp to simple hotel.

Arrive via Bangkok in Kathmandu's famous Yak & Yeti for two nights, a quick pitch at shopping/sightseeing. The rough part starts with the drive over monsoon-ravaged Kodari Pass to China. Camp and acclimate at 10,000 to 11,000 feet in a tented camp (comfortable) before reaching the Tibetan highlands. Continue higher into the plateau to Shigaze with a full day to explore Tashilumpo Monastery. Cross 16,700'-pass to Lhasa, capital of Tibet. Spend three extraordinary days visiting the Potala (former palace of the exiled Dalai Lama), the Norbulingska summer palace, and the monasteries. A series of three one-night stands before returning to the comforts of Kathmandu, and two nights in luxurious Bangkok. Add an optional 4-day extension to Nepal's Tiger Tops Jungle Lodge.

March-April & July-August, 15 days (from U.S.), $4,275 + air. 1986 departures: Mar. 31, Jul. 28.

Lute Jerstad Adventures International, P.O. Box 19537, Dept. A, Portland, OR 97219. (503) 244-6075.

PAKISTAN

SPECTACULAR BEAUTY AND ANCIENT CULTURES

"High Adventure" organizer Shirley Duncan personally leads this journey in North Pakistan and brings to it unique experiences. She arranges meetings with the people—from the Prince of Chitral, the Rani (Queen) of Hunza, and the Wali (King) of Swat, to Kalash tribesmen and refugees in an Afghan camp. An author, lecturer, and photographer, Duncan specializes in Asian culture and history.

Flying to Rawalpindi and Gilgit, you drive along the newly opened Karakoram Highway—formerly the Great Silk Road, Marco Polo's route—to Hunza, an idyllic crime-free society where people live to great ages. "You will be overwhelmed by the beauty and charm of this tranquil Shangri-La," Duncan predicts. Drive over the 7,000 ft. Shangla Pass into the green valley of Swat, tour the archaeological site of Butkara and see the colorful Mingora Bazaar. Visit Peshawar (remember Gunga Din?), and fly to Chitral. Here you visit a village and watch the traditional dances of the Kalash tribe, a people who dress in black homespun with shell-decorated headgear. Near the Khyber Pass, legendary gateway to India, you visit an Afghan refugee settlement. No trekking and no high altitudes on this tour, limited to 20 participants. "The best trip I have ever had," writes one world traveler. Stopovers allowed in Europe and Istanbul. Optional tours to Turkey and Petra (Jordan), also Syria.

October, 18 days (from U.S.), $3,395 including air from New York. 1986 departure: Sep. 30.

High Adventure Tours, 4000 Massachusetts Ave., N.W., #1426, Washington, DC 20016. (202) 686-0023.

PAKISTAN

THE LAND OF LOST LEGIONS

For almost one month, experience the life of the tribes of the Himalayan regions of Hunza and Punial, the Hindu Kush, and Baluchistan—speak with the elders, watch traditional dances, listen to the local music, and occasionally, sleep in village homes. The trip is led by Ashraf Aman, the first Pakistani to reach the summit of K2—the world's second-highest peak.

ASIA

Begin in Seoul with overnights in Colombo, Karachi, and Rawalpindi. Fly to Gilgit and take a jeep ride to the remote home of the charming Raja of Punial, where you dine and camp on the floor. On to Karimabad. Spend three nights with a Hunza family and meet the town's older residents—many live to be 125. Then

Afghan refugee tents—*Capers Club 400, CA.*

ride a minibus into north Hunza, 33 miles from the Chinese border (now open) and spend the night with a Wai tribal family (few remain). Near the entrance to Khyber Pass—the escape route for many Afghan refugees—visit the Qissa Khawani storyteller's bazaar. Near Trisch Mir, one of the highest mountain peaks of the Hinku Kush, meet the isolated Kalash tribe. Continue on to Baluchistan, ancient caravan crossroads, with its nomadic tribes from the adjacent borders of Afghanistan, Iran, and Russia. Home via Sri Lanka and Seoul.

April & July, 32 days (from U.S.), $5,888 including air. 1986 departures: Apr. 6, Jul. 6. In 1987: Apr. 5, Jul. 5.

Capers Club 400, P.O. Box 5489, Beverly Hills, CA 90210. (213) 657-0916.

PAKISTAN

TREKKING TO HUNZA

This strenuous (Grade B-3) 21-day itinerary to Hunza and back, with some rough river crossings and 10 trekking days, is definitely for the hardy. The former princely state of Hunza lies in high mountains where China, Russia, and Pakistan meet. Arrive and depart Islamabad, then fly to Gilgit if weather permits—or drive the Karakoram Highway (15 hours and an extra charge). Travel in this remote region can be unpredictable—be prepared to add a week to your schedule to accommodate delays, all part of the adventure.

Pakistan's Hunza Valley—*Mountain Travel, CA.*

Each day's hike lasts from three to six hours, starting at 9,750 feet and reaching 12,500 feet. Cross the moraine-covered Batura Glacier, trek along shepherds' paths, see yaks grazing in meadows, meet the friendly "Hunzakuts"—all within sight of the fantastic Batura peaks rising over 25,000 feet. In Karimabad, Hunza's capital, explore the 500-year-old palace of the Mir before driving back to Gilgit for overnight at an inn, and departure. Nine nights camping, remainder in guest houses and hotels, plus time to explore Islamabad and the old British-era Rawalpindi.

July-August, 21 days, (from U.S.), $2,290 + air. 1986 departures: July 12, Aug. 2.

Mountain Travel, 1398 Solano Ave., Albany, CA 94706. (800) 227-2384 or (415) 527-8100.

ASIA

PAKISTAN   **TREKKING TO CONCORDIA**

Concordia, one of the most sublime mountain sites in the world, is in the Karakorum Range, surrounded by six peaks over 25,000 feet high—one of the six being K2, second highest mountain on earth.

The trip begins with a flight from Islamabad to Skardu, with an aerial preview of sights to come as you dart through the narrow gorges of countless peaks. Continue 52 miles by jeep to Dassu and the trailhead. With porters, cook crew, and guides, the expedition winds up the Braldu River valley, climaxed by a 20-mile walk through the spectacular Himalayan corridor flanked with high peaks on both sides. You cross the Biafo Glacier and Choctoi River before the journey up the Baltoro "which will remain in your thoughts for years to come," according to Mike Covington of Fantasy Ridge. During five days at Concordia you face a chain of 26,000'-peaks and hear the creaking and groaning of buried ice rivers, melting ice, and rolling rocks. You join Mike's Broad Peak Expedition (a 75-day ascent) for return to Islamabad. The trek ends with several days in Islamabad or Rawalpindi. (Open to 12 trekkers; may be followed by a trek to Nepal.)

September-October, 35 days, about $3,200 + air from U.S.

Fantasy Ridge Mountain Guides, P.O. Box 1679, Telluride, CO 81435. (303) 728-3546.

THAILAND   **DIVING THE SIMILAN ISLANDS**

Board the 50-foot *Andaman* Explorer in Phuket, Thailand, for your overnight cruise to the Similan Islands, some of the most remote in the world, and awaken the next day to a delightful choice of diving locations. There is the classical coral garden, with its intricate branches of coral and clouds of reef fish, including many exotic Indian Ocean species. Or opt for the eastern side of the islands, where you see massive basalt boulders covered with soft and hard corals (diving is deeper here).

The diving is unlimited and is, as See & Sea tells us, "unspeakably remote—an adventure for those who have been to many destinations and are looking for something truly offbeat." The dedicated crew of four do a great job. The boat has three double-bed alcoves with electric fans, and two single berths. Sightseeing and traditional Thai food in Bangkok complete the trip before and after.

October-April, 16 days, $2,500 + air. 1986 departures: Oct. 25, Nov. 29, Feb. 22, April, 26.

See & Sea Travel Service, Inc., 680 Beach St., Suite 340, San Francisco, CA 94109. (800) 348-9778 or (415) 771-0077.

THAILAND   **BARGE, MINIBUS, FERRYBOAT, AND ON FOOT**

Bring a sleeping bag and prepare to rough it on this 2-week journey in Thailand, with an optional 2-week extension in

Malaysia. You travel by barge, minibus, and foot from Bangkok to the Golden Triangle (where Thailand joins Laos and Burma)—then on to Singapore for journeying by train, bus, coastal ferryboat, and trishaw through the Malay Peninsula.

The real adventure begins after leaving Bangkok for northern Thailand. Here you start a not-too-strenuous 5-day walk to isolated hill-tribe villages. Sleep and eat in village huts, encountering such tribes as the nomadic Akha, known for their bright costumes, extravagant headdresses, and traditional way of life. Trails lead through bamboo forests and poppy fields, and past sparkling

In a dugout canoe on the KOK River in Thailand—*Adventure Center, CA.*

waterfalls and turgid rivers. In Mai Sai on the Burmese border you overnight on the green banks of the Mekong River in the heart of the Golden Triangle, the wild region of opium runners. At Nakong Sawar you board a converted rice barge to cruise slowly downstream to villages where you sample the life of river dwellers by swimming, sunning, and viewing temples and markets. The Malaysian extension is similar—with train, bus, and ferryboat travel to islands, coconut groves, superb beaches, and old seaports. A few nights in tourist hotels.

Year round, "The Golden Triangle & Malaysia," 18 days, $435-$460 + air; 32 days including extension, $780-$796 + air. 1986 departures: Jan. 18, Feb. 15, Mar. 15, Apr. 12, May 24, Jun. 28, Jul. 26, Oct. 11, Nov. 15, Dec. 13, Dec. 20. In 1987: Jan. 17, Feb. 14, Mar. 14, Apr. 11.

Adventure Center AG, 5540 College Ave., Oakland, CA 94618. (800) 227-8747 or (800) 228-8747; also (415) 654-1879.

ASIA

THAILAND   **FROM ELEPHANT SAFARI TO TROPICAL SPLENDOR**

Travel by overnight train, bus, elephant (three days), bamboo raft (two days), ferry, express boat, and by air. All are required for transporting your group (up to 15) from Bangkok to north Thailand, through the hill country and jungle, down the Nam Haw River, to an idyllic tropical island, and back to Bangkok!

In the northern mountains—probably the most breathtaking scenery in all of Thailand—you discover beautiful waterfalls and a forest alive with birds and monkeys. You meet Tibeto-Burmese hill people—nomads who sport brightly embroidered costumes and massive silver jewelry. Stilted huts in villages provide accommodations for this part of the journey—most often in the chief's house. The anxieties of western life seem distant as you live with these friendly, open people who still practice spirit worship and rely on medicine men and Chinese herbal remedies. It takes two days on a thatch-roof bamboo raft to leave the tribal villages and reach a car and plane back to Bangkok. The remarkable journey ends with two nights at the tropical island resort of Ko Samui with its untouched beaches, the best coconuts in Thailand, and clean, efficient bungalows with all the amenities.

December, 16 days (from U.S.), $1,590 + air. 1986 departure: Dec. 19.

Mountain Travel, 1398 Solano Ave., Albany, CA 94706. (800) 227-2384, or (415) 527-8100.

THAILAND   **AN ASIAN EXPLORATION**
BURMA
NEPAL   Spend three weeks comparing Oriental customs, cuisine, and colorful costumes on this exotic itinerary that takes you through three enchanting Asian countries. You have a week to explore each country's unique charms, starting with Bangkok, Thailand, then on to Burma, and finally the Himalayan kingdom of Nepal.

Trip highlights include visits to lavish temples, bustling bazaars, and elegant palaces, meeting friendly, gentle people throughout. In Thailand, join religious pilgrims at the famous shrine of the Holy Footprint of the Lord Buddha and explore the magnificent ruins of Korat and Chiang Mai. In Burma, view the spectacular Pagoda of Rangoon, the leg-rowing fishermen of Lake Inle, and the pagoda studded plain of Pagan. And in Nepal, visit the Tibetan Handcraft Center, view Mt. Everest and other spectacular peaks, and day hike into the beautiful Pokhara countryside. What a grand way to unravel the mysteries and majesty of the Far East!

November-February, 22 days (from U.S.), $1,990 + international & domestic air. 1986 departures: Feb. 8, Nov. 1, Dec. 20.

Wilderness Travel, 1760-AT Solano Ave., Berkeley, CA 94707. (800) 247-6700 or (415) 524-5111.

THAILAND   **OF TRIBES AND TREASURES**
BURMA
Travel by elephant, bamboo raft, plane, minibus and riverboat—sleeping in native huts, on houseboats and in hotels ranging from

First, visit crowded, bustling Beijing—"the center of the world" according to citizens of the Middle Kingdom. See the major sights and still have time to visit the local stores (refrigerators and pedal sewing machines are hot-selling items). Then warm up your cycling legs with a ride up the winding mountain road to the Great Wall, the 3,750-mile long fortification built over a 2,500-year period to keep out invaders. Bus back to Beijing. A breathtaking flight into Tibet passes over soaring mountain peaks to Lhasa, at 12,000 feet. Cycle for 10 days (32 miles a day) in the pristine Lhasa Valley, stopping to see temples, monasteries, and palaces. The trip is for 20 experienced riders with bi-lingual guides, a bus to carry baggage, and overnights at new and old hotels. (Special Trans-Himalayan tour, cycling the Friendship Road from Lhasa to Kathmandu, scheduled Sep. 18 at $4,900 including r.t. air from Seattle.)

April-October, 21 days (from U.S.), $2,925 + air. 1986 departures: Apr. 23, May 15, Jun. 12, Jul. 10, Aug. 7, Sep. 18, Oct. 9.

China Passage, 168 State St., Teaneck, NJ 07666-3516, (201) 837-1400.

TIBET

EXPLORING AN ANCIENT KINGDOM

Lovers of "Lost Horizon" and fans of the exotic, read on. This 2-week trip takes you through the mystical legends, lifestyles, and Himalayan landscapes of fascinating Tibet. From Hong Kong, fly to Chengdu and then on to Lhasa where your week-long Tibetan adventure begins. Visit Xigaze and Gyangze, and return to Lhasa to further explore this capital city with 1,300 years of cultural and religious history, before your flight back to China. This package includes overnight stays at deluxe hotels and comfortable guest houses, most meals, and expert guides.

Discover the ancient Potala Palace—home of the Dalai Lama—and the world's tallest standing structure at 12,321 feet atop Mt. Putou. See pilgrims gather at the magnificent Jokhang, Tibet's oldest shrine. Wander through the colorful bazaars for unusual jewelry, rugs, and crafts. See many treasures of Tibetan art as you mingle with lamas and locals in the mountain-perched monasteries. Explore the serene gardens of Chengdu's Wuhou Temple before flying to Hong Kong to shop and sightsee—then home.

May & September, 16 days (from U.S.), $3,610 + air. 1986 departures: May 19, Sep. 29.

Inner Asia, 2627 Lombard St.-AB, San Francisco, CA 94123. (800) 551-1769 or (415) 922-0448.

TIBET

THE ULTIMATE PILGRIMAGE

Follow in the footsteps of the Buddhist and Hindu pilgrims and Tibetologists on this 35-day journey via Beijing or Kathmandu through the Himalayas to Mt. Kailash in western Tibet. The Kailash Range runs from Kashmir to Bhutan. Conditions are rugged and accommodations and food are simple, as you experience the majestic mountains en route to the sacred lake and holy mountain, visited for more than 1,000 years by pilgrims from all over Tibet.

The expedition is led by Subhu Sengupta, and by Yogi Ramaiah, a noted Hindu leader. Group members are welcomed as authentic pilgrims. Observe the Orthodox Tibetan Buddhists, who do three or 13 rounds of Mount Kailash (32 miles) and Lake Manosarovar, to wash away sins. The atmosphere of devotion is special.

July-September, 35 days (from U.S.), $9,250 including air. 1986 departures: Jun. 24, Aug. 1. In 1987: Aug. 1.

Odyssey Tours, 1821 Wilshire Blvd., Santa Monica, CA 90403. (800) 654-7975 or (213) 453-1042.

TIBET
CHINA

THE ROAD TO LHASA

Get a taste of Tibet where you spend 12 days on this 20-day sojourn through China via overland vehicle. First, spend three days in exotic Kathmandu before motoring north over the Himalayan divide to the Tibet border. Continue via Xigaze, Tibet's second largest city and the seat of the Panchen Lama, past the

Ceremonial cart in the streets of Kathmandu— *Jim Wills for Guides For All Seasons, CA.*

magnificent panorama of the northern flanks of Mt. Everest. Ride through the remote Tibetan hinterland, crossing a 17,600' pass to the capital of Lhasa. Visit the Potala Palace, Jokhang Temple, the Ganden Monastery and summer home of the Dalai Lama while in the "city of sun." Return to Kathmandu for an overnight, passing through the fabled turquoise Yamdrok Lake and the fortress city of Gyantse. Then head for home.

You may select one of two hotel packages for your stays in Kathmandu. These accommodations are not included in the price, although meals and tent lodgings on the overland trek are part of the package.

October & November, 20 days (from U.S.), $2,865 + hotel/meals Kathmandu + air. 1986 departure: Nov. 1. In 1987: Oct. 24

Guides For All Seasons, P.O. Box 97-AG, Carnelian Bay, CA 95711. (800) 457-4574, (916) 583-8475 or (916) 583-7797.

TIBET
NEPAL

GATEWAY TO TIBET

The 1,300-year-old Potala Palace in Tibet—*Judi Wineland for Overseas Adventure Travel, MA.*

With Nepal as your gateway, journey across a border only recently opened into Tibet, a thinly-populated area of high plateaus and massive mountains bordered by the Himalayas on the south and the Kunluns on the north. Travel by land vehicle into remote areas for most of this 23-day trip, with time set aside to explore the terrain and meet the local people.

Among the highlights: Norbu Lingka, the largest garden in Tibet; the 1,300-year-old Potala Palace; Sera, Drepung, Mendoling, and Samye monasteries; and the Tomb of the Kings. Spend several days in Lhasa, Tibet's capital, where you have a chance to shop and explore. You stay in local homes as well as hotels and guest houses.

July-October, 23 days (from U.S.), $3,500 + air. 1986 departures: Jul. 18, Aug. 29, Oct. 3. In 1987: Jul. 17, Aug. 28, Oct. 2.

Overseas Adventure Travel, 6 Bigelow St. #102, Cambridge, MA 02139. (800) 221-0814 or (617) 876-0533.

TURKEY

EXPLORING EASTERN TURKEY

With special interest in photography, the culture and history of the area, and meeting the people, Shirley Duncan, organizer of High Adventure Tours, brings rich understanding to this 20-day sojourn in an ancient land. You travel a part of the Old Silk Road—(yes, Marco Polo was here)—gaze at snow-capped Mt. Ararat—(have scholars really sighted remnants of Noah's Ark?)—and cross the Tigris and Euphrates rivers—(this was possibly the site of the Garden of Eden).

The tour begins with Ankara, Hattusas and Black Sea cities. You visit lovely Lake Van and spectacular Namrut Dag—2000-year-old hilltop funeral site with huge statues. Also visit the fairytale land of Cappadocia with its strange geological formations, rock-cut churches, and underground cities with multiple floors and a labyrinth of tunnels where thousands of Christians lived during Arab raids. See Harran where Abraham stayed, villages, palaces, crusader castles, mosques, bazaars, museums—all are part of the visit which Shirley herself leads. Travel is by private coach, and hotels are first-class or best available. Optional extensions offered to Petra and Jordan, as well as western Turkey.

September-October, 20 days (from U.S.), $2,995 including air from New York. 1986 departures: Sep. 12.

High Adventure Tours, 4000 Massachusetts Ave., N.W. #1426, Washington, DC 20016. (202) 686-0023.

UNITED ARAB EMIRATES

ARABIA—LAND OF CONTRASTS

At the bottom of the Persian Gulf, bordered by Saudi Arabia, Qatar, and Oman, the U.A.E. presents enormous contrasts. Sand, sea, and reddish brown scarps now mingle with skyscrapers and plush beach and mountain resorts. Oil, since the 1960s, has changed the area's face. Yet the quiescent ways of Bedu nomads persist. By minibus and landrovers, long-time resident Alison Simms leads eight participants on a 16-day journey from coastal city Dubai to booming capital Abu Dhabi, across the Hajar Mountains to the Gulf of Oman, stopping by Bedu nomadic encampments, and oases that have attracted settlers for over 6,000 years, and then back to the Persian Gulf.

You progress from several nights at the luxurious seaside resorts of Jebel Ali and Khor Fakkan, to camping under the stars beside a stream in the Hajar Mountains and on the sand dunes of the infamous Empty Quarter.

Visit souks, archaeological sites, and remote settlements. You'll see camel races in the Wadi, swim in an oasis at al Ain, and cross an immense sea of sand to the "Rim of the World." A farewell feast takes place aboard a shaikh's private dhow, cruising the Dubai Creek.

November-December, 16 days (from U.S.), $2,775 + air. 1986 departure: Nov. 28. In 1987: Nov. 27.

Cross Cultural Adventures, Inc., P.O. Box 3285, Arlington, VA 22203. (703) 532-1547.

U.S.S.R

MOUNTAINEERING IN THE PAMIRS

One of the most little known mountain regions in the Soviet Union, is the remote Pamirs, called "the roof of the world." The Pamirs are in the very heart of Central Asia on Marco Polo's "Silk Road" where the borders of the U.S.S.R., Afghanistan, Pakistan, and China meet. Nomadic Kirghiz herdsmen have settled on high meadows, and glaciers irrigate the apricot orchards of Tadzhik farmers below.

First fly to Moscow then to Osh and Daraut Kurgan, an old fortress city. Drive on to the base camp at Achik-Tash, where your Grade E-2 trek begins. On a 30-day trip experienced climbers take the Lipkin Rovta and ascend Peak Lenin (23,406') and other peaks along the Zaalai Ridge. Instruction will be given to those less experienced, and nonclimbers may hike to spectacular high-altitude valleys.

July, 30 days, $2,875 + air. 1986 departure: July 27.

Mountain Travel, 1398 Solano Ave., Albany, CA 94706. (800) 227-2384 or (415) 527-8100.

YEMEN

EXPLORING AN ANCIENT LAND

A great power in the ancient world, Yemen retreated into itself more than a millenium ago. On this 16-day journey with a specialist in its history, culture, art, and architecture, the exceptional role Yemen played in the ancient Near East comes to light. Its cities contain the world's first skyscrapers—stone and mud-brick towers. You see monuments to the Queen of Sheba and stop at the university where algebra was devised. Elaborate turbans and kilts worn by men reflect the ancient culture, as do the heavily-veiled women in crowded souks. Other women are proudly unveiled and wear brightly colored pantaloons and turbans.

Fly from New York via Amsterdam to Sana'a, capital of the

Yemen Arab Republic and the hub of your travel to a dozen other cities in various directions. Highlights include fantastic rock-cut dwellings in hill-towns, walled fortresses, a remarkable rock palace, small mountain-top villages, a port on the Red Sea, mosques, archaeological finds and royal artifacts in the National Museum, and the luxurious Taj Sheba Hotel in Sana'a. Truly a journey through history.

March & September, 16 days (from U.S.), $2,990 + air. 1986 departures: Mar. 28, Sep. 5.

Society Expeditions, 723 Broadway East, Dept. ATA, Seattle, WA 98102. (800) 426-7794 or (206) 324-9400.

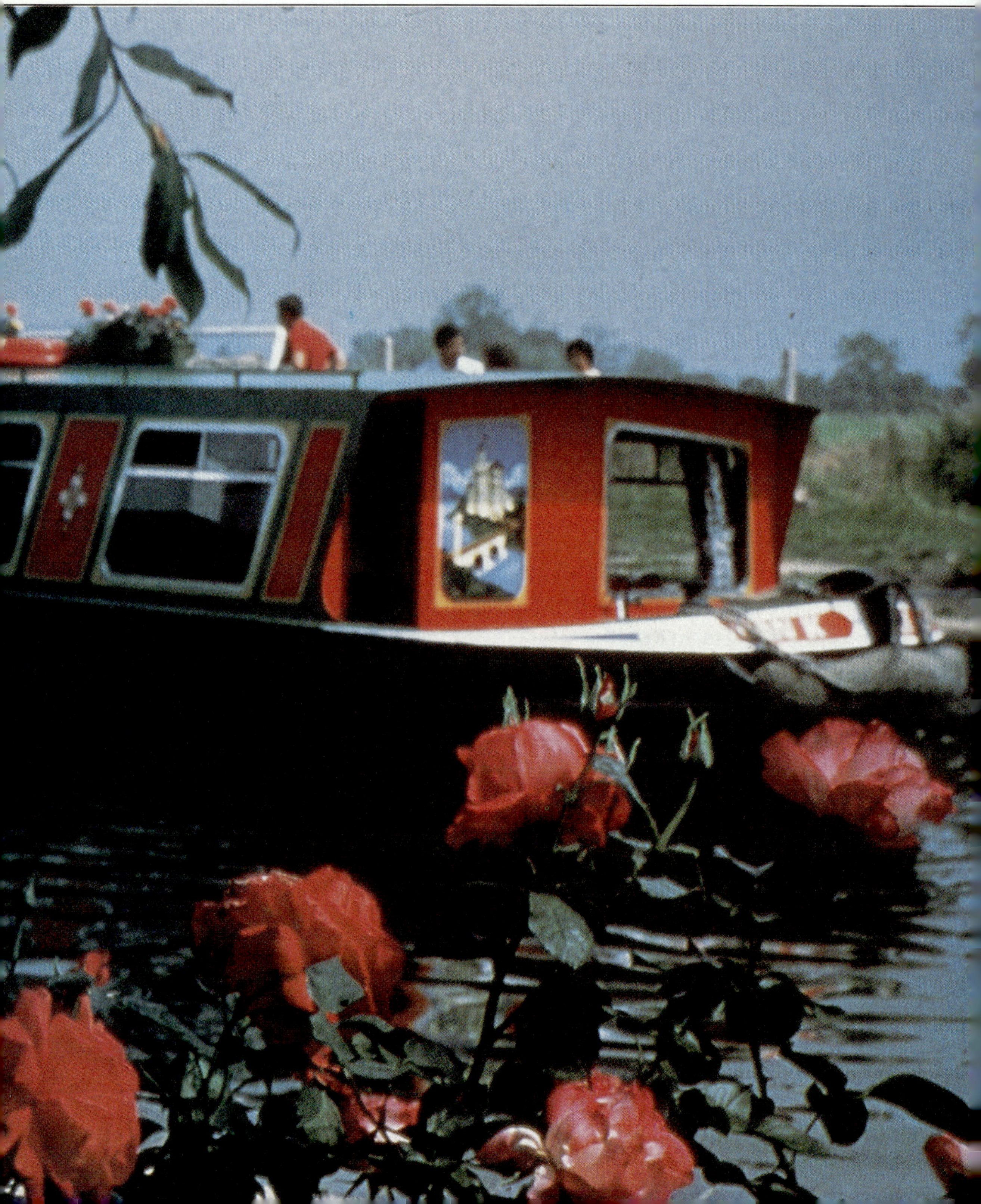

EUROPE

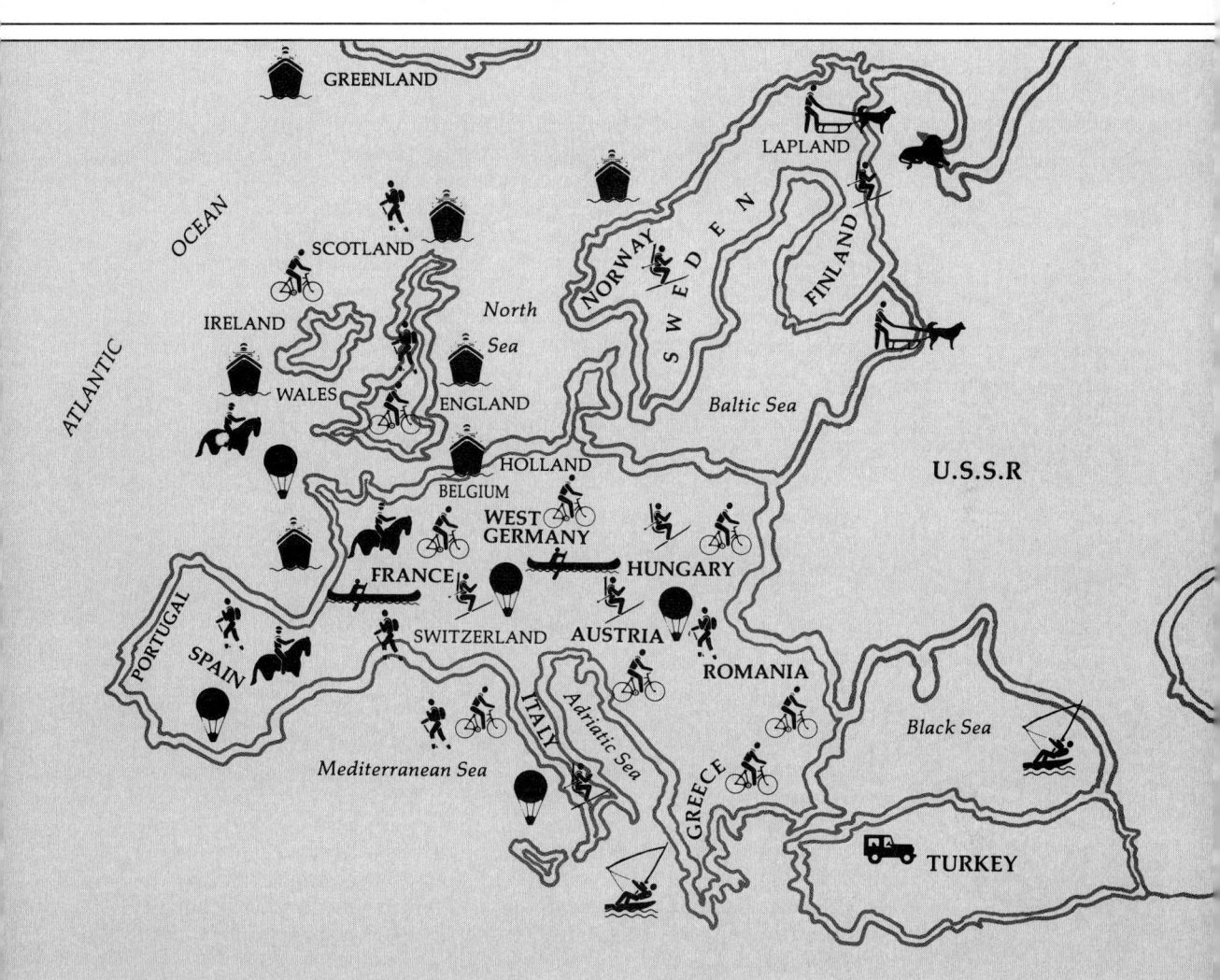

Tires filled—check. Brakes tight—check. Chain oiled—check. You're ready to roll, and so is your 12-speed Peugeot. Start pedaling through France's rolling hills, Austria's Alps, Holland's flat tulip fields, or Britain's lanes. Whether you take in the culture, the countryside, or the fine cuisine in any of two dozen countries, Europe is "fantastique!"

A bicycle is only one mode of transportation. Cruise the canals of France or England on a luxury barge. Paddle from castle to castle on a West German river. Sail past fjords and glaciers in Norway on the route of the Vikings. Or dogsled through Finland, float in a balloon over Salzburg, or ride horseback through the Loire Valley.

A maxiwagon will transport you across Europe and beyond on a camping safari. Travel by luxury train through the Scottish Highlands. Cruise the Greek Islands by yacht. Take a mule safari in the Swiss Alps. Or let your feet do the trekking in the Alps, England, and points in between.

These trips will give you a whole new view of Europe, exciting for the palate as well as the eye. You'll be reluctant to say good-bye, ciao, au revoir, or auf wiedersehen.

Barging in Shakespeare country—*Floating Through Europe, NY.*

AUSTRIA

ALOFT OVER SALZBURG

Whether on the ground or in the air, views of Salzburg are superb from every direction. You have the best of both vantage points during a week of ballooning with The Bombard Society, experts for nearly a decade in showing travelers the sights from aloft. Each morning you take off from a different scenic location north of the majestic Alps, drifting through an open area where the foothills meet the gently rolling countryside dotted with lakes. Celebrated picnic lunches are complemented by delightful settings, and afternoons are spent exploring the impressive sights—baroque villas, castles, gardens, spas, sparkling fountains, Mad King Ludwig's spectacular Bavarian palace, and of course, the delightful shops.

The week begins each Tuesday with three days at the 800-year-old Goldener Hirsch, a historic hotel which now combines modern comforts with the warmth of Austrian hospitality. The lovely 15th-century Schloss Fuschl in a dreamlike lakeside setting surrounded by pine-covered hills is our home for another three days. Not only do the Austrians serve superb meals, they also welcome balloonists with genuine friendliness.

September-October, 7 days, $3,980 + air. 1986 departures: Every Tuesday.

The Bombard Society, 6727 Curran St., McLean, VA 22101. (800) 862-8537 or (703) 448-9407.

AUSTRIA

HIKING ALONG THE DANUBE

Hike through rolling, wooded hills and valleys of Muhlviertal, the old watermill area of Upper Austria, for a truly delightful walking trip. Start with two nights in Vienna and a cruise on the Danube to Grien, followed by six days of exploring on foot. End with transfer to Salzburg for departure or for a day's (optional) visit. A van transports the luggage, and an English-speaking guide accompanies your group. Walks require from four to seven hours each day, and 4-star hotels provide overnight accommodations.

These walks are for nature lovers and history buffs alike. Cruise to Withering and visit the baroque monastery, church, and historic castle. Near Sandl, wander through the park—home of lynx, marmots, and many types of deer. Sample the product at the brewery in the medieval town of Friestadt, and visit a typical Austrian farm. After each day's walk, relax or swim in the hotel garden. You walk away from the farewell dinner in Sandl with a ceremoniously—presented walking medal.

May-September, 10 days, $320 + air. Salzburg extension $60-$100 + air. 1986 departures: Every Friday.

Directions Unlimited, 344 Main St., Mt. Kisco, NY 10549. (800) 533-5343, (914) 241-1700 or (212) 828-8334.

AUSTRIA

NORDIC SKIING—VILLAGE TO VILLAGE

"Cruise the untouched snow in a beautiful wide open valley moving between charming gasthofs and hearty restaurants" on this

8-day cross-country ski trek that's definitely not for those craving the high life of the resort. You ski through a remote alpine valley with a style all its own—greeted by cozy inns, hearty meals, and the friendly faces of farmers and villagers. You will not meet other North Americans. Each day you receive tips on technique from your guides, Ned Baldwin, an accomplished telemark skier and the author of four books on wilderness skiing, and Holly Blefgen, an instructor in downhill cross-country skiing. At night, relax by the fire with schnapps and good stories.

From Munich, motorcoach to the Steiermark region for a week's skiing, four hours a day. Gently descend from village to village, following little rivers through wooded flats, farmers' fields, and open meadows. More ambitious skiers can take advantage of the surrounding alpine slopes. Visit the castle in the walled town of Oberwolz. A grand celebration is held in historic Salzburg before returning to Munich.

February-March, 11 days, $1,195 + air. 1986 departures: Feb. 13, 20 & 27, Mar. 6 & 13.

Butterfield & Robinson, Inc., 70 Bond St., #300, Toronto, Ont., Canada M5B 1X3. (416) 864-1354.

Ballooning over Austria—*The Bombard Society, Va.*

AUSTRIA

ON HORSEBACK

"This is a great summer ride—we start at the foot of the highest mountain in the District of Salzburg and ride up to six hours each day for a week. It never gets too hot because of the altitude, as we pass through dark forests, quaint villages, below the glaciers of the Hohen Tauern Range, and across the alpine pass over high meadows to Kitzbuhl, then back to Neukirchen," writes FITS Equestrian founder Wolfgang Hallauer. "The cordial Austrian hospitality and their fabulous food make it a superb trip."

Riding into a quaint Austrian village—*FITS Equestrian, CA.*

There are some stiff climbs on this itinerary, which covers a variety of terrains and speeds and reaches altitudes of 6,000 feet. Participants should be experienced trail riders in good physical condition. Riders (never more than 16) from many countries participate. Stock is all well-trained, experienced trail horses. You overnight in cozy alpine inns and pensions.

June–September, 8 days, $460 + air.

FITS Equestrian, 2011 Alamo Pintado Rd., Solvang, CA 93463. (805) 688-9494.

EUROPE

AUSTRIA **BIKING ALONG THE DANUBE**

Fly to Salzburg or Munich for overnight at a castle before taking off on a 7-day cycling journey through upper Austria's picture-book countryside. You pedal a 3-speed Austrian Puch bicycle from 15 to 20 miles each day—unescorted—en route to historic towns and quaint villages, with luggage transferred to hotels. Travel at times by steamer, ferry, train, and on foot.

A smooth river towpath leads to Ottensheim and the famous baroque church there. Then on to Linz and its beautiful city center. The Danube Steamer takes you to the riverside resort of Grein, and a train carries you on to Aschach. Follow the path along the Blue Danube and cross it by ferry to Neustift, with time for a swim on Lake Rannasee. Cyclists end the romantic journey with an escorted walk, a river cruise, and a candlelight dinner, each rider wearing a well-earned medal. Back to Salzburg and home.

May-September, 8 days (from Austria), $190-$205. 1986 departures: Every Friday, May 18-Sep. 21.

Directions Unlimited, 344 Main Street, Mt. Kisco, NY 10549. (800) 533-5343 or (212) 828-8334 or (914) 241-1700.

AUSTRIA **AUSTRIAN ALPS TREK**

Jack and Donna Melill, former managers of the Rainier Guide Service (in Washington), consider the Austrian Alps the world's best hiking and climbing area. They guide a small group, no more than 12, on high scenic trails off the beaten path on this 2-week trek. Overnights are arranged at huttes (mountain inns) or at hotels.

Fly to Munich to meet your group and continue by bus to Neustift, a famous hiking and skiing center—your base for several days of hiking and an overnight trek. You'll take the tram up Stubai Glacier (11,343') for a short hike or alpine skiing. On subsequent days, hike to Franz-Senn Hut, then to the valley, and drive over Brenner Pass to Selva, in Italy, for hiking the Dolomites. A day in Venice offers total contrast (San Marco Square, a gondola on the Grand Canal, and all), then back to the mountains for hikes in the Stubai Valley, a day in Innsbruck, and return to Munich.

July, 15 days (from U.S.), $782 + air & meals. 1986 departure: Jul. 15.

World Adventure Travel/Tenzing Treks U.S.A., 2836 S.E., Suite A, Mercer Island, Washington 98040. (206) 232-2700 (ask for Jack).

AUSTRIA **MEANDERING IN THE ALPS**

Mountain rambling is less punishing than trekking but exhilarating and invigorating nonetheless. Meander from one mountain hut to another—you'll be observed by mountain goats, deer, and grazing cows—and take in the cultural life (concerts, galleries, museums, historic sites) in Innsbruck and Salzburg, where the trip begins and ends.

On the 12-day ramble (Grade B-2), with accommodations and

by experienced guides and a vehicle transports the luggage. (A self-guided option is also offered, as are tours in Denmark, Holland, and Ireland.)

June-September, 15 days, $1,450 + air. 1986 departures: Jun. 22, Aug. 2, Sep. 6.

World On Wheels, 650 Onwentsia Ave., Suite C, Highland Park, IL 60035. (312) 433-8660.

ENGLAND

PEDALING THROUGH TUDOR TOWNS

Quaint Tudor towns, gorgeous grass-scapes, castles, ancient Celtic camps, vineyards, and wildflowers are some of the rustic riches on these cycling adventures in southwest England bordering Wales. Itineraries are carefully planned, yet flexible for following individual whims. "Each route is designed to put you in touch with people as you cycle independently," says trip-planner Bob Dowler. They range from 3 to 16 days, for up to six cyclists, and fit conveniently into a European trip. The service includes accommodations, guidance, and rescue, if needed. Ride from 20 to 30 miles each day while discovering past and present English charms.

Start at the Victorian town of Malvern for example, then pedal through the Herefordshire countryside with its rolling hills, grazing cows, and woods where Merlin himself may still reside. Next, cycle through Shropshire, shaded by the Welsh Mountains, and stop to sample the local (and potent!) village cider. Hereford, with its magnificent cathedral, is next before winding up at the ancient market town of Ledbury, with its old world charm. Bring home memories of a jolly good vacation!

May & October, 5 days, (from England), $240. 1986 departures: Every Friday.

Bike Hikes, 82 Fuller St., Brookline, MA 02146. (617) 232-0198.

ENGLAND

WESTERN ENGLAND BY BIKE

With separate dates for adults and youth, AYH leads cyclists through the picturesque countryside of western England on a 16-day loop out of London. Pedal about 35 miles each day past rolling green hills, heather-filled fields, castles, and cathedrals. Visit Stratford-on-Avon and see one of Shakespeare's plays. Roam through medieval Salisbury with its Gothic cathedral. Tour the Roman baths and view the Georgian architecture in Bath. Attempt to unravel the mysteries of ancient Stonehenge.

It's a charming bit of old England, and rolling through it on a bike, talking with the people, and staying at hostels gives you a personalized feel for it. Hostel life, of course, means cooking your own meals, unless you prefer wandering into the local eateries for fish and chips or bangers and mash! Bring your own bicycle.

May-August, 16 days (from U.S.), $940 including air. 1986 departures: May 23 (open), Jun. 27 & Aug. 1 (youth), Jul. 11 & Aug. 15 (adult).

American Youth Hostels, P.O. Box 37613, Washington, DC 20013-7613. (202) 783-6161.

ENGLAND

HIKING IN LAKELAND

"Sunday strollers and more serious walkers alike enjoy themselves on our 9-day exploration of England's most beautiful corner, the tranquil Lake District," says Seth Steiner, director of Outdoor Bound Travel. Along with an Oxford-educated, personable local English guide, Steiner personally leads two lake country journeys—one easy-to-moderate and one moderate-to-

A B&B stop on the Lake District hike in England—Louise Reverby for Outdoor Bound, NY.

challenging—each summer. Both begin with an introductory briefing and slide show, giving the background you need for a rich experience in the Lake District.

Spend nine nights in the tiny village of Troutbeck-on-Windermere, crossing breathtaking countryside to explore Buttermere, Kentmere, and the 15th-century Ambleside, one of the major centers for the walking and climbing fraternity. Visit Grasmere, forever associated with William Wordsworth (take time to tour his tiny Dove Cottage); ramble through Hawkshead in the heart of Beatrix Potter country; sail aboard a scenic steamer to Howtown, then walk back, stopping for a swim along the way. Then it's on to three days in London, where you stay at a friendly guesthouse and see as many sights as you can pack in! All meals (including picnic lunches), airport transfers and transportation in the Lake District provided; breakfasts only in London.

June & July, 14 days (from U.S.), $1,295 + r.t. **air NYC $400.** 1986 departures: Jun. 29 & Jul. 13. In 1987: Jun. 28 & Jul. 12.

Outdoor Bound, 18 Stuyvesant Oval #1A, Dept. A, New York, NY 10009. (212) 505-1020.

Europe by bike—
EUROPEDS, CA.

ENGLAND

WALKING THE DEVON AND CORNWALL COAST

"These ancient provinces, surrounded by water and carpeted by wildflowers, offer some of the finest cliff walking in Britain," comments Perry Taylor of British Coastal Trails. "The coastal path gives easy access to the entire coastline of rocky headlands and quiet sandy coves, with dramatic views and uncrowded by summer tourists."

Taylor's tours in Devon and Cornwall start in Bristol with a sherry reception for becoming acquainted the first evening. For several days you catch spectacular coastal views as you visit Bolt Head and Gara Rock, and the medieval walled town of Totnes with its fine Norman castle. Stay at an old waterfront inn at Fowey, Cornwall's most picturesque town, and visit Mullion Cove (on the longer trips)—a sanctuary for sea birds with open clifftops studded with wildflowers. Padstow, once the haunt of pirates and near Tintagel of King Arthur's legend, and the misty wilderness of

Dartmoor complete the route. The tour is for 16 participants who walk about six miles a day. A luxury minicoach transports the people at various points as well as the luggage, and overnights are spent at charming village inns or hotels.

May-September; 8 days, $855; 12 days, $1,165. 1986 departures: May 17 & 24, Jun. 14, Jul. 2, Aug. 16, Sep. 10.

British Coastal Trails, 79-R Country Club Rd., Stamford, CT 06903. (203) 329-1612.

ENGLAND

PEDALING THROUGH HISTORY

"This itinerary, scheduled to coincide with Britain's colorful autumn foliage and cool weather, loops about 300 miles to some of the most famous castles, cathedrals, cultural centers, and colleges in the western world," according to Nantahala Outdoor Center whose summer cycling trips are in the Great Smokies.

Ride down lightly traveled country lanes (the hedgerows protect you from the wind), exploring at a relaxed pace of about 25 miles a day and settling in for the night at comfortable bed and breakfast places. Spend a week riding through the South Downs, the Wealden forest, the Wessex Downs immortalized by Thomas Hardy, and the Salisbury Plain. Then it's on to two or three days in the Cotswolds, the area of the classic English village, and through the Vale of Evesham to Stratford, then to Oxford. Sample highlights: Stonehenge, the Georgian city of Bath, Winchester Cathedral, a play by the Royal Shakespeare Company. Travel some of the distance by train. Rent a bike and saddle bags, or bring your own. A sagwagon accompanies the entire route.

September, 15 days (from U.S.), $995 + air. 1986 departure: Sep. 21.

Nantahala Outdoor Center, US 19W, Box 41, Bryson City, NC 28713. (704) 488-2175.

ENGLAND

YORKSHIRE/NORTHUMBERLAND WALK

Bounded by the Pennines on the west and the Cheviots on the north, northeast England is a land of contrasting beauty—a land that beckons exploration. On this 12-day walk you stroll delightful footpaths past mountain streams that cascade down tiny valleys, somber castles perched on high ridges, romantic ruined abbeys, and mellow stone cottages.

Your walking tour starts in Oxford, a graceful old city and Britain's first established learning center. Spend several days in the tiny villages of Thwaite and Muker, and walk Kisdonside to Kisdon Force. Stay in the market town of Helmsley—here your accommodations are in the old cobbled square under the 12th century castle. In the village of Hutton-Le-Hole, enter the high moors, carpeted with heather and gorse. In the city of York, walk atop the medieval walls and by narrow Elizabethan streets, and visit the York Minster, the largest cathedral in northern Europe. Finally, visit Farne Islands, a sanctuary for seals and a nesting site for seabirds, and walk along Hadrian's Wall as it climbs the basalt crags of the Great Whin Sill. Return to Oxford, pausing at the Stow-On-The-Wold and the Cotswolds before your flight home. The tour is limited to 16 participants who walk no more than five to six miles a day. A luxury minicoach transports the people at various points as well as the luggage.

>**June & August, 12 days, $1,185 approx. + air + lunches/afternoon teas.** 1986 departures: Jun. 21, Aug. 30.
>
>**British Coastal Trails Inc., 79-R Country Club Rd., Stamford, CT 06903. (203) 329-1612.**

ENGLAND
FRANCE

CYCLING THROUGH TWO CULTURES

"There's no need to choose between tasty French pastries and English steak and kidney pie on this bicycle journey through two cultures—there's time for both," says Quest Cycle co-founder Jason Takerer.

Spend several nights in fine hotels or bed-and-breakfasts and pedal your rented 10-speed at a leisurely 25 miles a day across flat valleys and medium-sized hills. Itineraries are flexible to accommodate all levels of experience and you may break off from the tour and design your own route if you wish. As you cycle through Kent, England's garden, take time to make brass rubbings in Royal Tunbridge Wells and to browse for antiques in Rye. Visit the Royal Greenwich Observatory, see the sound and light show at Ypres Tower, and imagine what medieval warfare must have been like on the site of the bloody Battle of Hastings. Then it's across the channel to the white cliffs of Normandy, where you feast on seafood in Dieppe, visit the cathedral Notre Dame in Rouen, climb chalk cliffs above the Seine, and take a day hike to Richard the Lion Hearted's fortress to view the same Gothic cathedrals he must have seen. When Chartres Cathedral looms in the distance, your holiday is complete. (Itinerary reversed on some routes.)

>**May-September, 9 days (from England or France), $1,175 Canadian ($870 U.S.) + air + some meals.** 1986 departures to be announced.
>
>**Quest Cycle Tours, c/o Hamilton Travel, 227 Bath Rd., Suite 2, Kingston, Ont., Canada K7M 2X6. (613) 549-4400.**

ENGLAND
SCOTLAND

CYCLING ON YOUR OWN

Discover the least urbanized part of England with its rolling gentle landscapes, picture-book cottages, marshes and fens, and quaint seaside towns. You discover history as well, and do it all by bicycle—on your own. American World Travel provides a personalized service for cyclists in two regions—East Anglia (Norfolk, Suffolk, Essex, Cambs, and the Fens), and in the Highlands of Scotland. The East Anglia itineraries depart from the main cycle base at Saxmundham, a 2-hour train ride from London. Or you may arrive at a Suffolk farmhouse for a week's stay, with your cycle awaiting you there.

Once you select your itinerary from a great variety of possibilities, you receive not only a 3-speed touring bicycle with panniers for luggage, wet weather clothing, and puncture repair kit—but also a complete map and route guide for the tour you choose, and bed-and-breakfast accommodation—all included in the tour price. You may start any day except Sunday. There is no sagwagon, but emergency repair service is available. There's something for cyclists of every range of ability and energy.

April-October, 8-15 days, $180-$315. 1986 departures: Daily except Sunday.

American World Travel, Inc., Dept. BH, 6950 Squibb Rd., Shawnee Mission, KS 66202. (800) 255-6165 or (913) 722-5929.

ENGLAND
SCOTLAND
WALES

WATERWAY HOLIDAY

Cruising the network of canals of England and Wales, or the Caledonian Canal of northern Scotland, gives you an intimate look at "the real Britain" and a delightful break from the usual 20th century travel. You generally cruise 10 to 15 miles a day at a top speed of 4 m.p.h. Boats can be picked up at points throughout the canal system, and are equipped with modern comforts and designed to make the ride safe, simple, and fun for the beginner.

UK Waterway provides two types of cruising—the "Skipper Yourself" boats and "Hotel" boats. Two or more reasonably energetic and agile people discover how easy it is to be skippers. The steering is generally by a simple tiller, and a route-planner map keeps you from getting lost. Villagers direct you to special features along the way. A guidebook describes the best places to stop for meals or to buy food to cook in the galley. For a totally carefree cruise, join others on a "Hotel" boat where a friendly crew treats you to top-class food. Moorings coincide with interesting

Canal barge crossing an aqueduct—*UK Waterway Holidays, MD.*

places to explore—or stay on board and relax with a good book. Whichever way you choose, it's liable to make you one of the growing waterway travel fans.

>March-October: "Skipper Yourself", 7 days $322-$495 for two, group rates; "Hotel" boat, 4 nights $735-$945 for two, 7 nights $298 for one.

>UK Waterway Holidays, 311 N. Charles St., Box 99, Baltimore, MD 21201. (800) 424-9822.

ENGLAND SCOTLAND

HIKING THE HIGHLANDS

The Scottish Highlands and the British historic Lake District, like the boots you will have to bring, are made for walking. Legends of Bonnie Prince Charles and Nessie herself abound. A guide well-versed in Wordsworth, Coleridge, Sir Walter Scott, Beatrix Potter, and the like is more than a luxury. It is a must.

A veteran of arctic and highland expeditions, Angus Erskine leads each day's craggy climb, usually involving an ascent of some 3,000 feet. The toughest climb, near the end of the 17-day trip, when your legs are ready for anything, is up Ben Nevis (4,406'). Loch Lomond and Loch Ness are on the itinerary, as are Glenfinnian (*Chariots of Fire* filmed here), Hadrian's Wall, Balmoral, and Glencoe, Scotland's most dramatic glen. Be ready for 7-hour hikes.

>June & September, 17 days (from U.S.), $1,190 + air. 1986 departures: Jun. 15, Sep. 7.

>Mountain Travel, 1398 Solano Ave., Albany, CA 94706. (800) 227-2384 or (415) 527-8100.

EUROPE

CAMP AND EXPLORE 12 COUNTRIES

You don't need to have a bundle in your billfold to see the best of Europe. Trek Europa offers a flexible itinerary and affordable rates on its two-month trek through 12 countries—England, Belgium, Holland, West Germany, Switzerland, Yugoslavia, Turkey, Greece, France, Italy, Austria, and Liechtenstein. You camp your way across in the company of a dozen fun-loving young people (ages 18-35).

Depart London and begin your circular route in Amsterdam via miniwagon. You spend nearly two weeks in Greece—four days touring the Greek Islands and four days in Athens. Other highlights include the fortress town of Dubrovnik on the Adriatic, the exciting French Riviera, romantic Rome, exotic Istanbul, the vineyard-rich Rhone Valley, and ever-chic Paris. Visit the Gallipoli War Graves, Vatican City, Black Forest, Dachau Concentration Camp, and other noteworthy sites. You have other adventurous options—a canal cruise, whitewater rafting, waterskiing, and para-gliding. Bring your own sleeping bag—Trek Europa handles the rest.

>April-September, 56 days (from London), $1,499-$1,835 + air. 1986 departures: Beginning Apr. 5, alternate Saturdays.

>Trek Europa, P.O. Box 127A, Staten Island, NY 10309. (800) 221-0596 or (718) 948-2122.

EUROPE

EUROPE

SKI ADVENTURES

"Every skier dreams of a winter adventure to some place far away where the snow is perfect, the air crystal clear, and where each morning brings an exciting new possibility," says Leo Le Bon of Mountain Travel. His skiing staff has chosen 10 such European winter adventures, all ranging from 9 to 14 days—all truly "dream tours."

You have four different types of tours to choose from. *Classic downhill* offerings include stays at the world's finest resorts in France's Chamonix and Val d'Isere/Tignes, and in Italy's Monte Rosa. Also in the Alps, *downhill touring randonee* combines downhill and cross-country, giving you access to backcountry far from the lifts. The equipment is lightweight and specially designed for ascents as well as descents. *Cross country touring* in Norway and Lapland is through unskied, virgin terrain—forests, parks, and glaciers—while *cross-country trail skiing* takes advantage of the well marked and prepared trails that connect towns along either the Swiss-French border, the Oslo Fjord in Norway, Switzerland's Engedin, and the High Tatra Mountains in Czechoslovakia. On these trail systems the lodges range from quaint country inns to modern hotels.

January-April, 9-14 days, $940-$1,240 + air. 1986 departures: Downhill—Jan. 9 & 25, Feb. 8, 13, & 15, Mar. 1, 6, 15, & 29; Randonee—Apr. 3 & 11; Cross-country touring—Feb. 21 & Apr. 4; Cross-country trail—Jan. 17 & 31, Mar. 14.

Mountain Travel, 1398 Solano Ave., Albany, CA 94706. (800) 227-2384 or (415) 527-8100.

Dog sledding in the Far North—*Mountain Travel, CA.*

FINLAND/LAPLAND

AN ARCTIC SKI ADVENTURE

The Lapps developed skis over a thousand years ago as a way to follow their herds, and adventurous skiers of all levels find that Lapland, with its April snow and frozen lakes, is still a delightful skiing experience today. This trip takes you into the most scenic part of Lapland, where gentle hills rise up from the flat plains (it's never mountainous) and where the forest comes to its end far above the Arctic Circle. You ski over marked routes as well as untracked country. Watch reindeer being herded, and keep your eye out for colorful Lapp clothes with bands of yellow, green, blue and red signifying the four seasons.

Fly through Oslo to Tromso, Norway, for an overnight. Next day, drive to your ski base, Lake Kilpisjarvi, a tiny village on the Finnish-Norwegian border. Stay in a newly remodeled hotel that provides an interesting bit of civilization in the wilderness. Enjoy afternoon and evening ski tours, exploring different areas of the countryside daily. Evenings, slip into a sauna, have a hearty dinner, and enjoy drinks around the fireplace. If weather permits, an overnight ski tour is included.

April, 10 days (from U.S.), $1,090 + air. 1986 departure: Apr. 4. In 1987:

Mountain Travel, 1398 Solano Ave., Albany, CA 94706. (800) 227-2384 or (415) 527-8100.

FINLAND LAPLAND

DOG SLEDDING/REINDEER SAFARI

Imagine roaming the North with Dancer, Prancer, and Vixen. Or answering the call of the wild with a dog sled sightseeing tour. This 15-day winter wonderland expedition begins in Helsinki, where you board an overnight express to the Lapland capital, Rovaniemi. Mark your Artic Circle crossing with a champagne toast, then bundle up as you board a sleigh for the 3-day reindeer safari. That night discover the "Lapp" of luxury at a sauna and cozy log cabin at Vikajarvi. Ride to Hietajarvi for ice fishing at a base camp with an outdoor shelter—back to Vikajarvi for another sauna and a chance to compare notes with reindeer herdsmen.

Dog sledding is next after return to Rouvaniemi. Later, fly to Ivalo, have a delicious Lapp dinner, and return to Helsinki. It's witnessing Mother Nature at her whitest and wildest. Not to mention that you will be one of the select few on earth awarded an official reindeer driving license.

December-April, 15 days (from U.S.), $1,495 + air.

Arctic Explorers, Professional Building, Rt. 9, Parlin, NJ 08859. (800) 631-5650 or (201) 721-2929.

FRANCE

CYCLING ON THE NORMANDY COAST

This bicycling jaunt for connoisseurs covers all the highpoints of the Normandy countryside and coastline. From Paris, a bus takes you directly to Lisieux in the heart of Normandy. Setting out through the gently rolling countryside, you absorb lasting memories...apple orchards...hard cider and brandy...the elegant Belle Epoque Grand Hotel in Cabourg immortalized by

Proust…the D-Day beaches…Bayeux's beautiful cathedral and tapestry…camembert and goat cheese…rocky inlets and small fishing ports…a superb seafood dinner in Cherbourg…the dramatic seascapes at Cap de la Hague.

Julian and Jane Archer, who originated luxury cycling tours, are an historian and restaurant reviewer and personally lead each of their trips. You cover an average of 40-45 miles a day along promontories and beaches (a sagwagon carries the gear), have ample time to explore the innumerable sites of interest along the routes, and enjoy 3-star restaurants as well! Can combine with Loire Valley Tour. Also other itineraries in France.

July, 7 days, $650 + air. 1986 departure: Jul. 5.

Lucullan Travels, Ltd., 402 29th Street, Des Moines, IA 50312. (515) 243-4089.

A cyclist in the Loire River Valley— *EUROPEDS, CA.*

FRANCE

A BICULTURAL BICYCLE TOUR

Taste the cultures of France and Germany as you cycle through France's Alsace region, bordering Germany's legendary Black Forest. Here Bavarian sauerkraut, sausage, and wine merge with French know-how to give you some of the best and most unusual cuisine in a country of expert chefs. A sagwagon gives an assist with luggage and tired bikers, and bilingual guides smooth the way. You lodge and dine in France's finest.

Meet in the capital of Strasbourg before transferring to Marlenheim, the beginning of the Route du Vin. Cycle local roads, following the Vosges foothills and stopping for wine tastings. Take a winding road into the low, rounded mountains, where intimate resorts are set amid spectacular views of forests, lakes, and streams. After wine, what else but cheese? Begin the Route du Fromage, passing through villages of cobbled streets, carved balconies, and colorful windowboxes. Ride along the Fecht River to Munster, where you lunch on fresh Munster cheese dipped in caraway seeds. Meander through Colmar, admiring its pure Alsation architecture, sidewalk cafes, and museum. Ride to Chateau d'Iseenbourg, an elegant 19th century mansion—enjoy its gardens and take a dip in the pool. Return to Paris or Strasbourg for your flight home.

June-September, 9 days, $1,350 + air. 1986 departures: Jun. 16 & 30, Sep. 1 & 15.

Progressive Travels, Ltd., P.O. Box 775164, Steamboat Springs, CO 80477. (800) 245-2229.

FRANCE

PARIS TO THE MED BY BICYCLE

"This 21-day itinerary which takes riders from the hustle and bustle of Paris to the blue Mediterranean—610 miles of pedalling—is our longest and most popular tour," writes Peter Boynton of EUROPEDS.

See the very best that rural France has to offer in history, art, architecture, cuisine, landscape, and friendliness as you and 17 others make your leisurely way—seldom riding more than 36 miles a day—south from the capital. Highlights include: Chartres and the Loire Valley, Alexander Calder's home and studio, Bordeaux wine villages, the walled city of Carcassonne, and a 3-day layover in the tiny, 17-family hamlet of Baran. Among your accommodations—an old hunting lodge above horse stables in the Poitou region, a 350-year-old farmhouse, castle hotels and a 16th century bishop's residence. Bring your bike or rent a 12-speed Peugeot for $100. A sagwagon is always available, and you're accompanied by a leader and mechanic. Children are welcome; continental breakfast and dinner included daily.

June, 21 days, $2,145 + air. 1986 departure: Jun. 12.

EUROPEDS, 883 Sinex Ave., Pacific Grove, CA 93950. (408) 372-1173.

FRANCE

CYCLING IN CHATEAUX COUNTRY

Calling all cyclists and connoisseurs of all things French! These nine days in the Loire valley specialize in culture, cuisine, and countryside. Depart Paris by train for Angers to start your daily 35-mile rides over nearly level roads (easy for first-timers) eastward toward Orleans. Relax overnight at comfortable country inns or chateaux-hotels and feast on veal, fish, or chicken prepared with heavenly sauces and served with local wines. Vans transport luggage to each night's destination.

You pedal past fields, forests, and quaint Renaissance towns. See the famous chateaux at Chenonceaux, Chambord, Blois, and Amboise. Your bilingual guide describes the feats of Joan of Arc and other notables as you roll past battlefields and historic sites.

After a farewell celebration in Orleans at journey's end, you'll have little wonder why this region was the French nobility's playground.

June-September, 9 days, $1,295 + air. 1986 departures: Jun. 15, Jul. 6, Aug. 10, Sep. 1.

Bicycle France, Ltd., 2104 Glenarm Pl., Denver, CO 80205. (303) 296-6972.

FRANCE

CYCLING THE LOIRE VALLEY

Touring this country since 1972, Bike Tour France knows how to design flexible itineraries to fit whatever time you have for a cycling interlude on a visit to France. You may join the tour for a week, for 16 days, or anywhere in between. Or, request a special itinerary for your own group almost anywhere in France. Bike Tours France is considered by some to be "without equal" in the Loire Valley region, one of the most popular areas for cycling. BTF provides necessary ground transportation, hotel accommodations, all breakfasts and some other meals, use of an excellent bike, the best

Pedaling through a tunnel of trees in France—*Bike Tour France, NC.*

maps, full tour documentation, T-shirts, visits to French homes, and tour leaders of "unparalleled experience," says BTF.

The Loire Valley tour averages 31 miles a day. Along the way members visit cathedrals, museums, famous chateaux, gardens, charming towns and small villages, ending with an optional visit to Chartres and a celebration dinner in Versailles. "Some of the best biking I have ever experienced," comments a Dayton, Ohio physician.

June & September, 7-16 days, about $62/day, or $997 for the full tour. 1986 departures: Jun. 14 & Sep. 27.

Bike Tour France, Dept. C, Box 32814, Charlotte, NC 28232. (704) 527-0955.

FRANCE

CYCLING THE NORTH BRITTANY COAST

Explore narrow back streets lined with rows of half-timbered houses, enjoy lip-smacking Breton crepes and fresh-caught seafood, spend a night in a luxurious 16th-century manor house hidden in a dense pine forest, pedal around the car-free island of

Cycling a causeway to Mont St. Michel—EUROPEDS, CA.

Brehat with its smoothly paved roads, and tour dramatic Mont-St. Michel and the walled city of St. Malo, on this 14-day visit to the northern coast of Brittany.

You cover about 32 miles a day for 10 cycling days, on rented 12-speed Peugeots (fee is $100) or bring your own bike. EUROPEDS allows great flexibility—customize your tour (following an incredibly detailed map)—or simply take a day off and travel by van. Limit is 18 riders and you are accompanied by a leader, van driver, and mechanic. First-class hotels where available, and some excellent restaurants along the way. This trip links with a South Brittany Coast itinerary for those wishing more than two weeks to explore this wonderful culture.

September, 14 days, $1,398 + air. 1986 departure; Sep. 3.

EUROPEDS, 883 Sinex Ave., Pacific Grove, CA 93950. (408) 372-1173.

FRANCE

CYCLING IN PERIGORD AND THE DORDOGNE

Fly to Paris and Bordeaux, and transfer by chartered bus to Ste. Foy-la-Grande, on this 2-week trip to cycle through the Perigord region and Dordogne Valley of southwestern France ending with two final days in Paris. Averaging 35 miles a day, you stay at comfortable inns with most dinners and breakfasts provided. A van transports the luggage.

Ride through lush vineyards to quaint Saussignac on your way to Moulin de Malfourat where you get an extraordinary panoramic view of the countryside. Cycle past Gothic churches, castles, and elegant chateaux through the Dordogne Valley. Visit the Vezere Valley's prehistoric settlements and caveman paintings. Explore Rocamadour, a centuries-old village set in a rugged cliff, and Collognes la Rouge, built of red sandstone. "One of the most magical vacations of my life," remarks a Washington, D.C. cyclist who also commends the "food, wine, and incomparable beauty" of the entire region. CCT offers two other choice cycling routes in France—through the Loire Valley, and along the coast of Brittany and Normandy. Other European destinations include England, Ireland, Holland and Belgium.

June-October, 15 days (from U.S.), $1,229 + air. 1986 departures: Jun. 26, Aug. 28, Sep. 18.

Country Cycling Tours, 140-AG West 83 St., New York, NY 10024. (212) 874-5151.

FRANCE

BIKING THE RHONE VALLEY

Some bike tours are for people who enjoy roughing it, but Bill McBride has created a different kind of cycling experience. "Our trips offer sounds, colors, and the local people." In the South of France, discover unspoiled hamlets and two-dollar wines, Roman coliseums and French bullfights, roadside swimming holes, and scenes immortalized by poets and painters.

From Paris, take the TGV south to Avignon and transfer to Orange. Next day start cycling through the towns of Provence during "festival." Cafe sitting and people watching are favorite pasttimes, with music everywhere! A day's ride brings you to the Drone region with its tiny, ancient towns. Continue south to Avignon, the world-renowned wine region, for tastings and dinner in a candlelit courtyard. A many-splendored festival unfolds on the banks of the Rhone. Another spectacular festival takes place at Arles, the ancient Roman walled city, once home to Van Gogh.

Then cycle southwest to Camargue, a land of flamingoes, straw-thatched cottages, and cowboys. Take in the International Music Festival in Aix-en-Provence and visit Cezanne's studio before returning to Paris for your flight home.

July, 10 days, $1,390 + air. 1986 departure: July 21.

McBride's Earth Ventures, 6608-C St. James Dr., Indianapolis, IN 46217. (317) 783-9449.

FRANCE

RHONE VALLEY/PROVENCE—ON WHEELS

Connoisseurs of French cuisine and lush countryside head for this 10-day cycling journey through the Rhone Valley and Provence

A medieval castle backdrop for bikers—*Bill Wildberger for Bicycle France, Ltd., CO.*

region of France. Meet your group and bilingual guide in Paris before transferring to Montelimar, where the daily 35-mile rides begin, en route to Cassis. Spend nights in charming country inns or hotel chateaux serving fabulous French cuisine which changes from nouvelle to Mediterranean as you progress southward. A support van for luggage and repairs accompanies the group.

Pedal down the Rhone Valley past lavender fields and rolling hills on your way to explore the medieval town of Les Baux. See the Roman coliseum in Arles, the Augustus theatre in Orange, and the aqueduct at Pont du Gard. Meet the French when you stop for wine-tasting in each region. View the Palace of the Popes at Avignon and visit Aix-en-Provence with its fountains and tree-canopied Cours Mirabeau. Accept your cyclist's award at the farewell Bouillabaise celebration on the shore of the Mediterranean Sea. A great way to capture the rapture of France.

May-October, 10 days, $1,345 + air. 1986 departures: May 6 & 18, Jun. 3, Sep. 12 & 23, Oct. 4.

Bicycle France, Ltd., 2104 Glenarm Pl., Denver, CO 80205. (303) 296-6972.

FRANCE

THE LOIRE VALLEY ON HORSEBACK

In centuries gone by the Loire Valley was the favorite playground of French kings and nobility. Their magnificent chateaux were built when French culture flowered and the rest of the world sought to copy it. One can imagine them traveling on horseback from one chateau to another—or off hunting after wild stags or boar. (Some of the boars' descendants still live among the dark oaks).

This is your chance to ride, as did the kings, through the picturesque valley. With a French guide and no more than 12 riders—all of whom have solid knowledge of riding basics and some cross-county experience—you ride out each day through majestic forests and vineyards rich with grapes. Visit the famous chateaux which have become partly museums and stay as pampered guests with some of the private owners. Spend other nights at luxury hotels or rustic inns. Dining will be as memorable as your daily rides. The valley is famous for the finest of French foods. The trip starts and ends in Paris. (For another ride, in another area, Bitterroot Ranch in far off Wyoming will provide details on a week in Alsace.)

May-September, 8 or 11 days, $1,100 or $1,520 + air. 1986 departures: Jun. 8 & 18, Sep. 14 & 24.

Equitour/Bitterroot 27, East Fork, Dubois, WY 92513. (800) 545-0019 or (307) 455-2778.

FRANCE

CAVES AND CASTLES

Under the guidance of Dr. Ian Tattersall, Curator of Anthropology for the American Museum of Natural History, 15 travelers discover the best of France—its prehistoric caves, medieval castles, chateaux, and gastronomic delights. Fly to Paris and Bordeaux, then travel by motorcoach for 10 days, before returning to Paris to visit museums and walk through the Marais district. Stay in first-class hotels and restored chateaux (most meals included). Expect a great deal of walking, some over rough terrain.

A visit to the Lascaux Caves in Les Eyzies (if allowed) and the newly opened replica begins the exploration. Also visit Grand Roc, with its long tunnels; Cap-Blanc Rock with walls decorated by carvings of bison and horses; and other caves, castles, and medieval towns in the Dordogne Valley. Become familiar with Sarlet, Brive-la-Gaillard, Turenne, Rocamadour (hanging precariously on a cliff), Cahors, Pech-Merle, and surrounding villages. A sumptuous farewell dinner in Paris at the Musee du Vin (cellars of a former Benedictine monastery) marks the end of the exceptional tour.

May, 16 days (from U.S.), $3,880 + air. 1986 departure: May 2.

Discovery Tours, American Museum of Natural History, Central Park West at 79th St., New York, NY 10024. (212) 873-1440.

FRANCE

THE GREAT BALLOON ADVENTURE

The wind gently wafts you beyond treetops, with an unobstructed view of the French countryside, as you dangle in a basket from a huge, colorful balloon. Delighted country people in the vineyards and villages below shout greetings. The eventual landing is celebrated by a gourmet picnic and champagne, while waiting for the chase car to catch up and take the aeronauts back to town.

Burgundy, with beautiful rolling countryside, picturesque farms, and sleepy market towns—and the Loire Valley and its chateaux, manorhouses, and intricately decorated palaces—provide the two exotic locations for these aerial escapades, which balloonist Buddy Bombard organized nearly 10 years ago. His van picks you up at the Crillon Hotel in Paris for transport to luxury hotel headquarters, where there's time to settle in before starting off on your first balloon ride. Spend five days in Burgundy—or a week in the Loire. Mornings are for exploring the region by land, afternoons for exploring it by air, evenings for celebrating. What a glorious way to visit these history-drenched regions of France!

May-October, 5 days in Burgundy, $1,770; 7 days in the Loire Valley $2,970 or ½ week, $1,770. 1986 departures: Weekly.

The Bombard Society, 6727 Curran St., McLean, VA 22101. (800) 862-8537 or (703) 448-9407.

FRANCE

A PAINTER'S WORKSHOP

Paint and sketch the magic of a landscape and culture that inspired painters such as Van Gogh and Cezanne, Monet and Renoir, Miro and Picasso. Your inspiration comes from the picturesque seaside ports and the medieval hilltowns, and from the masters themselves as you visit the museums and observe their works.

From Paris, transfer to Nice and continue through peaceful villages and renowned artist havens before your return to Paris. Each morning, paint, sketch, and pick up pointers from your instructor, Jackie Kirk, an artist and instructor of watercolor at the College of Marin. Afternoons attend workshops and visit local museums including the Jeu de Paume and the Louvre in Paris, Chagall and Matisse museums in Nice, the Fondation Maeght in

Haut-de-Cagnes, the Musee de L'Annonciade in St. Tropez, and more. Spend nights at inns selected for their historic charm. Finish off your trip with a final showing of your work and a farewell dinner. The tour includes a bilingual guide, all breakfasts, eight lunches, and eight dinners.

May & June, October, 18 days (from U.S.), $1,890 + air. 1986 departures: May 9, Jun. 20, Oct. 2.

Wilderness Journeys, Box 807-AG, Bolinas, CA 94924. (415) 868-1836.

FRANCE

A PERSONALIZED STROLL

Take a dip in the medicinal mudbaths—it's only one of the many ways to immerse yourself in the countryside on this walking tour through southwestern France. Your guides, Rod and Maryvonne Buntz, meet you in Paris for a 6-hour train ride to Dax in the south. They accompany you on your choice of walks through their favorite off-the-beaten-path spots. Have dinner with them one evening at their 17th-century country house near the river Adour. Visit the wine cellar of their friend at Chateau Lignac in Bordeaux. Stop at a

Hiking in France's chateau country—*Mountain Travel, CA.*

mushroom farm belonging to another friend and sample the Saumur wine. The Buntz's bring along a rare personalized touch and an insider's feel for this rural corner of France.

On the tour you see the Cognac vineyards and wine cellars of St. Emilion, stop at small restaurants, visit a duck market, meet local shepherds, visit Basque villages, and walk through a fairytale castle still inhabited by its owners. The trip winds up in the Loire Valley, with stops at the chateaux of Usse-Villandry and Chenonceaux, before returning to Paris, and home.

June & September, 18 days (from U.S.), $2,090 + air. 1986 departures: Jun. 8, Sep. 7.

Mountain Travel, 1398 Solano Ave., Albany, CA 94706. **(800) 227-2384 or (415) 527-8100.**

FRANCE **CRUISING CANALS BY LUXURY BARGE**

Barging under a draw bridge on a French canal— *Michael Kenna for The French Canal Boat Company, CT.*

"The pleasures of a gentle nomadic life, the comfort and cooking of a luxury hotel, and the privacy of your own home"—that's how one writer describes his cruise aboard *Le Papillon*. Everything is first class on this former cargo barge, cut down to 96 feet to allow access to the smallest of France's locks, and refitted to accommodate six guests and a crew of four.

The week-long cruises in spring and fall are on the Canal du Midi. In summer *Le Papillon* cruises some of the navigable waters in Burgundy on the Canals du Nivernais, Bourgogne, Centre, Rhone au Rhin, Seille and the River Saone. Your departure date determines the exact location for boarding. An accompanying minibus ferries you to neighboring chateaux and vineyards—or you may simply relax on the flower-laden deck under the shade trees lining the canal banks. Another option: jog or bike along the towpath, rejoining the barge at the next lock.

April-November, 6 days, $7,800 for 1-6 persons + air. 1986 departures: Sundays.

The French Canal Boat Company, 285 Briar Brae Rd., Stamford, CT 06903. (203) 322-1370.

FRANCE

GOURMET CYCLING THROUGH THE DORDOGNE

Cycle past chateaux, castles, and caves on this picturesque route through the Dordogne River Valley, nestled snugly between the famous wine regions of Burgundy and Bordeaux. Considered France's most beautiful rural landscape by many, it's a region where mankind has lived for 40,000 years. The shimmering river flows westward, its banks lined with poplar and willow trees, rimmed with vineyards. Paved country lanes wind past chestnut groves and cows grazing on slopes above picturesque villages. Hilltop fortresses watch over the tranquil scene.

Meet in Argentat, on the Perigord border, and cycle along the banks of the Dordogne, stopping in a lush meadow for a gourmet picnic of local foods. Move on to Rocamadour, a cliffside village, and Sarlat, a reconstructed medieval town. At Les Eyzies-de-Tayac, view caves covered with stunning prehistoric paintings. In Bastide country, fortified towns recall the feuds between the English Plantagenets and the French Capetiens. You dine at several Michelin starred restaurants along the way. Lodgings are in chateaux and inns; bike rentals are included as are most meals.

May-October, 9 days, $1,290 + air. 1986 departures: May 16 & 30, Jun. 13, Aug. 29, Sep. 12 & 26, Oct. 10.

Progressive Travels, Ltd., P.O. Box 775164, Steamboat Springs, CO 80477. (800) 245-2229.

FRANCE

A LUXURIOUS CRUISE

For a luxurious, gourmet cruise through the Alsace countryside (from Strasbourg), or in the rural province of Franche-Comte (from Besancon), board the deluxe, 8-passenger charter craft *Panache*. "Each of our hotel barges," explains Continental Waterways, "features spacious wood-panelled salons, umbrella-shaded sundecks, and comfortable cabins with private baths." A private motorcoach accompanies the barge for daily excursions.

In Alsace you cruise through spectacular countryside to Hochfelden with its timber-facaded homes and shops. Then to Saverne in the Vosges Mountains. Other highlights: the storybook villages of Riquewihr and Ribeauville, Saverne and its majestic chateau, Bouxwiller with its famous crystal factory, the villages of Arzwiller and Schneckenbusch, the castle of Luneville, and the crystal house of Baccarat. In the enchanting Franche-Comte region, visit Dole's 15th century houses, cruise under dramatic limestone cliffs to Baume-les-Dames, and through spectacular woodlands along the River Doubs. Visit the Chateau of Belmont with its 16th century kitchen still intact, and the 17th century castle at Montbeliard.

April-November, 6-day charter, $1,400-$1,750 per person. 1986 departures: Wednesdays.

Continental Waterways Ltd., 11 Beacon St., Boston, MA 02108. (800) 227-1281 or (617) 227-3220.

FRANCE

CRUISING AND FLOATING

Everything is five miles an hour or less, whether you're floating on waters of the canals or on air way above. For a week of cruising the canals of Burgundy, you live on a luxury hotel boat transformed from a cargo boat or barge. Your floating hotel carries bicycles for cycling lanes along the way, and a deluxe minicoach is on hand for excursions to medieval villages, chateaux, churches, and vineyards. As for meals, be ready for freshly-baked croissants, an epicurean lunch on deck, and a five-course Provincial French dinner.

On one of this company's cruises you float from village to village each day, but in the early morning or evening, climb into the basket of a hot-air balloon to soar over the luscious landscape. Exhilarating as it is up in the air, coming down to earth again is a buoyant event with the knowledge that a delicious Burgundian meal is in the offing. Four or seven days of ballooning without cruising is also a possibility.

April-November, hotel boat, 7 days, $1,200-$4,500/person; charter, $2,800-$39,000.

Horizon Cruises, Suite 200, 16000 Ventura Blvd., Encino, CA 91436. (800) 421-0454, (800) 252-2103, or (818) 906-8086.

FRANCE

CRUISE TO FONTAINEBLEAU

Cruising on a deluxe hotel barge is a splendid way to see Chablis, a majestic region of famed wines, historic towns, and celebrated chateaux. The *Lafayette*, a newly built 22-passenger flagship, will take you there in style, with four-course candlelit dinners, the finest of cabins, and a superb chef and experienced crew.

The six-day cruise begins with a champagne welcome in Auxerre, capital of Chablis. Visit St. Germain Abbey, which houses France's oldest mural paintings. Then down the Yonne River to Vezelay and its famed Basilica. In Sens, see France's oldest Gothic cathedral (12th century), and indulge in delicious pate d'escargots from the local market. Visit the magnificent chateau in Vaux-le-Vicomte, and the waterside village of Moret-sur-Loing, made famous by the Impressionist painters. Then cruise through the forest at Fontainebleau, visit Marie-Antoinette's palace, and see the stately formal gardens. Optional (and extra) on this cruise: hot-air ballooning. (For a cruise through the Upper Loire and Sancerre, try the 24-passenger *Escargot*.)

April-November, 3 & 6 days, $620-$1,640 + air. 1986 departures: Every Wednesday & Saturday.

Continental Waterways Ltd., 11 Beacon St., Boston, MA 02108. (800) 227-1281 or (617) 227-3220.

FRANCE

A BARGE CRUISE FROM ALSACE TO LORRAINE

Explore the hamlets and villages in the foothills of the Vosges Mountains on this luxury barge, the *Stella Maris*, which cruises the Canal de la Marne au Rhin with eight guests and a crew of four. Your route through Alsace and Lorraine takes you past everchanging vistas filled with wildflowers, birdlife, and hints of history.

Buffet lunch on board a hotel barge—*Floating Through Europe, NY.*

Meet in Strasbourg, capital of Alsace, where sightseeing includes visits to the red sandstone Gothic Cathedral and the quarter called "La Petite France." In the afternoon, cruise the plains of the Rhine Valley to picturesque Waltenheim. Next, tour the vineyards of the Vosges foothills and visit the fairytale villages of half-timbered houses. Stop in Saverne to explore the Chateau Rohan with its museums of archaeology, fine and decorative arts. Climb through wooded landscapes to visit the crystal factory in Lutzelbourg, riding on an "incline," a device for raising boats up hills. In

Lorraine's pleasant countryside, you reach the garrison town of Luneville and the Duke of Lorraine's chateau. In Nancy, visit the Place Stanislas, Musee des Beaux Arts, Musee de L'Ecole, and explore the baroque buildings, gardens and shops. Top off your tour with a grand gala aboard your vessel.

April-October, 7 days, $1,095-$1,395 + air. 1986 departures: Every Sunday.

Floating Through Europe, 271 Madison Ave., New York, NY 10016, (212) 685-5600.

FRANCE

DECKED-BOAT PADDLING

For superb whitewater paddling, spend a week with Nantahala Outdoor Center in southern France (a departure from their Appalachian base) navigating everything from small creeks to high volume rivers. Anticipate Class III-IV water, chilly temperatures (the rivers are glacier-fed), and be ready with a good roll. The trips, not for novices, begin and end in Grenoble.

Intermediate decked boaters first paddle the Drac, nestled in the high alps, then the Guissanne, a tiny creek. Overnight at a canoe-kayak club camp before tackling the big, wide Durance with large waves, great for surfing and playing. Evenings relax at the main camp at Embrun, near the culinary offerings of villages. Advanced

Paddling on the Ubaye River in France—Mary Ellen Hammond for Nantahala Outdoor Center, NC.

paddlers run the lower Ubaye River (paddle beneath a 2,000-year-old Roman bridge), and tackle the Verdon Gorge, called the "Grand Canyon of France"—cramped between 1,000'-cliffs. Huge boulders, crystalline blue water, and a stretch that goes underground, keep you alert. The week ends with windsurfing and sunning on the lake below the Verdon, or simply enjoying Moustier-St. Marie, the quintessential provincial French village at the foot of the gorge.

> **June, 8 days, $850 + air & train.** 1986 departures: Jun. 19 (advanced), Jun. 29 (intermediate).
>
> **Nantahala Outdoor Center, U.S. 19W Box 41, Bryson City, NC 28713. (704) 488-2175 (ask for Janet).**

FRANCE

BARGING THROUGH BURGUNDY

"Cruising gently through Burgundy in our 74-year-old, 99-foot ship, the *Virginia Anne*, has been likened to the pleasure of traveling in a luxury passenger ship early this century in the golden age of elegance and romance," says Frontiers International, a company known for providing luxury vacations with a distinctive flair.

For a 3- or 6-day cruise from Corbigny to Mailly-la-ville, hop a train in Paris to Laroche-Migennes where you're transported to your barge in Corbigny. Travel the beautiful Canal du Nivernais in Burgundy—108 miles, 114 locks, and three tunnels take the waterway across the divide between Yonne and the Loire Valley. Pass lush pastures and woodlands, hilltop villages and busy markettowns, and via minibus visit places of interest—Roman remains, castles, the medieval hill village of Vezelay, and the Morvan National Park. Bicycles are also available, so plan to explore the canal towpaths and nearby towns and get some exercise at the same time. For those who want to see more of France, there are two longer journeys through France offered in the spring and fall.

> **March-November, 3-6 days, Charter only: $3,150-$7,400 or approximately $525-$1,233 per person + air.** 1986 departures: Wednesdays & Saturdays.
>
> **Frontiers International, Pearce Mill Rd., Wexford, PA 15090. (800) 245-1950.**

FRANCE

CANALS OF BURGUNDY

A spectacular cruise through the Cote d'Or introduces you to Burgundy, a land of fine wines, vineyard castles, Flemish-Burgundian art treasures, and gourmet specialties (including moutarde Dijon). Two understatedly elegant and well-furnished river barges, the *Litote I* and *II*, offer a combined weekly capacity for 42 pampered passengers.

After an escorted trip from Paris to Dijon on the high-speed TGV train, you start the leisurely river journey at the farming town of Pouillenay. Visit Semur-en-Auxois (a beautiful medieval town), and the monastery at Flavigny. Other highlights of the route: Beaune (wine capital of the Cote d'Or), the famous Hospices founded in 1441, the old priory in La Bussiere, a 12th century winery at Clos de Vougeot, Dijon and the Palace of the Dukes of Burgundy. An alternate route takes you from Dijon to Chagny. (For a cruise in the Bordeaux and Midi region, try an 8-passenger barge, the *Mark Twain*.)

April-November, 3 & 6 days, $590-$1,580 + air. 1986 departures: Every Wednesday & Tuesday.

Continental Waterways Ltd., 11 Beacon St., Boston, MA 02108. (800) 227-1281 or (617) 227-3220.

A French fisherman mends his nets—*Rod Buntz for Mountain Travel, CA.*

FRANCE

HOTEL BARGE CRUISING

A week's canal cruise in the Brittany and Loire regions, or in the Charente River/Cognac district, is offered from April to October by European Canal Cruises. It's "a memorable experience, superbly managed with class and style," in the words of an enthusiastic traveler. Providing gourmet meals prepared by Cordon Bleu chefs, and with twin-bedded cabins (private facilities) for eight guests, both barges—the *Duchesse Anne* and the *Royal Cognac*—meet passengers at points easily reached from Paris.

Each day's excursions take in historic sites, museums, chateaux, wineries, and Cognac producers. Bicycles are on board for pedaling through the villages and countryside. Even a game of tennis or golf can be arranged along the way. It's a glorious way to experience the delights of France's western provinces. For further travel in the scenic region before or after the cruise, luxury minibus travel coordinates with cruise dates, providing stays in small, country hotels and inns, private homes, chateaux, and castles.

April-October, 7 days, $1,320 + air; charter rate, $10,030. 1986 departures: Sun. & Wed.

European Canal Cruises, P.O. Box 71075, Seattle, WA 98107. (800) 367-0303.

FRANCE
SWITZERLAND

WILDERNESS SKIING

The French call it Ski Sauvage, leaving trails behind to cross vast natural areas of untracked snow, surrounded by immense glaciers and rugged peaks. With Le Grand Ski's certified guides, European experts in off-trail adventure skiing and mountain climbing, you join a group of no more than six to test your limits in magnificent snowscapes, where steep chutes plummet into deep open bowls. Your guides take you to fresh powder, even in inclement weather, select the terrain that best challenges your abilities, offer pointers on alpine ski techniques and are fully equipped and trained for mountain safety procedures.

Among Le Grand Ski's packages which SOBEK offers are ski weeks with three world-famous resorts as your base. Val d'Isere, with neighboring Tignes, is the world's largest ski complex (more than 100 lifts), and surrounded by cosmopolitan hotels, chalets, restaurants, and clubs. Chamonix, at the base of Mont Blanc, has long challenged mountain climbers and great skiiers with up to 9,2000 vertical feet of off-trail skiing, and also offers gourmet dining, cafes and cinemas, a casino, and covered swimming pools. Zermatt, reached by cog railway features incredible glacial skiing under the Swiss Matterhorn, and a spectacular descent into Italy.

January-April, 7 days, Chamonix, $820 + air. 1986 departures: Every Friday, Jan. 10-Apr. 4 + Sat. Feb. 15 & 22; Val d'Isere, 7 days, $960 + air. Jan. 3 & 17, Feb. 15 & 22, Mar. 14; Zermatt, 7 days, $1,160 + air. Feb. 28; Ski-Mountaineering, 14 days, $1,200 + air. Apr. 4, 11, & 18.

SOBEK (Le Grand Ski), Box AG, Angels Camp, CA 95222. (209) 736-4524.

FRANCE
WEST
GERMANY

GOURMET BIKING IN ALSATIA

Treat your eyes to the scenery of Alsace—the winding narrow streets and flower-bedecked "Romantik" houses. Evenings treat your palate to gourmet Alsatian and French cuisine on this cycling journey through one of Europe's loveliest areas. It's a trip for cyclists who are not out to beat any long distance records but are seeking congenial company, beautiful countryside, and friendly conversation over superb meals in intimate surroundings.

With your guide, begin in Karlsruhe, Germany, and pedal over vineyard-covered hills to Schweigen, on the border. Visit pottery shops, cycle thorugh the Haguenauer Forest, pass through miles of unspoiled landscape, with big farms, tiny villages, and an abundance of churches. Along the way visit St. Ulrich's Chapelle to major (and some minor) archaeological sites in mainland Greece. Your activities are varied on the route, which starts and ends in Athens. Some days, ride 20 to 49 miles, while other days you visit historical points via bus or swim in crystal clear waters. All breakfasts, several dinners, comfortable hotels, and a luggage van are provided. Bring your own bike or rent one.

View the famous Lions' Gate and excavations at Mycenae and explore the theatre where the ancient classics were first heard at Epidauros. Take a scenic cog-rail train up the gorge to Kalvarita and sail through the sea caves of Keri on the Island of Zakinthos. In Delphi, however, it's far too late to ask questions of the long-gone oracle.

May & September, 23 days (from U.S.), $1,249 + air. 1986 departures: May 8, Sep. 4.

Classic Bicycle Tours, P.O. Box 668J, Clarkson, NY 14430. (716) 637-5970.

GREECE / TURKEY

SAIL THE GREEK ISLES AND TURQUOISE COAST

Expect sailing, swimming, sun, archaeological sites, and the legendary hospitality of the natives as your everyday fare on this 2-week cruise through the Greek Isles and the Turquoise Coast in Turkey. Other highlights include tours of medieval monasteries and castles, dolphin sightings, nature walks, village celebrations, shopping for carpets and weavings, or simply swimming in the surf. Combine all this with the energy and enthusiasm of your captain, Nick Thompson, who left his engineering career behind in London to become a professional yacht skipper in the Aegean!

From Athens, fly to Rhodes to board a 48-ft. yacht. Spend most of the first day crossing the blue Aegean to Kas, surrounded by Lycian rock tombs and an amphitheater. Cruise to the modern harbor of Kalkan and nearby Patara, now an extensive city of ruins. Follow the coast to the northwest to reach Olu Deniz, the jewel of the Turquoise Coast. Here you stop for a swim in a cobalt-blue lagoon. Next is the coastal town of Fethiye, the small island of Baba Adisi, the sheltered bay of Ekingik, and Marmaris, a resort town. After several more stops in Turkey, cross to the Greek island of Kos, volcanic Nissiros, and the indented islet Simi before heading back to Rhodes for an overnight in a hotel, a farewell dinner, and flight home.

June & September, 17 days (from U.S.), $1,450 + air. 1986 departures: Jun. 14, Sep. 5.

Wilderness Travel, 1760-AT Solano Ave., Berkeley, CA 94707. (800) 247-6700 or (415) 524-5111.

GREENLAND

AN ARCTIC JOURNEY

Imagine a 16-day journey to the Arctic, up the West Coast of Greenland, under a sun that does not set, and where summer is one long day filled with vistas of snow-capped mountains, deep-blue seas, incredible icebergs, and deep fjords with blooming meadows and a surprising array of flowers. Cruise for seven days and explore remote villages that hark back to the old days, while at the same time adapting to new ways of life and modern technology. The climate is arctic and subject to sudden changes, but less so in Disko Bay. Yet, temperatures rise to 50-59 F. and even to the 80's, and without any humidity!

Exploring fjords on a Greenlandic Trawler—Dominic Capezza for Greenland Cruises, Inc., NY.

Depart from Montreal and stop off at Frobisher Bay on Baffin Island before reaching Greenland for a 2-day stay at Godthaab/Nuuk, the country's capital. Here you learn much about Inuit life from knowledgeable guides, at the museum, and in meetings with artists and locals. Cruise from Godthaab far north, to within 935 miles of the North Pole. The rest of the stay is hotel-based in Jakobshavn and includes fjord exploration in a Greenlandic Trawler, and a helicopter flight to the Ice Cap. The fully escorted trips are limited to 24 passengers.

June-August, 16-18 days, $3,350-$4,400 including air. 1986 departures: Jul. 8 & 22 (from Montreal); Aug. 17 (from L.A. via Copenhagen); Jun. 22 (from NYC via Iceland & Copenhagen).

Greenland Cruises Inc., 10 Park Ave., 24S, New York, NY 10016. (212) 683-1145.

GREENLAND

CRUISING ABOVE THE ARCTIC CIRCLE

Experience Greenland's majestic world of gigantic icebergs, Viking ruins, and remote coastal settlements, and cross the Arctic Circle. This odyssey into the "land of the midnight sun" opens up dramatic sights and cities seen by few non-natives, yet you tour by ship and plane in comfort with a small group.

Meet longtime explorers Skip and Susan Voorhees in Montreal, and proceed to Frobisher Bay then to Godthaab, Greenland's capital; Qorqut, at the end of a fjord; and Narssarssuaq, with Viking ruins dating back to the time of "Eric the Red." Hike, photograph, or leisurely observe the marvelous variety of birds and plants. Then it's off for a five-day cruise north to Jakobshavn on Disko Bay above the Arctic Circle. Here you hike across tundra to a promontory to view glaciers, icebergs, and at your feet the delicate Arctic wildflowers. Fly to Sondrestorm Fjord over the Greenland ice cap and back across to Godthaab.

July, 13 days, $3,490. 1986 departure: Jul. 15.

Special Odysseys, P.O. Box 37-G, Medina, WA 98039. (206) 455-1960.

HOLLAND BELGIUM

A TWO-COUNTRY CRUISE

Enjoy an intimate view of the 15th through 17th century glories that flowed into one long and golden age of Renaissance art and culture on this luxury barge cruise through the canals of Belgium and Holland. "It's the only two-country barge cruise in Europe," according to its organizer. On the luxurious *Juliana*, with a crew of seven pampering 24 guests, you glide under dainty white bridges through a splendid system of locks, and wind peacefully past fields of flowers and clusters of working windmills.

A hotel barge in Holland—*Floating Through Europe*, NY.

Fly to Bruges for a champagne welcome, dinner, and a meeting with the *Juliana*, your home for the next six days. Spend the first afternoon at the Groeninge and Memling Museums, then head out on an afternoon cruise on the Ghent-Oostende Canal to Deinze on the River Leie. Stop at the 16th century pink castle of Ooidonck and in old Ghent for a look at Van Eyck's "The Adoration of the Mystic

Lamb." In Antwerp visit the Royal Museum of Fine Arts, and in Delft tour the Delftswork factory and the Prinsenhof Museum. Conclude with a farewell dinner cruise through the canals of Amsterdam.

May-October, 7 days, $1,050-$1,495 + air. 1986 departures: Every Sunday.

Floating Through Europe, 271 Madison Ave., New York, NY 10016. (212) 685-5600.

HOLLAND BELGIUM WEST GERMANY

CYCLING IN THE LOWLANDS

Cycling's the way to see Holland and the lowlands across its borders. It's a biker's paradise with flat terrain, excellent biking networks, and picturesque scenes. These 5 to 10 day excursions give you a choice of Holland's provinces in the north, south, east, and center of the country, as well as across into West Germany and Belgium. All are unescorted, with overnights at country hotels and luggage transported each day by van.

Depending on the region you choose, you'll explore castles, watermills, and fishing villages, stop by the famous Van Gogh collection, and sample cheese in Edam. Heathlands and ancient villages (like Tilburg) appear along the routes, as well as winding rivers, and country mansions. You can cycle below sea level in the east, and ferry across the Rhine on the German tour. Windmills, clogs, and tulips turn up wherever you are on this cycling Dutch treat.

Year round, 5-10 days, average $32-$42/day. 1986 departures: Daily (unescorted).

Directions Unlimited, 344 Main St., Mt. Kisco. NY 10549. (800) 533-5343 or (212) 828-8334 or (914) 241-1700.

HOLLAND WEST GERMANY

A DUTCH BIKE DELIGHT

Everyone bicycles in Holland, and it's easy to pretend you're one of the locals—riding over wonderfully flat, picturesque terrain. Choose from 1- or 2-week tours, all averaging 32 miles a day with frequent stops for sightseeing and snacking. Your Dutch guide is bilingual. In the Dutch countryside you pass prismatic fields of tulips, daffodils, and hyacinths; idyllic dairy farms dotted with thatch-roofed cottages; quaint villages where craftsmen create Delft pottery and wooden shoes; and North Sea beaches. Tour the sparkling canals of Amsterdam, and indulge a sweet tooth with pastries and chocolates.

For the slightly more athletic, IBT offers a rougher tour through Bavaria's rolling hills. Pedal past vineyards and through fairytale-like towns of Gothic and Renaissance charm. Order a plate of bratwurst or weiner schnitzel for true happiness. In addition to typical hotel accommodations, you stay in romantic castles. Tour price includes overnights, breakfasts, and van for luggage. Transport your bike free on KLM, or use one of IBT's, free.

April-September, 1 or 2 weeks, $1,100 to $1,625 including air from NYC. 1986 departures: Apr. 20, May 3 & 11, Jun. 8 & 22, Aug. 3 & 17, Sep. 14 & 28.

International Bicycle Tours, 12 Mid Place, Chappaqua, NY 10514. (914) 238-4576.

HOLLAND
WEST
GERMANY

CYCLE WITHOUT HILLS

Cycling through Holland and West Germany with friends or family is made easy by Allen Turnbull whose headquarters are in far-off Virginia. He specializes in self-guided trips—7-day-loop itineraries on flat, flat terrain, which you may start any day. Travel to Arnhem, 50 miles south of Amsterdam, to pick up your 3-speed bicycle for biking in Holland or down the Rhine into West Germany. "It's a cyclist-friendly area," Turnbull says. Overnight lodging, dinner, and breakfast are included in his packages. Luggage is transported by van to each night's destination. Cyclists on these trips won't starve. A typical Dutch breakfast includes breads, rolls, juice, jam, eggs, sausage, ham, and cereals, and dinners are equally hearty.

Pedal past windmills and thatched cottages, ride through flower fields and quaint villages, explore forests, cross dunes, or visit museums on your daily 30- to 45-mile trek. You won't be cycling alone. In Holland 14 million people have 11 million bikes.

May-October, 7 days, $325 (family discounts) including bike rental. 1986 departures: Every day.

Bike Virginia, Inc. P.O. Box 203, Williamsburg, VA 23187. (804) 253-2985.

HUNGARY
ROMANIA

BICYCLING BEHIND THE IRON CURTAIN

"Cyclists discover that the lands behind the 'Iron Curtain' are vibrant, exciting countries full of colorful folklore, history, unique cuisine and beautiful countryside," reports Tom Sheehan of Off the Deep End. This cycling adventure takes you from the horse-filled "Great Plains" of Hungary to the mysterious Transylvanian Alps (legendary home of Count Dracula!) and from the magnificent city of Budapest to historic Bucharest.

Bring your own bike or purchase an 18-speeder. Stay at deluxe and first-class hotels (including a lakeside resort and typical roadside inn), and enjoy the finest of local cuisine, traditional native feasts, and bar-b-ques. You will be accompanied by a local tour guide, Off the Deep End staffers, and a sagwagon (carrying the luggage and available when you need a rest as well). Riding can be strenuous, covering 35-55 miles a day, over some hilly terrain.

May, 15 days (from U.S.), $1,165 + air. 1986 departure: May 23.

Off the Deep End Travels, P.O. Box 7511-F, Jackson, WY 83001. (800) 223-6833 or (307) 733-8707.

IRELAND

EMERALD ISLE CYCLING

Count the 40 shades of gorgeous green on this 14-day cycling adventure through scenic Sligo and Donegal counties in the northwestern part of the Emerald Isle. Travel by chartered bus from Dublin to Sligo where your daily 30-mile treks begin. Each evening listen to Irish tunes as you relax at a cozy country inn. A guide and a luggage van accompany the group and most meals are included in the price.

EUROPE

Ride along a jagged coastline to quaint fishing villages and wave to the natives who may still speak the ancient Irish language. Explore coves, sandy beaches, castles, ancient camps, and "fairy forts." Cycle around the picturesque Rosguill Peninsula on the Atlantic Drive, one of the most scenic roads in all of Ireland. Return for a 2-day stay in Dublin to shop for tweeds, visit the Abbey Theatre, and swap stories with the friendliest people. Says one cyclist: "This was my first experience with CCT and will not be my last—a unique vacation that will long be remembered." Other CCT destinations include England, France, Holland, and Belgium.

July-August, 14 days (from U.S.), $1,149 + air. 1986 departures: Jul. 17 & 31, Aug. 14.

Country Cycling Tours, 140-AG West 83rd St., New York, NY 10024. (212) 874-5151.

ITALY

WALKING THROUGH TUSCANY

Art and nature lovers rate this 12-day adventure through Chianti country a real find. From Pisa, you transfer to Florence for three days to take in the sights, shop, and linger in world-famous museums. Then it's six days of moderate hiking through scenic hilltop Tuscan towns. Finish your trek in Siena, the most well-preserved medieval city in all of Europe. Back to Pisa for departure.

An expert guide, comfortable accommodations, memorable meals, and fine Chianti wines are part of this package. Ramble through vineyards, oak woods, and olive groves. Explore ancient Etruscan villages, Renaissance palaces, and old family estates. Stay overnight in a country villa and a 10th-century convent. Meet the friendly local folks at wine-tastings. Discover Siena's magnificent

Walking streets in Florence—*Alan Cameron for Wilderness Travel, Ca.*

Campo, striped Cathedral, and quaint winding streets. A wonderful way to catch the flavor—and fever—for Italy.

May and September, 12 days (from U.S.), $1,190 + air. 1986 departures: May 4, Sep. 28.

Wilderness Travel, 1760-AT Solano Avenue, Berkeley, CA 94707. (800) 247-6700 or (415) 524-5111.

ITALY

A ROMAN HOLIDAY BY CYCLE

Discover the romance of Italy with nine days touring the beaches on bicycle and a weekend on foot in Rome. After a relaxing stay in Rome, climb on your bike and head out the Appian Way to the ancient town of Lavinium. At Nettuno, cycle through Cicero National Park on a quiet beachside road to Mt. Cicero, frolicking grounds for Ulysses. Cycle along more fabulous beaches to Terracina, whose tropical-like beauty earns it the name of "Gateway to the Sun." At Formia visit the tomb of Cicero. Other stops include the Isle of Ischia, with its ancient thermal baths; Naples, host of the volatile Mt. Vesuvius; Pompei and its ruins; beautiful seaside Sorrento; and the island of Capri, with its spectacular Blue Grotto. Return to Rome for flight home or spend an extra day visiting the Amalfi coastline.

Travel by bike opens up communication, Bill McBride believes. "You become part of the scene—you belong." His tours are loosely structured to allow following your own special interests at your own pace. Spend nights in comfortable hotels and country inns, with long and leisurely dinners and a briefing on the next day's ride.

August, 11 days, $1,490 + air. 1986 departure: Aug. 18.

McBride's Earth Ventures, 6608 St. James Dr., Indianapolis, IN 46217. (317) 783-9449.

ITALY

CYCLE THROUGH CHIANTI COUNTRY

"We leave behind the din of the crowds and the tourist clamor as we strive to find a new level of appreciation and insight that goes deeper than the 'Eurail Pass' awareness," explain the leaders of Butterfield & Robinson European bicycle tours. "The unknown hotels you'll always remember, the little road built just for you, the vineyard owner with a phrase that puts the whole country in perspective—these are the extras we offer."

Your cycling tour through Tuscany, home of Chianti wines, begins at the fabulous Villa La Massa, where your 12-speed bicycle is waiting. Cycle along the valley of the Arno River to the vineyard-laden hills for wine tastings at castles, villas, and farms. Spend two nights at an incredible villa overlooking the valley. In Panzano, sample more local wines as well as olive oil and homemade cheeses. Pass ancient castles, fattorias, and pieves, as you cycle toward the 14th century "Towers of Nobility" in San Gimignano. Explore the market, then head to Volterra and Siena. Here you explore the countryside or take a guided tour down the cobblestone lanes. Top off your trip with a celebration in the flowered garden of Villa Scacciapensieri.

>May & June, September & October, 9 days, $1,395 + air. 1986 departures: May 24, Jun. 14, Sep. 13, Oct. 11 & 18.

>Butterfield & Robinson, Inc., 70 Bond St., Suite 300, Toronto, Ont., Canada M5B 1X3. (416) 864-1345.

ITALY

FLOATING OVER TUSCANY

It's bound to be "amore" at first flight on this grand 7-day balloon adventure. From Rome, travel to Siena for a week at the luxurious Park Hotel, a former patrician palace dating back to the 16th century. Then it's up, up, and away each morning, flying over colorful landscapes with charming villas, vineyards, castles, and cathedrals. Wave to friendly Italian faces as they watch you drift along.

Lunch each day at a quaint, walled, medieval town. Afternoons—visit ancient villages and fabulous museums or drive through Chianti country. Back to Siena for festive dining and strolling Gothic streets to the Piazzo Del Campo. Breathtaking beauty and the spirit of the Renaissance engulf you. The experienced Bombard Society also flies over the Swiss Alps and the French countryside.

>May, 7 days (from Italy), $3,980 + air. 1986 departures: Every Tuesday.

>The Bombard Society, 6727 Curran St., McLean, VA 22101. (800) 862-8537 or (703) 448-9407.

ITALY
SWITZERLAND

PATHS IN A REGION OF LAKES

Walking in the Swiss/Italian Lakes Region—Butterfield & Robinson, Inc., Ont., Canada.

"In our 20 years of travel experience we have been constantly refining our concept—the discovery of hidden Europe," George Butterfield explains. The sophisticated traveler visits one area carefully, he believes, rather than seeing eight countries in as many days. This delightful walk through a glorious region of finger lakes with plant life, forgotten villages, and rock-strewn fields, mixed with lively Italian spirit and cool Swiss touches, confirms his theory.

Meet in Milan for a ride by private coach to a lakeside hotel in Luino, a quaint resort town. Take a cruise on Lake Maggiore before dinner. Walk to the Swiss border town of Ponte Tresa and float past tiny villages on the ferry to Lugano. Still to come on the relaxed journey: the ski resort of Lanzo, peaceful in summer months...valley paths between Lakes Lugano and Como...a ferry to Bellagio...a final evening at a lakeside hotel in Varenna...then return to Milan. The 9-day, proceed-at-your-own-pace tour with about four hours of walking per day includes accommodations at charming villas and hotels.

June-September, 9 days, $1,415 + air. 1986 departures: Jun. 5, Sep. 18.

Butterfield & Robinson Inc., 70 Bond St., Suite 300, Toronto, Ont., Canada M5B 1X3. (416) 864-1354.

NORWAY SCOTLAND IRELAND WALES

VOYAGE OF THE VIKINGS

Follow the routes first taken by the Vikings centuries ago on this 15-day cruise that docks in Norway, Scotland, Ireland, and Wales. Dr. Thomas D. Nicholson, the director of the American Museum of Natural History and an astronomer and mariner, as well as anthropologists and historians, are on hand to lecture about the legendary Vikings, Norwegian arts and crafts, geology, and the rare birdlife you encounter en route.

The cruise starts out in Oslo, where you board the *Illiria*, one of the finest small passenger cruise vessels in the world (only 74 cabins). First, sail through the breathtaking fjords of Norway, calling at several remote North Sea islands on the way to Wales and Ireland. Some of the other highlights: Oslo and Thor Heyerdahl's balsa raft, the bird sanctuary at Runde Island, the fjords and glaciers of the Norwegian coast, the colonies of seabirds on the island of Noss, the Bronze Age site of the Standing Stones of Callanish, the 12th-century St. David's Cathedral in Wales, Caernavon Castle. Finally dock in Dublin, and catch a flight home, or take the post-cruise extension through Ireland for eight days.

August, 15 days (from U.S.), $3,663-$7,645 + air; extension: 7 days, $689. 1986 departure: Aug. 12.

Discovery Tours, American Museum of Natural History, Central Park at 79th St., New York, NY 10024. (212) 873-1440.

PORTUGAL

AFFORDABLE FORTNIGHT

Is your travel budget slim? Not enough funds available for two weeks in Europe? Look again. These 15 days in northern Portugal's alpine valleys, remote vineyards, and wild, dramatic landscapes give you a meet-the-people adventure combined with hikes and easy climbs—at an affordable price. The tour is called "The Unknown North."

Starting in Oporto, drive to the rugged Geres National Park and stay for a week at a family-run pension. Stags, eagles, wolves, and wild horses inhabit the park. Ruins remain from the days of the Celts and Romans. Climb the granite peak of Pe do Cabril (4,048') one day, or hire saddle horses for the half-day trek. Drive to Boega for several days, staying on a 23-acre estate in a delightful 16th century manor house with a 20th century freshwater pool for swimmers. Back to Oporto by train. Before departure there's time to visit the old town and wine lodges of the Vila Nova de Gaia, and to take the single track railway to the Upper Douro for lunch at the region's most famous vineyard. Though at one point you cross the Lethe, River of Forgetfulness, the holiday will be one to remember.

April-November, 15 days, $440-$460 (most meals extra), + air. 1986 departures: Apr. 20, May 4, Sep. 21, Oct. 5 & 19. In 1987: Apr. 19, May 3.

Adventure Center AG, 5540 College Ave., Oakland, CA 94618. (800) 227-8747 or (415) 654-1879.

SCOTLAND   THE HIGHLANDS BY LUXURY RAIL

Elegant dining aboard the *Royal Scotsman*, Frontiers International, PA.

Breathtaking scenery, gastronomic excellence, historical railway carriages, superb service—The Royal Scotsman, a new luxury train with the feel of a luxury hotel, has it all—and more! Glide through the unspoiled beauty of the constantly changing panorama, relaxing in the restored elegance of antique coaches and pampered with outstanding service. The train has eight coaches, some from the late Victorian and Edwardian period. They carry an average of fewer than four persons per coach. The private compartments are double the size of any known in Europe. The luxury train opened its service in 1985, offering a prestigious journey that combines yesteryear with today.

Starting in Edinburgh, your route follows little-used railway lines running through the enchanting mountains and glens of the Scottish Highlands. You cover 1,000 miles in six days (or may choose a 3-day trip) and travel from the gently rolling farmlands and estates of eastern Scotland, through the rugged beauty of the central mountains, to the spectacular coastal scenery of the western highlands. The train makes frequent stops for photography and sightseeing and settles in each night in the quiet countryside. Along the way the 9-person crew wines and dines the passengers in the elegant 1891 dining car—the oldest railway dining car in use in the world.

April-October, 3 & 6 days, $1,380-$3,330 + air. 1986 departures: Every Tuesday and Friday.

Frontiers International, P.O. Box 161, Pearce Mill Rd., Wexford, PA 15090. (800) 245-1950; in PA (412) 935-1577.

SCOTLAND

CYCLING HIGHLANDS AND ISLANDS

"When you travel a lightweight 10-speed touring bike, you really experience the unique majesty of the Scottish highlands and islands," says Hamish Tear. Led by a Scottish guide, these 2-week cycling tours take you to mist-enshrouded hills, stormy coasts, lofty peaks, remote lochs, and quiet country towns. You cover an easy 25-35 miles a day, pedaling from village to village with 14 other cyclists. That leaves lots of time and energy for exploring, visiting with people along the way, or strolling out to find the heather on the hills. A sagwagon is along for baggage and tired-person transport. You may choose between more active and less active routes.

Each tour begins and ends in London. Overnights on some tours are at cozy bed-and-breakfast places, at luxurious hotels on others. You travel to your base at Aviemore and to tour starting points by train—a nice mixture of rail and bike. The six cycling itineraries differ. Head into the Isle of Skye and the Whisky Trail on one. Others take you to the castles of Grampian, the Sleat and Moidart forgotten glens, the Northwest Highlands of Garry and Duich, and other beautiful places.

June-September, 15 days, $988-$1,545 + air. 1986 departures: Jun. 8 & 21, Jul. 5 & 9, Aug. 2, 16, & 30.

Hamish Tear Expeditions, Ltd., P.O. Drawer 459, Vail, CO 81658. (303) 926-3286.

EUROPE

SPAIN

BALLOONING IN IBERIA

Add a 1- or 2-day adventure to your holiday on the Costa del Sol with a never-to-be-forgotten ride in a hot-air balloon. From Marbella it's just an hour's drive to Ronda to meet your pilot for early morning coffee and pastries and to watch the 90-ft. tall balloon being inflated. Then it's up and away, gently floating with the wind, close to the ground. Drift over the lush Andalusian countryside while a chase car follows to the landing—an occasion for champagne toasts to the aeronauts of the day. You're back by mid-morning, ready to complete the day with golf, tennis, pool or Mediterranean swimming, or whatever in this subtropical paradise.

World Balloon Tours can help with hotel reservations and will route you to casino entertainment and superb seafood and other Andalusian specialties.

   May-October, daily flights, $150/day + air.

   World Balloon Tours Ltd., 311 Bannock St., #C, Denver, CO 80223. (303) 469-1243.

SPAIN

The Scottish Highlands—Mountain Travel, CA.

EASY HIKES AND ANCIENT TOWNS

There are two Spains—one with tourists and the other without. Northern Spain falls into the latter category, although not for lack of beauty or history. It has plenty of both. Ancient towns, Romanesque art treasures, Basque fishing villages, labyrinthine mountain gorges, and Hemingwayesque streams brimming with the fish he loved to catch, make northern Spain a rugged undiscovered paradise.

These two and a half weeks of minibus travel and easy hiking (Grade A-1) begin in Madrid and end in Barcelona—the only two modern cities you see. A hearty 34-year-old Basque mountaineer (the first Spaniard to climb Mt. Everest) leads the group along mountain trails populated by a lot of goats and few people. Civilized highlights include medieval Avila, ancient but lively Salamanca, Altamira with its cave paintings, and the sights in San Sebastian and Pamplona. The rest is countryside, fishing villages, beaches, Ordesa National Park, and the badlands of the Pyrenees. With luck, untouristed Spain can remain a well kept secret.

June & September, 18 days (from U.S.), $1,490 + air. 1986 departures: Jun. 8, Sep. 20.

Mountain Travel, 1398 Solano Ave., Albany, CA 94706. (800) 227-2384 or (415) 527-8100.

SPAIN

Riding along the Andalusian Coast— FITS Equestrian, CA.

RIDING THROUGH SPAIN

Stop just dreaming of castles in Spain—go visit them, traveling the way Don Quixote did—on horseback. Your Portuguese military saddle is well-padded with fur, making six hours of riding easy and comfortable. (Picnic lunch stops followed by siestas in the shade of olive trees help keep your strength up as well!).

FITS Equestrian offers several itineraries in Spain, including one where home is an old mill converted to a guest house…a base for your castle explorations. There is a 2-week ride through the cobblestoned streets and along the Atlantic coast of Andalusia, and a 1-week trip exploring the fabled "white towns" and villages near Sevilla. Perhaps best of all is a 30-day ride across Spain from top to bottom. People from many countries participate, and while you needn't be an expert rider you must have solid riding skills, be in good physical condition, and be able to handle all types of terrain and all gaits. (FITS offers other itineraries in Spain and other countries.)

Year round, 9-30 days, about $90 per day + air. 1986 departures: Every week.

FITS Equestrian, 2011 Alamo Pintado Rd., Solvang, CA 93463. (805) 688-9494.

SWEDEN — CROSS COUNTRY UNLIMITED

No one cross-country skis like the Scandinavians, and no place has better skiing than Scandinavia. People of all skiing ability schuss to their hearts' content for a reasonably-priced week in one of the last pristine wilderness spots in all Europe. The famous Fjallnas Fjallhotel is your base. Tucked in the snow-covered forests and mountains of northern Sweden, near the Norwegian border, it offers a friendly atmosphere and warm hub for days of breathtaking panorama viewing and refreshing exercise.

After a hearty Swedish breakfast every morning, step outside into "The Way of the Kings," Europe's biggest cross-country ski area, strap on your skis, and venture into the snow. With 280 miles of good touring tracks, you will not lack for trails. It's wide-open space…your only companions are the reindeer, moose, and musk oxen that roam the area. Choose your own guided tours—up to 25 miles a day—then home to saunas, friendly people, and fine food.

February & March, 9 days (from U.S.), $750 + air. 1986 departures: Feb. 28, Mar. 7.

Ryder/Walker Alpine Adventures, Dept. A, 96 Gainsborough St., Suite 303W, Boston, MA 02115. (617) 267-5783.

SWITZERLAND — BALLOONING OVER THE ALPS

With the largest fleet of balloons in the world, Buddy Bombard has been taking travelers aloft in France for nine years. Now his multi-flowered air machines float over the peaks, glaciers, and rolling pastureland of the Swiss Alps during the month of August.

A week of ballooning revolves from two luxury hotels with elegant, old-world charm—the Bellevue Palace in Bern, and the Palace in Lucerne. With each day's flight scheduled in the late afternoon, mornings are filled with exploring old walled towns, towers, imposing castles, and farm villages, and with excursions by steamer on Lake Lucerne and by rail or cable car to dazzling mountain views. Aeronauts glide over pastureland dotted with small wooded areas, placid lakes, and picturesque villages—with the mighty Alps in the near distance as a magnificent backdrop. It's a spectacular way to experience the fabulous scenes of Switzerland!

July & August, 7 days, $3,980. 1986 departures: Tuesdays.

The Bombard Society, 6727 Curran St., McLean, VA 22101. (800) 862-8537 or (703) 448-9407.

SWITZERLAND **HIKE THE SWISS/ITALIAN ALPS**

Experience the grandeur of the Alps and the panorama of tranquil Swiss valleys with fellow outdoor enthusiasts from all over the world on an 8- or 16-day hiking adventure planned by Ryder/Walker. Begin the morning with a hearty breakfast, then choose one of two hikes varying in difficulty. The hikes are strenuous, ranging from six to 15 miles per day, with at least one peak of 10,000 feet, so you should be in good physical condition. There are expert guides to assist you with years of accumulated mountaineering and hiking experience. Overnight stays are in luxury hotels.

Choose from Saas-Fee, Zermatt, Pontresina, Kandersteg, Cortina (Italy), or a combination of any two. The charming mountain village of Saas-Fee, for example, provides steep and challenging terrain with trails weaving through lush valleys. Or perhaps sample the trails at Zermatt, the grand old man of mountain towns. Here you can explore glacial expanses or tread the tops of glorious summits. A third offering, Pontresina, one of the highest wind sheltered valleys of the Upper Engadine, is a scenic resort with over 100 miles of hiking paths.

Hiking in the Swiss/Italian Alps—
Ryder/Walker Alpine Adventures, MA.

June-September, 8 or 16 days, $775-$1,500 + air. 1986-87 departures: Every Friday.

Ryder/Walker Alpine Adventures, Dept. A, 96 Gainsborough St., #303W, Boston, MA 02115. (617) 267-5783.

SWITZERLAND CIRCLING LAKE GENEVA

If you've always dreamed of cycling in Switzerland and have a week's vacation (or want an add-on for another trip), here is the opporunity to explore magnificent Lake Geneva in only five days, riding three to seven hours a day and carrying your luggage in saddle bags attached to your Swiss-made bicycle.

Begin the 118-mile ride in Lausanne, pedalling out through quaint market-towns, vineyards and past flower-bedecked piers on the lakeside. Cross the border into France and cycle through medieval towns and tiny fishing villages. Back into Switzerland via Vevey and Montreux. Enjoy lake fish specialties and regional dishes along the way, and wind things up with a farewell fondue dinner back in Lausanne. Cyclists must be in good condition. The trip is fully guided, uses tourist class hostels (rooms with private baths), and includes continental breakfasts.

May-September, 7 days, $398 + air. 1986 departures: Nearly every Sunday.

Forum Travel International, 91 Gregory Lane, #21, Pleasant Hill, CA 94523. (415) 671-2900 or (415) 946-1500.

SWITZERLAND IN THE BERNER OBERLAND

"This route through the Central Swiss Alps, in the shadow of the majestic Jungfrau Group, offers the most spectacular terrain in all of Europe," promises Peter Boynton, creator of EUROPEDS. Reasonably well-conditioned hikers cover 85 miles in 9 days at a leisurely two to four miles per hour, along the remarkable Swiss trail system, marked and manicured with utmost precision.

Begin in genteel Gstaad, cross north-south ridges from valley-nestled village to village, and get a remarkable climber's eye view of pristine glaciers and jagged ancient peaks. Rub elbows with the rugged mountaineers who actually make it to the top, and spend two nights enjoying the sociable atmosphere of comfortable Swiss Alpine Club huts. Sometimes the going gets a litte steep, but the abundant waterfalls, verdant valleys, glimmering glaciers, and enchanting mountain architecture more than reward your effort! Link this trip with other Alpine hikes or cycling in France, if you wish.

August, 12 days, $1,100 + air. 1986 departure: Aug. 2.

EUROPEDS, 883 Sinex Ave., Pacific Grove, CA 93950. (408) 372-1173.

SWITZERLAND HIKING IN THE ALPS

With a 15-day Swiss Holiday Card in hand for unlimited train, boat, and bus travel and discounts on cable cars, chairlifts, and mountain cog railways, you have a passport to hiker's heaven. With a choice of alpine trails to follow each day and a first-class family-run mountain inn beckoning each evening, you have the ultimate Swiss Alps holiday!

Cecil Dobbins, a guide of 20 seasons, takes hikers from 5 to 75 years of age on 2- or 4-week hikes in three spectacular regions—the Valais (Zermatt and Saas-Fee), Bernese Oberland (Grindewald), and Lake Lucerne. Spend all or only part of the day on the trail. Take a cable car above the vee line and hike down on graded, well-maintained trails for up to 12 miles. It's a chance to walk the lush alpine meadows and absorb incredibily beautiful vistas most people see only on postcards. Zurich is the arrival and departure point for the alpine hikes.

June-September, 2 or 4 weeks, $1,310 or $2,620. 1986 departues: Jun. 15 & 29, Jul. 13 & 27, Aug. 10 & 24, Sep. 7.

Alpine Adventure Trails Tours, 783 Cliffside Dr., Akron, OH 44313. (216) 867-3771.

SWITZERLAND ESCAPADE AROUND LAKE LUCERNE

Keep fit and rediscover a more leisurely rhythm of life in a group of friendly people on this 7-day bicycle tour through the fabulous city of Lucerne and its surroundings. Spend most overnights in the comfort of hotels in the city, picturesquely situated at the north end of the lake of four cantons.

You are greeted in Lucerne by your leader and cycling companions and matched up with a 7-gear Swiss touring bicycle. Average 15 to 27 miles per day, traveling over small hills on moderate terrain. Along the way, pass pleasant hillsides dotted withn Bernese-type farmhouses, rich green forests, fertile meadows, and historic monasteries, chapels, and churches. Highlights include visits to Hergiswil, a summer resort; a tour of a glass-blowing factory; a trip to the health resort of Schwarzenberg (2,772'). You'll have a chance to take a rack railway up Mount Rigi for an overnight in Kaltbad. And, of course, you won't want to miss a ride up the steepest cog-wheel railway in the world to Mount Pilate (7,000'), where you'll have a magnificent view of Lucerne and a scenic panorama of the alpine ranges. You'll return home with unrivaled memories!

May-October, 7 days, $750 (or $570 with budget-class hotels) + air. 1986 departures: May 19, Jun. 2 & 30, Jul. 28, Aug. 25, Sep. 22, Oct. 6.

American World Travel, Inc., 6950 Squibb Rd., Shawnee Mission, KS 66202. (800) 255-6165 or (913) 722-5929.

SWITZERLAND MULE SAFARI IN THE ALPS

This 63-mile trek in the mountains of the Valais canton in southwest Switzerland, the Matterhorn country, is made on the back of a mule and on foot—one mule for two people. Caravans with 20 participants travel for a week from one mountain valley to another, over mule paths to picturesque mountain villages, where they stop overnight at country inns. It's the Switzerland of your dreams—meadows carpeted with wildflowers, bright blue sky against snowy mountians, passes at 7,000 feet, larch forests, rushing streams, and mountain fauna.

The sure-footed, friendly mules (they never refuse a lump of sugar!) provided the only transport between the villages and the outside world in past generations. Today the villagers welcome them back along with their riders from faraway. No previous experience is needed. Just be physically fit and enjoy open air, exercise, fun, and adventure. The route begins and ends at the Sion railway station with bus transfer to Grimentz or Haute-Nendaz at the start, and back again at the finish. Minimum age: 12.

June-September, 7 days, $598 + air. 1986 departures: Nearly every Sunday. (In July, only Jul. 3.)

Forum Travel International, 91 Gregory Lane, # 21, Pleasant Hill, CA 94523. (415) 671-2900 or (415) 946-1500.

SWITZERLAND — SKI TOURING THE HAUTE ROUTE

Chamonix and Zermatt, two foremost mountaineering and skiing centers and two of the most popular, can get downright crowded. Beat the lift-lines by traversing the awe-inspiring, 40-mile-long Chamonix-to-Zermatt Haute Route, a series of rigorous high mountain passes and interlocking glaciers that wind through the renowned summits of France, Switzerland, and Italy. It's an exhilarating adventure—with overnights in mountain huts.

After several days of "acclimatizing" in quaint Chamonix, begin a week's trek. Traverse the Argentiere Glacier, descend through the Col des Escandies, continue the Haute Route through Col de la Chaux and ascend to the Cabane des Dix below the impressive north face of Mont Blanc. Ski the finest peak in the western Pennine Alps and descend to the famous Vignettes Hut. The final day's famous descent beneath the walls of the Matterhorn to Zermatt leads to hot baths and gourmet meals at a sumptuous 4-star hotel.

April, 14 days, (from U.S.), $1,350 + air. 1986 departure: April 19.

Ryder/Walker Alpine Adventures, Dept. A, 96 Gainsborough St., Suite 303W, Boston, MA 02115. (617) 267-5783.

SWITZERLAND — FLAVOR OF ITALY IN A WALKER'S PARADISE

In the Southern Swiss Alps find all the flavor of Italy and a hikers's paradise of glaciers, snow-capped peaks, granite canyons, swift mountain streams, alpine meadows carpeted with wildflowers and butterflies, and romantic stone-hewn villages. This hiking trip follows a unique itinerary through three of Switzerland's most culturally-intact and visually-distinct regions.

Begin in Ticino, the Yosemite of Switzerland. Hike across the Alps into the lovely Val Bavona and Val Maggia, exploring granite-hewn villages and sampling rich Merlot wines. After a brief sojourn in Lugano, journey into the rare beauty of the Val Bregaglia, with it stupendous alpine spires, forests of chestnut, and its 3,000 year descendants—warriors and artisans. Ascent into Les Grisons by hiking in the "eternal snows of the Bernina Range" among the Romansh-speaking peoples of the Upper Engadine. This is untouristy Switzerland at its best. Accommodations in country inns, palazzos, and Swiss alpine huts. Trip includes visits to Chur, St. Moritz, Lugano, Lucerne, and Zurich.

July & September, 16 days (from U.S.), $2,361 including air. 1986 departures: Jul. 12, Sep. 13.

Wilderness Journeys, P.O. Box 807-AG, Bolinas, CA 94924 (415) 868-1836.

SWITZERLAND — THE ALPS OF SUMMER

Discover some of the lesser known mountains and valleys with Swiss guide Lydia Garret-Lipp. Every August she meets Americans in her homeland to lead them on day trips off the beaten track, and to share her knowledge of local customs and lore. This leisurely 2-week tour is flexible enough to offer a choice of exhilarating, high-mountain hikes and easier scenic walks, plus opportunities to chat with innkeepers and with the people in one picturesque village after another. No special skills are required, but you should be in good health.

After a welcoming fondue dinner in Bern, travel through the Wallis region near Zermatt by train, postal bus, and cable car, for five days of excursions from Saas-Fee. Then in Italian-speaking Ticino, walk the Strada Alta (High Road), observe cheese-making, and pass meadows along the way. From Cavigliano, walk or hike into the romantic valleys and stop for a swim in a mountain stream or Lake Maggiore. Other stops: Locarno, Andermatt, Disentis, and Fluelen, where you board a steamship for an excursion on Lake Lucerne in the heart of Switzerland to the old town of Lucerne. A last mountain excursion via the world's steepest cog railway to Mt. Pilatus ends with a farewell raclette dinner in Lucerne.

August, 15 days, $1,150 + air. 1986 departure: Aug. 9.

Swiss Hike, c/o Garrett-Lipp & Associates, Inc., P.O. Box 3236, Lacey, WA 98503. (206) 491-6836.

SWITZERLAND WEST GERMANY — BIKING THROUGH THE RHINE VALLEY

How about spending most nights in dormitory-style lodging, preparing your own meals, and pedalling 40-50 miles a day over some rough terrain? Pack up your bike, tool kit, and travel gear—and get ready to spin your bicycle wheels through some of Europe's most scenic towns and landscapes.

This 25-day journey begins in London, then on to France, pedalling along the vineyard-lined banks of the River Mosel. In Germany you follow the Rhine, and stay in a castle hostel set in the mountainside town of Bachrach. Then cruise downriver, gazing upon still more castles that line the route. Cycle through the dramatic Black Forest, then on to explore the peaks, glaciers, and picture postcard villages that make up the Swiss Alps. Enjoy a 2-day stopover in Grindelwald, the famous Swiss sports center, where you have time to hike, ride a cable car, or relax in a sauna. Back to London and home.

August-September, 25 days (from U.S.), $1,550 includes air. 1986 departures: Aug. 8 (adult), Jul. 25 (youth), Sep. 5 (open).

American Youth Hostels, P.O. Box 37613, Washington, DC 20013-7613. (202) 783-6161.

SWITZERLAND
WEST
GERMANY

RIDING THROUGH THE RHINE

American Youth Hostels, known for its youth tours, now provides adult-only trips as well. One departure is for adults, another for youth, and a third trip for families on this 25-day cycling tour of the Rhine Valley. Participants supply their own equipment and 10-speed bikes, and are rarely beginners. A day's

Visiting Bern on a bike trip in Switzerland—*American Youth Hostels, D.C.*

ride averages between 40-50 miles on some rough roads. Evenings, relax at cozy youth hostels where the group prepares dinner with local cheeses, wursts, and other specialties.

Begin in London and stop in Luxembourg en route to Germany's Rhine Valley and scenic Switzerland. Pedal down the vineyard-lined banks of River Mostel, where the alpine peaks form a dramatic background. Stroll along the famous promenade in Heildelberg and tour historic Trier. After a Rhine River cruise, spend the night at Bacharach castle. Then cycle through the enchanted Black Forest region. At Grindelwald, the Swiss sports center, hike, ride a cable car, or relax in a sauna before you return to London for a flight home filled with "wunderbar" memories!

>**July-September, 25 days (from U.S.), $1,495 + air.** 1986 departures: July 26 (youth), Aug. 9 (adult), Sep. 13 (open).

>**American Youth Hostels, 1332 I St., N.W., Suite 800, Washington, DC 20005. (202) 783-6161.**

WALES

A WELSH WONDERLAND

"This former stronghold of the Celts, one of the few areas spared by the invasion of the Anglo-Saxons, remains much as it was centuries ago," comments Bayard Fox of Equitour/Bitterroot. See for yourself on this week-long, 125-mile horseback ride as you visit isolated farmhouses, pass moorlands and meadows where sheep graze, and meet friendly Welsh people who take the time to share their songs, folk tales, and unusual language, though it will be some time before you'll master their spelling.

From London, drive to Cwmfforest in the Black Mountains, where you stay with your Welsh hosts in a pleasant 17th century farmhouse. Spend the first evening around the fireplace after dinner discussing the trip ahead. Next morning, you'll mount a horse from a fine stable of Hannoverians, thoroughbreds, and sturdy Welsh cobs. Then it's off through the forest to Llathony Priory, continuing through the Black Forest via Offe Duike and Mye on Wye. En route, picnic along the road and at pubs and absorb the rich countryside with its grassy rolling hills, wooded slopes, and peaceful lakes. Spend overnights in farmhouses, one near the abbey of Strata Florida. Hilly country brings you to Aberystwyth on the coast for your drive back to Cwmfforest and London. It's a delightful opportunity to meet the Welsh and explore a bit of the British Isles the way they used to be.

>**May-September, 8 days, $770 + air.** 1986 departures: May 24, Jun. 21, Jul. 19, Aug. 2, Sep. 13.

>**Equitour/Bitterroot 27, East Fork, Dubois, WY 82513. (800) 545-0019 or (307) 455-2778.**

WEST GERMANY

FLOATING DOWN THE NECKAR—IN LUXURY

Cruise the exquisitely beautiful River Neckar by luxury hotel barge, following a romantic valley of marvelously wooded landscape beneath castle-crowned slopes and hills. Like other cruises offered by this company, it is designed for the discerning traveler who appreciates the comfort of luxury floating hotels.

Meet in Heidelberg for a champagne welcome. Here you explore the nooks and crannies of this storybook, red-roofed town rising above the river. The next morning cast off on the 10-passenger Lys, manned by a crew of four, at the landmark six-arch bridge to begin the river-long panorama down to Stuttgart. Cruise to Hirschhorn, probably the most picturesque of all river towns. Moor at Eberbach, a former imperial residence, then head to Mosbach with its tiny cobblestoned streets and marketplace. Continue along the widening river, moving from dense woodlands and forests to the orchards and vineyards of Lauffen, a romantic walled town. Stop to meet the growers and sample the wine. Spend your final day cruising to Stuttgart, with a stop at Ludwigsburg, a cosmopolitan city of baroque, classical and empire architecture. All too soon, end the cruise with a farewell feast aboard the Lys.

June-October, 7 days, $1,295 + air. 1986 departure: Every Sunday.

Floating Through Europe, 271 Madison Ave., New York, NY 10016. (212) 685-5600.

WEST GERMANY

CANOEING THE NECKAR

Castle-to-castle canoeing is a new experience for most paddlers. On this castle-lined river you drift lazily along, land where you wish to explore the ramparts of a historic castle, sit down at a waterfront cafe for lunch, or picnic in a garden. At night you settle in at a manor house or castle that takes in guests, or in a quaint guest house. A van accompanies your group to carry luggage and take you on journeys through the countryside.

Meet in Stuttgart, then travel by bus to Bad Friedrichshal where your aquatic adventure begins. Five days of paddling takes you through some of the most beautiful scenery in southern Germany. The outing ends in Heidelberg, with time to explore its famous university and 16th century castle, and museums and marketplaces, before driving back to Stuttgart.

August, 9 days (from U.S.), $1,095 + air. 1986 departure: Aug. 30.

Off the Deep End Travels, P.O. Box 7511-F, Jackson, WY 83001. (800) 223-6833 or (307) 733-8707.

WEST GERMANY

BIKING THROUGH THE BLACK FOREST AND MORE

Effort and elegance are combined in these leisurely, yet exciting 8- or 10-day bike tours through the wineries, resorts, and cultural-historical sights of the Upper Rhine Valley, the Black Forest, and Lake Constance. The pace is leisurely (average of 30 miles a day), though bikers should have some experience. Each group of cyclists (maximum of 19 per group) is provided with specially-designed, 10-speed cruising bicycles, and is accompanied by a biking guide, a van, and a bike trailer for the temporarily faint-hearted. You sup and overnight in carefully selected country inns, many of which have swimming pools—a welcome sight for the sore of leg.

Begin in Buchschlag outside of Frankfurt. Pedal through dense forests to a baroque hunting castle. Visit the medieval King's Hall, a Carolingian architectural treasure. In Heidelberg, stay at the famous Hotel Zum Ritter, and visit the castle. Then off to Baden-Baden, Germany's most elegant spa and gambling haven. The tour includes the wine-growing region of Baden and a spectacular view of the Rhine River. (Also self-guided hiking trips offered through this wonderful area.)

May-September, 8 or 10 days, $625-$850 + air. Frequent departures.

Forum Travel International, 91 Gregory Lane, #21, Pleasant Hill, CA 94523. (415) 946-1500 or (415) 671-2900.

WEST GERMANY AUSTRIA

CYCLING TO SALZBURG

Between Heidelberg in Germany and Salzburg in Austria there's excitement for both the eye and the palate. Pedaling 36 miles a day along backroads, past castles, walled villages, lakes, and famous rivers, you have the delight of sampling specialties of a new region about every 40 miles.

Rothenburg, Dinkelsbuehl, and Munich are among the 12 picture-book towns and cities on the two-wheeling trek. Detailed maps and itineraries give you historical and cultural pointers. Explore a Benedictine monastery. Visit a tapestry museum. Wander through medieval towns. Go swimming, sailing, or kayaking near Salzburg with the Alps as a backdrop. Bring your own bike (free on international flights) and pedal with the group or at your own pace when you wish. A sagwagon carries luggage or cyclists who need a day off.

July, 15 days, $1,495 + air. 1986 departure: July 12.

Gerhard's Bicycle Odysseys, 4949 Southwest Macadam, Portland, OR 97201. (503) 223-2402.

WESTERN EUROPE

Traveling on a "road" in Venice— Trek Europa, NY.

DRIVE, SIGHTSEE, AND CAMP

Even on a limited budget you can discover Europe's highlights on this 21-day tour through the major cities and magnificent countryside of Belgium, Holland, West Germany, Switzerland,

Austria, Italy, Monaco, and France! It's a trek full of contrasts from the bustle of Paris to the breathtaking Bavarian Alps. You cruise the canals of Venice in a gondola, windsurf on the French Riviera, explore the fairytale town of Salzburg, and discover cathedrals, ancient ruins, and gelato stands in Rome. Plenty of chances to meet the people—you shop in local markets and cook over your campfire.

The trip begins in London, then to Brussels. From here drive in comfortable maxiwagons with a guide and 11 other travelers, all between the ages of 18 to 35. Move on to Amsterdam, then down through Heidelberg and the Bavarian Alps. Visit the major Italian sites in Venice, Florence, and Rome. Finally, start your journey back north, passing through the romantic French Riviera, the vineyards of Grenoble, and Lake Geneva's lush wonderland. In Paris, take in the Eiffel Tower and the exhilarating nightlife, then head back to London with souvenirs and newfound friendships in tow.

April-September, 21 days, $525-$673 + air & meals. 1986 departures: Apr. 12 & 26, May 10; Every Saturday May 24-Sep.20.

Trek Europa, P.O. Box 127A, Staten Island, New York, NY 10309. (800) 221-0596 or (718) 948-2122.

WESTERN EUROPE / NORTH AFRICA

DRIVE AND CAMP

Outdoors lovers and value seekers: Take note of this 5-week exploration of eight Mediterranean and North African countries! Depart from London, then head to Spain where you hop aboard a minivan with a group of 12 between the ages of 18 and 35. Stop in Madrid, Granada, and Seville before traveling to Portugal and Gibraltar. Continue on to Morocco, Tunisia, and Algeria, then drive north through Avignon and Paris back to London for a flight home. (Or reverse the route.) "Camping is the key to keeping our itineraries flexible," says Trek Europa. "It creates a fun back-to-nature feeling that's at the heart of our holidays." You camp each night (bring a sleeping bag) and cook hearty meals over the fire.

Trip highlights include the Left Bank in Paris with its artists, cafes, and romantic charm; the well-preserved Spanish medieval town of Toledo; the bustling Marrakech Bazaar; the Koutoubia Mosque; the famous Kasbah. At the beautiful beaches of the Costa Del Sol you may join or leave the trip if your time is limited to two or three weeks. An unforgettable adventure for those who want to explore this fascinating area in a free and flexible way.

April-September, 35 days, $1,130-$1,325 + air. 1986 departures: Apr. 3, May 7, Jun. 16, Jul. 21, Aug. 18, Sep. 22.

Trek Europa, P.O. Box 127A, Staten Island, New York, NY 10309. (800) 221-0596 or (708) 948-2122.

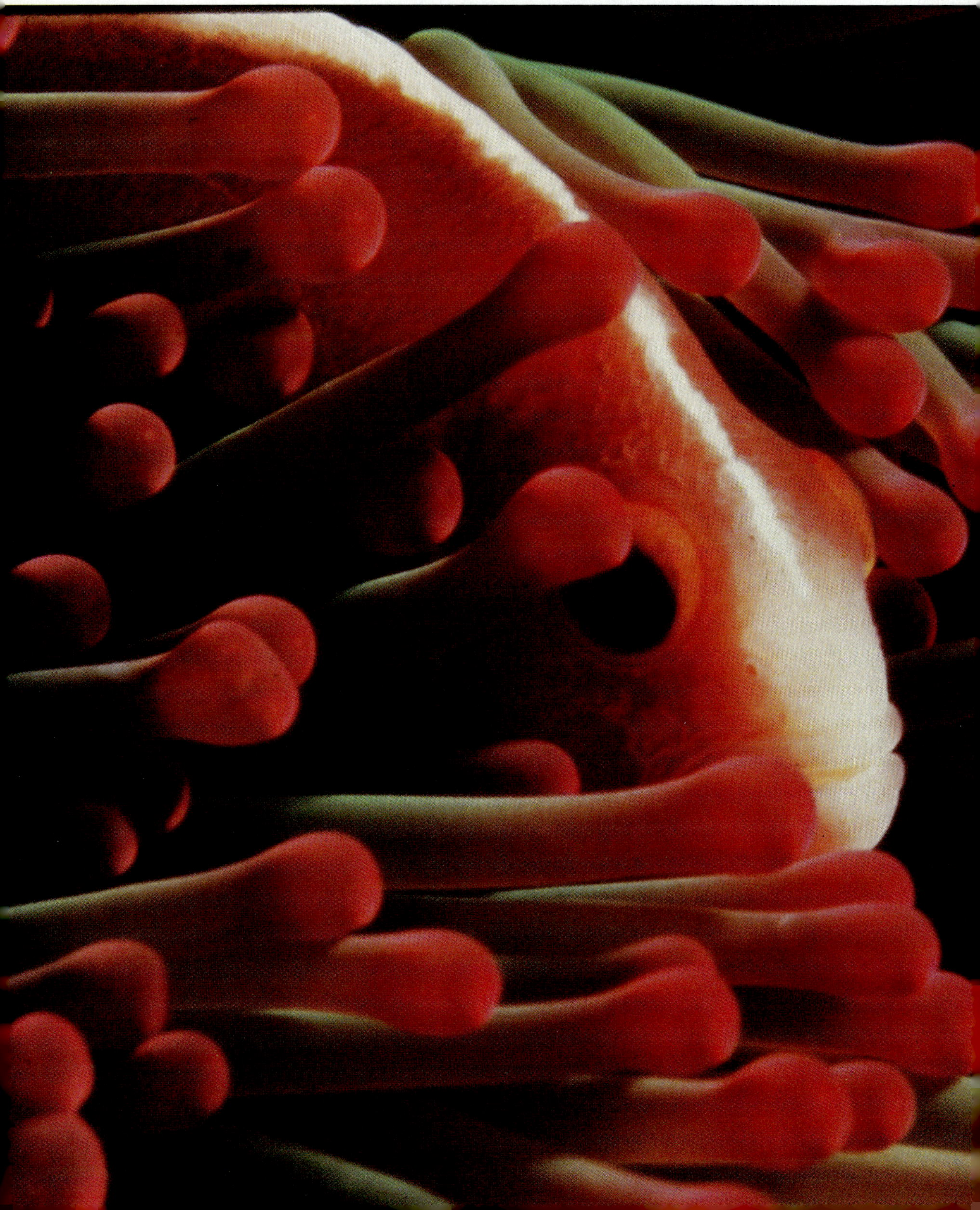

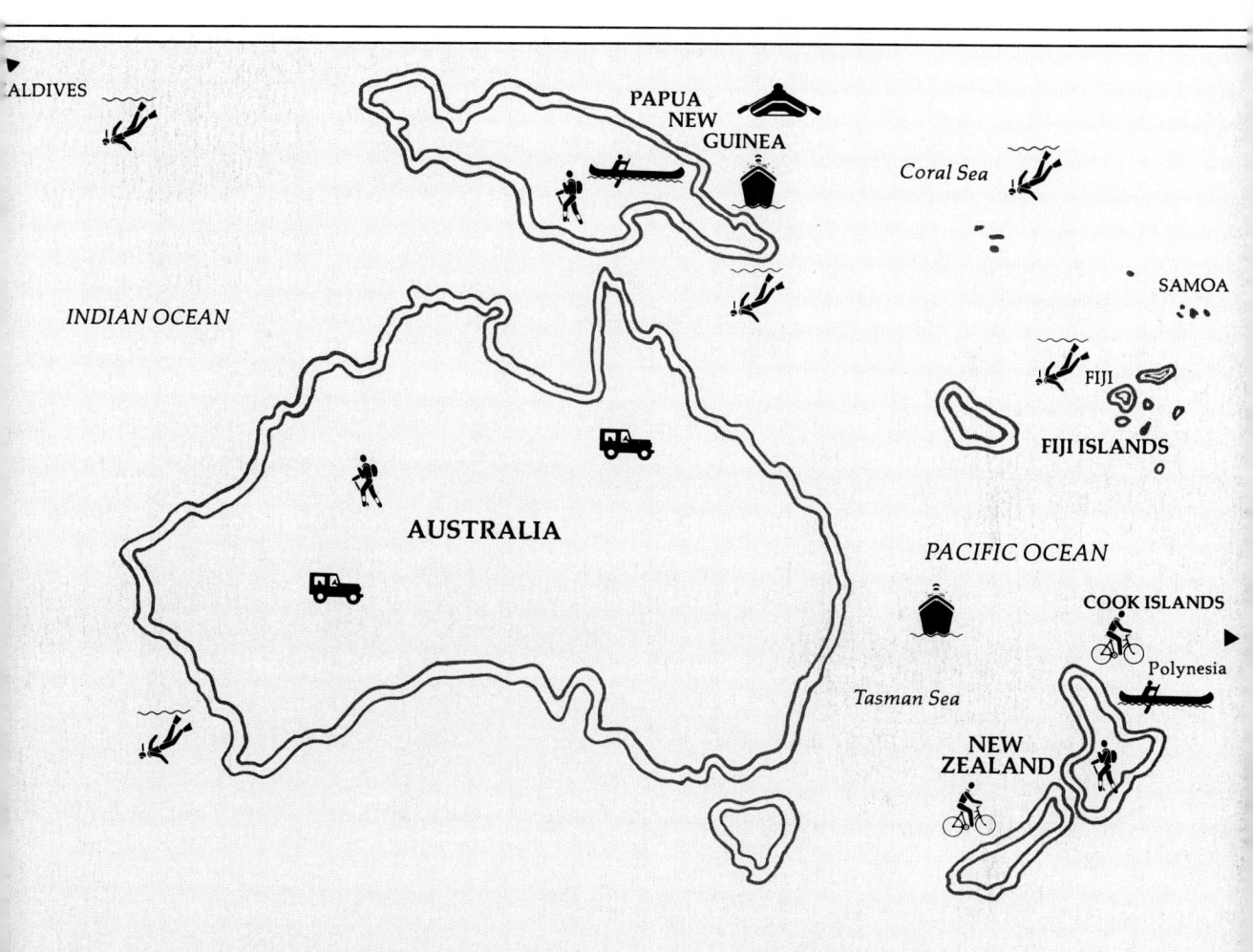

THE PACIFIC

The Pacific is a region of contrasts—deserts, snow-clad peaks, tropical islands, and crystal-blue waters teeming with strange and brilliantly colored fish.

Australia, a continent in itself, varies your holiday with snorkeling and diving, camping, cruising, swimming in jungle pools, examining aboriginal rock paintings, visiting cattle stations, hunting for opals, exploring the Outback and Red Centre, and much more.

In New Zealand interest centers on natural history—majestic fjords, primeval rainforests, waterfalls, exotic birds, high peaks. Travel by vehicle, bicycle, boat, or on foot. Walk the famous Milford Track. Helicoptor to the head of Tasman Glacier. Meet the Maori people. View the thermal geysers.

Sail or plane-hop to South Pacific islands, and dive on some of the worlds superlative reefs with blue holes, caves, and sheer cliff faces. With an anthropologist, explore the fascinating culture of Stone Age tribes in Papua New Guinea and trek from village to village in the Southern Highlands.

All this adventure is on the other side of the world but you'll find it's just this side of Paradise.

Clown fish in anemone in the Coral Sea off Australia—*Amos Nachoum for La Mer Diving Seafari, Inc., NY.*

AUSTRALIA

HIGH ADVENTURE

"We have created the ultimate in Australia High Adventure programs—a trip for those who really want to experience the Australian people, their land, and its natural features, culture, and unique animals," notes the director of Adventure Center.

Snorkeling on the Great Barrier Reef, Australia—*Adventure Center, CA.*

The 3-week trip called "The Ancient Land of Wonder" takes you to Sydney, the Great Barrier Reef, Kakadu National Park and the Top End, and the Red Centre.

First fly through Sydney to Proserpine and at Shute Harbour meet your crew and your floating safari camp for seven nights. Explore spectacular Whitsunday Passage, characterized by eucalyptus, pine, rainforests, and mangrove forests. Next, take a camping safari overland, examining ancient aboriginal rock art and an array of wildlife en route. Then enjoy a cruise on the Yellow Waters Lagoon and Jim Jim Creek Floodplain, a 1-mile hike along the floor of the Jim Jim Falls Gorge, and a raft trip to Twin Falls for sunning, swimming, and relaxation. Fly to Alice Springs, and head to Ayers Rock with a trek to nearby Kings Canyon and Georgefell Ranges. Finish off your Australian journey with a camel wagon ride through valleys and sand dunes before you return to Sydney for flight home.

Year round, 22 days, $1,290 + air & food. 1986 departures: Every Sunday.

Adventure Center AG, 5540 College Ave., Oakland, CA 94618. (800) 227-8747 or (415) 654-1879.

AUSTRALIA — DIVING THE CORAL SEA

"Clear, still water and incredibly rich reefs spiced with plentiful pelagic fish make for some of the world's finest diving," says Carl Roessler, the head of See & Sea, speaking of the Coral Sea, 200 miles from Australia's Queensland Coast and 100 miles beyond the Great Barrier Reef. Feed a shark pack, swim with huge manta rays, photograph a World War II wreck, as you dive again and again in water with clarity up to 200 feet.

See and Sea offers you a choice of two itineraries. The southern route takes you from Dart, Flinders, Diamond, and the superlative Marion Reefs to the astonishing marine life surrounding the Yongala. On the northern course, you journey to Bouganville, Osprey, and the unparalleled Cod Hole. Because of their isolation, you explore the reefs from the live-aboard, custom-built, 65-foot cruiser *The Reef Explorer* (sleeps 12). Enjoy luxury accommodations and excellent food, covering 500 to 700 ocean miles (mostly at night) in the course of your journey. The expeditions begin and end in Townsville or Cairns; however you can extend your vacation with two days of sightseeing and shopping in Sydney.

October-December, 14 days, $2,950 + air. 1986 departures: Oct. 5 & 19, Nov. 2, 16, & 30.

See & Sea Travel Service, Inc. 680 Beach St., Suite 340, San Francisco, CA 94109. (800) 348-9778 or (415) 771-0077.

AUSTRALIA — IN SEARCH OF THE GREAT WHITE SHARK

"This expedition is for a select group of five divers and underwater photographers who think the thrill in adventure travel is gone," says La Mer President Amos Nachoum, who is an expert underwater wildlife photographer. "We take divers on one of the world's greatest adventures—facing the White Shark in its natural environment."

The world's Great White Shark expert, Rodney Fox, leads this underwater safari which sails out of South Australia's Port Lincoln aboard a prawn trawler equipped with the same three shark cages used during the filming of *Jaws*. Spend endless hours observing and photographing shark behavior at close range through special viewing ports. As a special highlight, movie producer Stan Waterman (*The Deep*) will be along to photograph a documentary on the interaction of sharks and divers. Nachoum promises the expedition will leave you with enough memories, stories, and photographs to last a lifetime!

February, 12 days, $7,000 + air. 1986 departure: Feb. 16. In 1987: Feb. 15.

La Mer Diving Seafari, Inc., 823 UN Plaza, Suite 810, Dept. A, New York, NY 10017. (800) 348-3669 or (212) 599-0886.

AUSTRALIA — COACH CAMPING—BARRIER REEF TO BUSH

If you have a month to spare and the curiosity to explore, tempt yourself with this insider's look Down Under. You circle the eastern half of Australia by coach, from Melbourne, Sydney or Brisbane up the east coast, over to Darwin at the northern tip, down through the Red Centre—the outback and the bush—and back to your starting point. The coach captain is the guide, a hostess/cook does the campfire cooking, and overnights are in cozy sleeping bags in tents.

Aside from tours in major cities en route, there are many highlights: Camping on a tropical island... cruising Whitsunday Passage... snorkeling midst the coral of the Great Barrier Reef... the wilds of cowboy country... magnificent gorges and chasms... birds and wildlife in lagoons and billabongs... a swim in a jungle thermal pool... an aboriginal corroboree... poking around Alice Springs... exploring or climbing Ayers Rock... hunting for opals... seeing a cattle station... and much more.

Year round, 30 days, $1,421-$1,511 + air. 1986 departures: Feb. 15, Mar. 1 & 22, Apr. 12, May 17, Jun. 14, Jul. 19, Aug. 16, Sep. 13, Oct. 4 & 25, Dec. 27. In 1987: Feb. 14 & 28, Mar. 14 & 28.

Australian Pacific Tours, 5689 Whitnall Hwy., No. Hollywood, CA 91601. (800) 821-9513; (800) 227-5401 in CA or (818) 985-5616.

AUSTRALIA — THE LAST UNDERWATER FRONTIER

"This diving expedition off the atolls of Rowley Shoals in the Southern Indian Ocean and the Timor Sea lets divers with a pioneering spirit travel to one of the underwater world's last frontiers, accompanied by Eugenie Clark, a leading authority on marine biology," La Mer's Amos Nachoum tells us.

Fly to Perth on Australia's west coast and board the 70-ft. *Joddi Anne* to sail to the atoll, 170 miles west of Broome. Spend 12 diving days in virtually unexplored waters, spiced with scores of brillantly colored tropical fish, gorgonias, and an abundance of soft coral. Watch ocean white tips, manta, eagle rays, and swordfish float past. Enjoy the most electrifying dives of your life in 30-ft. tides! "All in all, it's a trip that stretches the frontiers of exotic dive travel," says Nachoum. And after you've tried the expedition, you can't help but agree!

August & September, 16 days, $3,200 + air. 1986 departures: Aug. 11 & 27, Sep. 11.

La Mer Diving Seafari, Inc., 823 UN Plaza, Suite 810, Dept. A, New York, NY 10017. (800) 348-3669 or (212) 599-0886.

AUSTRALIA — FROM THE BARRIER REEF TO THE RED CENTRE

Australia's three most spectacular natural attractions—the Great Barrier Reef, Kakadu National Park, and the Red Centre—are the focal points on this month-long whirlwind tour.

Join the coach camper in either Melbourne, Sydney or Brisbane, and continue north across the banana-clad hillsides of Queensland to the Gold and Coral Coasts, and on into the tropical rainforests, cane fields, and spectacular scenery of North Queensland. On Green Island, board glass-bottom boats for a close-up view of the 1,200-mile-long Great Barrier Reef, host to millions of colorful fish.

Continue inland through the rugged outback of the Northern Territory toward Darwin to spend a day. Then on to the Kakadu National Park, with its unique tropical wildlife, lagoons, and billabongs (Australian for arroyo). Spend two days conquering Ayers Rock and the mountain highlands of the Red Centre, then home via Adelaide. This giant loop uncovers the heart of Australia.

Year round, 30 days, $1,575 + air. 1986 departures: Mar. 15, Apr. 26, May 31, Jul. 12, Aug. 23, Oct. 4, Dec. 27.

Goway Travel Ltd., 40 Wellington St., East, 2nd fl. Toronto, Ont. Canada M5E 1C7. (416) 863-0799 or (604) 687-4004.

AUSTRALIA

RED CENTRE IN THE OUTBACK

As forbidding and magnificently austere now as it was when 19th century explorer Ernest Giles first charted the region, the Red Centre features vast, low-shrub plains, towering canyons, and spectacular red gorges. In your boat-equipped, four-wheel-drive expedition vehicle, you and 14 other adventurers set off for a 9-day journey into this wilderness with overnight stops at billabongs (waterholes) and other natural wonders.

Leaving Alice Springs, head into the Western MacDonnell Ranges and on via Goose Bluff to the Finke River, probably the oldest in the world. Visit Palm Valley with its 1000-year old palm trees. Drive through the George Gill and James Range, inaccessible on traditional tours, cross sand dunes, and rediscover the Lost City and Garden of Eden with its oasis pool hidden deep within. Then it's on to Ayer's Rock, a day of exploration, visiting the domes of the Olgas formed by the tides of an extinct sea, and return to Alice Springs by way of meteorite craters and a camel farm.

Year round, 9 days, $565 + air. 1986 departures: Jan. 4, Feb. 15, most Saturdays Mar.-Nov., Dec. 26. In 1987: Jan. 10, Feb. 7, Mar. 7, 21, & 28.

Australian Pacific Tours, 5689 Whitnall Hwy., N. Hollywood, CA 91601. (800) 821-9513, (800) 227-5401 (in CA) or (818) 985-5616.

AUSTRALIA

ROCK "N" REEF CAMPER

This 3-week overland trek by tour-coach brings out the multi-faceted character of Australia—from the coastline to the countryside. You tour the best of the Barrier Reef and Sunshine Coast, followed by a visit to the heart of the dramatic Outback.

First, drive from Sydney to Port Macquarie for your first overnight camp at the historical former penal settlement town. Follow the east coast to the beautiful coastal and mountain scenery, stopping in Brisbane for a panoramic view from Mt. Gravatt Lookout. Tour Fraser Island, the largest sand island in the world, with its tropical rainforest, fresh water lakes, and natural rock pools. In Gladstone, visit the largest alumina plant in the world. In Prosperine, join our launch for a cruise to Long Island, where you sun, swim, or just relax. Return to the mainland for visits to Townsville and Cairns, passing through lush rainforests and sugar plantations. Take a ride on a glass-bottom boat for a view of magnificent coral formations. Finally, visit the caves and paintings of Ayers Rock, and climb the magnificent monolith, then return to Alice Springs for your flight home.

Year round 18 days, $900 + air. 1986 departures: Monthly.

Adventure Center AG, 5540 College, Ave., Oakland, CA 95618. (800) 227-8747 or (415) 654-1879.

AUSTRALIA   **SAFARIS THROUGH THE CAPE YORK PENINSULA**

Northern Australia's Cape York Peninsula offers nature lovers an opportunity to see a multitude of flora and fauna—and a camping safari is one of the finest ways to see this wilderness at its best. Forum Travel offers several itineraries. We could write pages about each, so full of excitement and events is each one. However, we provide you with a brief summary.

On the 11-day deluxe "Platypus Safari," journey through the highland tropical rainforests, see aboriginal rock paintings, and discover grey kangaroos and dingos in the wild from your camp at Lakefield. Then on to the Great Barrier Reef for beachcombing and birdwatching. On an 18-day budget "Desert Adventure," cross the northern end of the Simpson Desert, camp in Alice Springs, and see the sun rise on Ayers Rock. Then on to Lake Eyre, the world's largest salt lake, and to Winton, home of Waltzing Matilda. The 14- or 20-day "Cape York Experience" includes a 4-wheel-drive journey to Australia's northernmost region, negotiating many crystal clear creeks and rivers, and cruising to Thursday Island in the Torres Straits (former home of the pearling industry). This journey ends in Cape Tribulation, which contains many of the most primitive and rare plants in the world.

April to October, 11 to 20 days. Platypus Safari, $1,795; Desert Adventure, $1,135; Cape York Experience, $965 (14 days), $1,226 (20 days).

Forum International Travel, 91 Gregory Lane #21, Pleasant Hill, CA 94523. (415) 671-2900 or (415) 946-1500.

AUSTRALIA   **SAFARIS, TREKS, AND NATURE HIKES**

Pacific Exploration Company knows the vast Australian Outback intimately, and specializes in nature, hiking, and outdoor tour programs to remote and scarce wilderness areas. Many trip combinations are possible for the traveler, eager for adventurous exploration. Judge for yourself.

Choose the Desert Overland Safari, and spend five days traveling by open vehicle through roadless Central Australia. Explore Ayers Rock and other unusual formations, observe wildlife such as camels and kangaroos, view aboriginal paintings, sleep in a swag (bed roll), and wake to a spectacular sunrise. The Lamington National Park Tour features graded walking tracks (easy to hard) through a lush subtropical rainforest, plus accommodations at a rustic lodge that offers guided nature walks, bird watching, and other naturalist programs. Still, a third tour takes you to the Great Barrier Reef by helicopter and sets you down on Heron Island, a nature reserve where you enjoy guided reef walks, sightseeing by glass-bottom boat, snorkelling and scuba diving, and bird and turtle watching.

March-December, 14-24 days, $1,235-$1,825 + air. 1986 departures: Multiple.

Pacific Exploration Company, Box 3042-T, Santa Barbara, CA 93130. (805) 687-7282.

<u>AUSTRALIA</u>

REDISCOVER THE RED CENTRE

Explore the spectacular gorges and mountain ranges west of Alice Springs—land that was discovered by the explorer Ernest

Touring Australia's tropics in an expedition vehicle—
Goway Travel Ltd., Ont. Canada.

Giles in 1872—on this overland Australian safari. Also called the Red Centre, the land is an ocean of dunes, desert flowers, and vast canyons punctuated by Ayers Rock—the world's largest monolith.
After your arrival in Alice Springs, spend a day exploring the

invertebrates, and scores of eagle rays gliding by in perfect formation. Dive any time of day or night in perfect temperature conditions. Stay on Fiji before or after trip with two boat dives a day ($150), or take an optional extension to Papua New Guinea.

Deep-sea diving in Fiji—*Amos Nachoum for La Mer Diving Seafari, Inc., NY.*

Year round, 15 days (from West Coast), $2,700 + air. 1986 departures: Mar. 29, Apr. 12, May 17, Jun. 21, Aug. 16, Sep. 13, Oct. 25, Nov. 15, Dec. 20. In 1987: Mar. 21, Apr. 11, May 23, Jun. 13 & 27, Jul. 18, Aug. 8, Sep. 5, Oct. 17 & 31, Dec. 19.

La Mer Diving Seafari, Inc., Dept. A, 823 U.N. Plaza, #810, New York, NY 10017. (800) 348-3669 or (212) 599-0886.

FIJI ISLANDS — ISLAND ADVENTURE FOR SHUTTERBUGS

Learn about photography from the "pros" and develop the photo album of a lifetime on this 2-week visit to romantic, colorful Fiji. The odyssey includes seven days at sea aboard privately-owned yachts. The trip is fully escorted by a noted, professional photographer who provides tips on shooting techniques and equipment care in the tropics; you will meet her upon departure from Los Angeles on May 11.

Start in Nadi, Fiji and transfer to Savusavu on the island of Vanua Levu for some relaxation by the pool or beach. Spend three days on a working copra (dried coconut meat) plantation, with thatch-roofed bures (cottages) serving as accommodations, and on out trips to surrounding area. Then board the yachts for a week of cruising. Plenty of time for snorkeling, beach combing, trolling for marlin, as well as photo opportunities aboard ship and on visits to remote island villages. Fly home from Nadi or plan an extended stay in Fiji or a layover in Hawaii.

May, 14 days (from L.A.), $1,960 + air ($914). 1986 departure: May 11.

Special Odysseys, P.O. Box 37-G, Medina, WA 98039. (206) 455-1960.

FIJI
SAMOA
COOK ISLANDS

THE WORLDS OF THE SOUTH PACIFIC

Experience the endless summer of the South Seas, urges Skip Voorhees. "See the islands as the Polynesians see them, away from typical tourist attractions." Jungle waterfalls, lush green mountain slopes, thatched tropical homes, white sandy beaches, tranquil lagoons, an underwater world of kaleidoscopic color, and remote villages—these are the ingredients.

The 19-day adventure starts by flying to Fiji for the ultimate. R & R at a copra plantation—time for tennis, snorkeling, deep sea fishing, beach combing and shelling. Fly on to Apia, capital of Western Samoa—picturesque with its "Bloody Mary" prototype, dugout canoes, open markets, barefoot businessmen, tapa cloth, turquoise lagoons. Pull away from Apia's lingering spell for several days in Rarotonga in the Cook Islands—wild orchids, barrier reefs, horseback riding along the beach, friendly people who love to sing. Then it's on to Aitutaki, a remote atoll where you stay at a traditional local hotel. As though this is not enough, an add-on may be arranged to the Kingdom of Tonga or Suva in Fiji.

Year round, 19 days (from U.S.), $980 + air. 1986 departures: Every Sunday.

Special Odysseys, P.O. Box 37-G, Medina, WA 98039. (206) 455-1960.

FRENCH POLYNESIA

ART ADVENTURE IN THE SOUTH SEAS

"Paul Gauguin, Robert Louis Stevenson, Herman Melville and dozens of other artists, writers and travelers were seduced by the enchantment of a South Seas adventure," writes Carol Katz, director of Wilderness Journeys. "We now give modern-day artists the same opportunity, by enhancing their travel through French Polynesia with informal workshop sessions in watercolor, painting, drawing, and writing techniques. The result is an illustrated journal of the South Seas experience." Jackie Kirk, an artist and watercolor instructor at her own school, leads the workshops.

Both amateurs and professionals participate in this expedition, which travels through the Society Islands, from Tahiti to Raiatea to Huahine to Moorea. In addition to workshop time, you hike, bicycle, paddle outrigger canoes, explore coral reefs and archaeological sites, participate in Polynesian dance festivals and, of course, swim and snorkel in the bluegreen lagoons. Travel is through off-the-beaten-track districts, spending most nights in Tahitian-style bungalows and enjoying French and Polynesian cuisine. The Arts Workshop is for credit; non-artists may do an island trek instead.

June & December, 16 days (from L.A.), $2,575 including air.

Wilderness Journeys, Box 807-AG, Bolinas, CA 94924. (415) 868-1836.

MALDIVES — DIVING IN THE INDIAN OCEAN

The Maldive archipelago, a chain of 19 atolls straddling the Equator in the Indian Ocean, is awash with tidal currents rich in nutrients. A center for most Indo-Pacific exotic fish species, every island is a living reef, and most are uninhabited and unaffected by pollution.

Divers fly to Singapore for a stopover, then to Male in the Maldives to board the 70-ft. ketch, *Rusalka*. A 42-ft. motor launch travels alongside to carry the gear. Capt. Max Herman is considered the most experienced sailor/diver in the archipelago, having lived there for eight years. Each day you have three to four spectacular dives in 200-ft. visibility to blue holes, caves, and sheer cliff faces plunging thousands of feet, teeming with clown trigger, butterfly, angel and surgeon fish and covered with soft and hard coral. In between dives visit exotic islands with palm trees and white sandy beaches, snorkel on shallow reefs, explore for shells, and take beautiful lagoon night dives.

January-May, October-December, 15 days (from U.S.), $2,900 + air. 1986 departures: Mar. 16, Sep. 19, Oct. 17, Nov. 7, In 1987: Jan. 16, Feb. 1, Mar. 15, Apr. 10, Oct. 16, Nov. 6, Dec. 20.

La Mer Diving Seafari, Inc., Dept. A, 823 U.N. Plaza, #810, New York, NY 10017. (800) 348-3669 or (212) 599-0886.

MICRONESIA — DIVE TRUK LAGOON TO PONAPE

The 20-year veteran of diving vacations, Sea & See, now offers one of the most exciting new dive programs in recent years, taking you from Truk Lagoon to Ponape for endless plunges in remote areas. On this 12-day cruise, dive your fill of the great sunken wrecks of the Japanese Fourth Fleet and untouched Oroluk Atoll, finishing up with Ponape's beautiful reefs, the Kaprohi Waterfall, and the ruins of Nan Madol.

Your vessel is the luxurious live-aboard cruiser, the 170-ft. *Thorfinn*, with its 13 double cabins, a luxurious salon, and even a hot tub, a delight for nondivers who also look forward to beach excursions, interludes of sailing, and fine dining. This is the ultimate way to dive the Truk Lagoon and the forgotten atolls to the east. If you prefer shore-based, shorter programs, See & Sea can tailor a vacation of any length for you to Truk, Ponape, and Palau, or any combination.

November-April, 14 days, $2,900 + air. 1986 departures: Jan. 17, Feb. 14, Mar. 14, Apr. 11, Nov. 21, Dec. 19. In 1987: Jan. 17, Feb. 14, Mar. 14, Apr. 11, May 9.

See & Sea Travel, Inc., 680 Beach St., #340, San Francisco, CA 94109. (800) 348-9778 or (415) 771-0077.

Exotic corals on the Great Barrier Reef off Australia— Adventure Center, CA.

NEW ZEALAND AN EXCEPTIONALLY SCENIC WALK

To study the natural history of New Zealand, participants sometimes travel by air, motorcoach, bus, or launch. But most days they walk—usually eight to 10 miles—through a wondrous land. They start the fascinating itinerary to the North and South islands with a day in Auckland and dinner with a New Zealand family.

With professional naturalists as guides, highlights include a 5-day trek in Urewera National Park to the traditional home of the "children of the mist" along the Whakatane River, a region steeped in Maori history and legend. Visit Maori settlements and explore thermal geysers and hot crystal springs. In the south, spend three days on Stewart Island, an ornithological paradise of kiwi, weka, kaka, long-tailed cuckoo, and other exotic birds. In Fiordland National Park, (by far New Zealand's largest), observe penguins, seals, and native parrots. Walk the Milford Track, spectacularly scenic with mountain passes, towering canyon walls, bush glades and waterfalls—and share meals and lodging in mountain huts with people from all over the world. On to Milford Sound, most majestic of fiords with primeval rainforests, deep lakes, giant ferns, and glistening waterfalls among snow-clad peaks. Next, Mt. Cook National Park, training ground for mountaineers, and optional flights to the head of Tasman Glacier, Westland National Park, and Franz Joseph Glacier—then to Christchurch and return to Auckland.

Year round, 23 days (from U.S.), $2,190 + air. 1986 departures: Jan. 11, Feb. 8, Mar. 8, Nov. 8, Dec. 13. In 1987: Jan. 10, Feb. 7, Mar. 7, Nov. 7, Dec. 12.

Nature Expeditions International, 474 Willamette, P.O. Box 11496, Dept. AG, Eugene, OR 97440. (503) 484-6529.

NEW ZEALAND CYCLING TO QUEENSTOWN

On this 17-day 600-mile cycling tour from Wellington to Queenstown on the South Island, you average 55 miles a day. But don't let this stop you. It's okay to walk up a hill, ride at your own pace, or take a lift in the support van. Besides, there are three rest days for relaxing or soaking up the sun and sights, and all but ten miles of the well-planned, scenic route are paved. Spend one night as a guest in a New Zealand home, others at fine lodges or bed-and-breakfast stops.

Explore Wellington before setting out along the Marlborough Sound. Cycle through lush pine forests and orchards to Nelson Lakes National park and the Lake Rotoroa Lodge with its old-world charm. Continue through the Buller Gorge, along the coast of the Tasman Sea, past the geological curiosity of the Pancake Rocks, to Westland National Park and spectacular glaciers and peaks. After a challenging route across the Southern Alps, take advantage of an optional scenic flight to Milford Sound then on to Queenstown and a farewell dinner.

March, 17 days, $1,450 + air. 1986 departures: Mar. 6, Mar. 26. In 1987: Jan. 8, Jan. 27, Feb. 15, Mar. 6.

Backroads Bicycle Touring, P.O. Box 1626-Q34, San Leandro, CA 94577. (415) 895-1783.

NEW ZEALAND NORTH ISLAND BIKE TOUR

Cycle New Zealand's smooth roads and byways on a 15-day tour of the North Island. Choose between camping and hotel accommodations. A van carries your luggage (or tired bikers). With the country's famous mountain peaks as backdrop, and in the company of a small group of cyclists led by two experienced

New Zealand panorama—*Adventure Center, CA.*

guides, make your way—no more than 41 miles a day—along the North Island's east coast. The trip begins in Auckland and ends in Wellington.

Along with biking, there's time to explore the world-famous geothermal springs around Rotorua and swim in the crystal clear lakes. Visit a dairy farm and the kiwi orchards, swim and sunbathe at Ohope Beach. At Te Araroa, the easternmost town in the world, early risers are the first on earth to see the sun rise. Explore the earliest European settlements near Tokomaru Bay and, in Gisborne, tour the historic city and learn about the Maoris and their aboriginal culture. Cycling the South Island in 18 days, Wellington to Queenstown, also a possibility.

January-March & October, 15 days, $625-$1,350 + air. 1986 departures: Jan. 13, Feb. 24, Mar. 24, Oct. 13 & 20.

Adventure Center AG, 5540 College Ave., Oakland, CA 94618. (800) 227-8747 or (415) 654-1879. CA only: (800) 228-8747.

NEW ZEALAND: EXPLORING NATURE'S FINEST BY FOOT

You don't need much more than hiking boots and a day pack to experience the startling beauty of New Zealand's unspoiled wilderness. Designed for nature enthusiasts, this 23-day escorted tour features a series of hikes and field trips in New Zealnd's scenic National Parks. Your tour escort handles equipment and transportation details, so you are free to spend four to six hours on the trails each day—hiking at your own pace.

Arrive in and depart from Auckland, the largest and most cosmopolitan of New Zealand's cities. Highlights of the tour include a 3-day, 20-mile hiking safari led by native Maori guides through the Urewera National Park rainforests; Tongariro National Park, known for its active volcanoes and geysers; whitewater rafting on the Tongariro River; an excursion on the glaciers of Mt. Cook National Park with a ski plane flight to Tasman Glacier; a boat ride on magnificent Milford Sound. Finally, spend five days hiking the famous Milford Track, an incomparable mountain area of dense rainforests, remote Alpine meadows, and cascading waterfalls, surrounded by towering peaks. The tour ends at Queenstown on the South Island before flying home.

November-March, 23 days (from U.S.), $1,790 + air. 1986 departures: Jan. 11, Feb. 8, Mar. 8, Nov. 1. In 1987: Jan. 10, Feb. 7, Mar. 7.

Pacific Exploration Company, Box 3042-T, Santa Barbara, CA 93130. (805) 687-7282.

NEW ZEALAND: ON YOUR OWN IN A MOTORHOME

Vacationers who love independent travel (not to mention breathtaking scenery!) will delight at this opportunity to explore the highways and byways of New Zealand in a deluxe motorhome, large enough to accommodate six people. The fully self-contained vehicles allow you to pull off by a lake or stream for camping or to enjoy the excellent facilities of more formal camping parks. When you rent a motorhome, you receive a travelpak—complete with road maps, camping directory, and sightseeing discounts.

Your drive through New Zealand can include many adventure extras as well. You can land by ski-plane on the rugged slopes of the Tasman Glacier or soar over scenic Milford Sound in a small plane (early in the morning for the best views). Raft or canoe down the Waitroa River, jet boat along difficult waterways where a normal propeller would snag, trek (new Zealanders call it tramping) along an excellent network of paths and tracks, stopping at conveniently located huts, or hop on a horse to explore the difficult terrain of the backcountry. All on your own, as you like it.

Year round; minimum 4 days; 3 berth: $32-$55/day; 6 berth: $48-$82/day; including insurance.

Mount Cook Line, 9841 Airport Blvd., Suite 904, Los Angeles, CA 90045. (800) 468-2665 or (213) 649-6185.

NEW ZEALAND / SOUTH PACIFIC

SAIL THE COOKS, TONGA, FIJI, NEW ZEALAND

The ocean-racing sloop *Tequila*, captained by D'Arcy Whiting, sets sail from Auckland and follows New Zealand's coastline of harbors, bays, and islands. The 46' yacht makes anchorage at such ports as Mansion House Bay, Percy Island, and Honora, New Zealand's most northerly port. Skipper Whiting is a well-known sailing personality and ensures that his guests experience the trip of a lifetime.

Also visit remote areas of the South Pacific on inter-island passages on board sloops and schooners. Tonga, Fiji, and the Cooks feature pristine waters, warm winds, and unique island cultures. One-week and longer sailings can be scheduled for groups of four or more, or join part of an ocean passage as an individual crew member.

New Zealand: Jan.-May, 10-21 days, $750-$1,425 + air; South Pacific: Year round.

Ocean Voyages. 1709 Bridgeway, Sausalito, CA 94965-1994. (415) 332-4681.

PAPUA NEW GUINEA

A JOURNEY TO THE STONE AGE

Interested in anthropology, art, or simply an out-of-the-ordinary adventure? You'll find all of this and more in Papua New Guinea with its Stone Age tribes, fascinating culture, and rich landscapes.

First, fly through Port Moresby and Madang, then take a traditional copra boat to the Pacific's Circle of Fire. Share in the Polynesian way of life—stay in a thatched hut, soak up the sun on the black sand beaches, or hike up the volcano's slopes. From there, and board your dugout canoe on the Sepik River and travel through lush jungle—a cultural treasure house. Here traditional tribal ways include a combination of animistic art, magic, and ritual. Visit the spirit houses with their elaborate carved and painted entrances, meet the Sepik villagers and see their sacred wooden images and masks. Visit an out of the way village on Blackwater Lake, then fly to the Western Highlands. Here witness a traditional "sing sing," a spectacularly costumed native festival. Wind down your journey with a relaxing raft trip through a beautiful limestone gorge and beneath rushing waterfalls on the Waghi River. Finally, return to Port Moresby for a farewell dinner.

July-October, 17 days (from U.S.), $1,690 + air. 1986 departures: Jul. 25, Oct. 31.

Wilderness Travel, 1760-AT Solano Ave., Berkeley, CA 94707. (800) 247-6700, or (415) 524-5111.

PAPUA NEW GUINEA

THE HIGHLANDS IN DEPTH

"On this comprehensive 16-day cultural and wildlife expedition, curious travelers who don't mind a little discomfort learn about the people, cultures, tribal art, and wildlife in a variety of New Guinea environments. Our trip focuses especially on the Sepik River, New

Exploring the villages of Papua New Guinea—David Tenenbaum for Wilderness Travel, Ca.

Guinea Highlands, and Trobriand Islands," says David Roderick, the president of Nature Expeditions. "It's a new treatment in travel—you learn on location, accompanied by an anthropologist with specific New Guinea expertise."

Expedition highlights include a 4-day stay on Trobriand Islands, where you observe the overseas canoe-trading system and the yam harvest festivals; three days aboard the houseboat *Sepik Explorer*, with a journey to the native village of the Aranbak people by river truck; a visit to the Baiyer River Wildlife Sanctuary where you witness the spectacular mating displays of the Lesser Bird of Paradise; and a meeting with the famous wigmen of Enga. Accommodations vary from first-class hotels to small ship cabins to rustic lodges. Transportation is by air, minibus, jeep, and small motor launch.

June-October, 17 days (from U.S.), $2,790 + air. 1986 departures: Jun. 20, Aug. 8, Sep. 13, Oct. 11. In 1987: Jun. 19, Aug. 7, Sep. 12, Oct. 10.

Nature Expeditions International, 474 Willamette, P.O. Box 11496, Dept. AG, Eugene, OR 97440. (503) 484-6529.

PAPUA NEW GUINEA

TREKKING IN THE SOUTHERN HIGHLANDS

"The fascinating tropical Southern Highlands of central Papua New Guinea were not explored by westerners until the last 30 years," says Bill Abbott, director of Wilderness Travel. "It's a wonderful way for hikers to experience the people, and their traditions and culture firsthand." The 17-day trek takes you back through time.

First fly through Port Moresby to Tari in the Southern Highlands and continue by dirt road to the village of Koroba, where you stay overnight. You hike from village to village through this mountainous region, carrying a light pack and staying in thatched guest huts. Porters carry group food and equipment. The Huli people (the "wigmen" wear elaborate headgear festooned with birds of paradise, feathers and flowers) make friendly hosts, eager to share their rich cultural heritage and traditional lifestyle of yam, taro, and banana cultivation. Hiking can be rigorous, sometimes along muddy, steep footpaths and rough tracks over several ridges at an altitude of 6,000 feet. You feel well-rewarded, however, when you make it across the forest and alpine meadows to a base hut beside beautiful Pindaunde Lake (11,000'). From there, if you choose, go on to conquer Mt. Wilhelm (15,000'), PNG's highest summit. Return to Port Moresby for farewell dinner and flight home.

July & October, 17 days (from U.S.), $1,690 + air. 1986 departures: Jul. 11, Oct. 17.

Wilderness Travel, 1760-AT, Solano Ave., Berkeley, CA 94707. (800) 247-6700 or (415) 524-5111.

PAPUA NEW GUINEA

EXPLORING REMOTE REEFS

"Papua New Guinea offers astonishingly prolific and virgin diving—some of her offshore islands feature incredible blue-water dropoffs capped with lush coral gardens and swarms of reef and pelagic fish," comments Carl Roessler of See and Sea. The land itself is a treasure-trove of primitive culture—the home of stone-age tribes who speak 700 different languages.

Choose from eight different lavish 12-day exploratory cruises to New Guinea aboard the 65-ft. Australian premier dive cruiser *Reef Explorer*. Your vessel takes you to remote islands, such as Hermit Islands and the Ningoes, where only a few intrepid adventurers have ventured into the marine depths. Explore remote reefs where you see such extravagant creatures as the pink deadly stonefish and the rare scorpionfish. See plunging dropoffs and shallow, coral-rich gardens and watch scores of turtles scatter in front of the ship. Choose an optional Sepik River Cruise extension to discover the wonders of the remote Papua New Guinea interior.

January-May, 12-18 days (from U.S.), $2,700-$3,750 + air. 1986 departures: Jan. 25, Feb. 10, 23 & 28, Mar. 9, 14 & 23, Apr. 6 & 20, May 8.

See & Sea Travel Services, 680 Beach St., #340, San Francisco, CA 94109. (800) 348-9778 or (415) 771-0077.

PAPUA NEW GUINEA

DIVE INTO A PACIFIC PARADISE

Sail aboard the 65-ft. motoryacht, *Telita*, for diving in waters with 100- to 300-ft. visibility and an extraordinary variety of rare tropical and pelagic fauna. Your expedition guides, Bob and Dinah Halstead (photographer with over 10 years of diving in New

Guinea, and chef extraordinaire), change their base every three months to provide the best diving opportunities. Their yacht is equipped with five double cabins, diving lockers, and a photographer's workbench.

From January to March they dive in the Solomon Sea off New Ireland, known for whale and shark migrations, manta rays, and dolphins. Other locations—April to June: Manus Island and the isolated atoll of Hermit island in the Bismark Sea, the site of 34 known WWII Japanese wrecks and rich flora and fauna. July to September: Kimbe and Rabaul, one of the wreck diving capitals of the world, with volcanic dropoffs and all tropical species. October to December: Alotau on Milne Bay in the Coral Sea where you spot the "gentle giant" whale shark and rare calico scorpion fish. Each 15-day tour includes 10 days of magnificent diving, and may be extended for a cruise on the Sepik River or a stay at the Karawari or Ambua Lodge in the highlands. Other special expeditions involve marine biology led by the world's foremost shark authority, Dr. Eugenie Clark, and an underwater photography expedition led by photographer and author Chris Newbert.

Year round, 17 days (from U.S.), $3,200 + air. 1986 departures: Jul. 24, Aug. 21, Oct. 30, Dec. 18. In 1987: Jan. 14, Mar. 4, Apr. 23, Jun. 25, Jul. 16, Aug. 2 & 16, Sep. 3, Oct. 15, Nov. 5, Dec. 17. Marine biology expedition, Jul. 24-Aug. 9, 1986, $3,750 + air. Underwater photography expedition, Aug. 21-Sep. 6, 1986, $3,500 + air.

La Mer Diving Seafari, Inc., Dept. A, 823 U.N. Plaza, #810, New York, NY 10017. (800) 348-3669 or (212) 599-0886.

POLYNESIA

THE CULTURE AND THE PEOPLE

Meet the people, their crafts, music, history, and lifestyle on this cultural expedition through the islands of Polynesia. Many of the islands are of volcanic origin, their sharp green peaks rising abruptly out of the sea; others are low-lying coral atolls, built up slowly over thousands of years. Their sand beaches and turquoise lagoons invite you to relax, enjoy, and join in the slow-paced life of the islanders.

Depart from Los Angeles for a brief stop in Papeete, Tahiti, a quaint south sea town inhabited by native Tahitians and sailors. Continue on to Huahine, a remote French Polynesian island, famous for its unique remains of Polynesian Maraes. Visit Rarotonga and Aitutaki in the Cooks, renowned for their natural beauty and colorful dancing. Then move on to Western Samoa, the cradle of Polynesian culture. Finally, visit the islands of Fiji, where friendly, hospitable people are still strongly attached to their traditions. You have many opportunities to explore remote islands, enjoy authentic person-to-person contact through village stays, and snorkel among some of the most beautiful coral reefs in the world. Dana Keil Ph.D., a former professor of anthropology at the University of Massachusetts and at Washington State University, is your guide for this amazing cultural journey.

December-March, July & August, 24 days (from U.S.), $2,190 + air. 1986 departures: Jan. 10, Feb. 7, Mar. 7, Jul. 11, Aug. 8, Dec. 12. In 1987: Jan. 9, Feb. 6, Mar. 6, Jul. 3, Aug. 7, Dec. 11.

Nature Expeditions International, 474 Willamette, P.O. Box 11496, Dept. AG, Eugene, OR 97440. (503) 484-6529.

POLYNESIA

ADVENTUROUS SPIRIT REQUIRED

Are you patient, flexible, willing to rough it? Most important, do you have an adventurous spirit? If your answers are yes, this 25-day cultural expedition is right up your alley. Be prepared for little privacy and casual accommodations at times—it's the best way to meet the people of these remote Pacific Ocean islands and share their lives. Eat as the locals do, learn traditional dances and songs, join reef-and-lagoon fishing outings, harvest bananas and coconuts. Enjoy amazing scenery as you snorkel among beautiful coral reefs, walk the sandy beaches and turquoise lagoons, and explore the volcanic mountains of Rarotanga—by vehicle and on foot. Among the other islands you visit: Aitutaki, Upola, Savaii, and Fiji.

Stay in wooden-framed houses on Fiji and in stucco homes in the Cooks. Be prepared to sleep dormitory-style during your village stays. In the cities, overnights are in first-class hotels. First fly to Papete, then continue to the Cook Islands, the islands of Upola and Savaii in Western Samoa, and to Suva and Nadi in Fiji. Your trip ends at the Regent of Fiji.

January & August, 25 days (from U.S.), $1,990 + air. 1986 departures: Jan. 4, Aug. 2. In 1987:

Nature Expeditions International, 474 Willamette, P.O. Box 11496, Dept. AG, Eugene, OR 97440. (503) 484-6529.

THE SOUTH PACIFIC

DISCOVER PARADISE ON EARTH

"I find it almost impossible to think of the Lost Islands of the Pacific without wanting to put aside whatever I'm doing and set out at once," says T.C. Swartz, director of Society Expeditions. Here, there remain many opportunities for the kind of discovery Stevenson wrote about and Gauguin painted. "We take you there—to pristine beaches, to villages where inhabitants have never seen cars, to quiet lagoons where the water is clear and clean. It's the closest thing to paradise on earth."

Travel in the company of cultural experts aboard the expedition ship *Explorer*, which provides luxurious living quarters, fine food and dining and a complete new fitness center with its own sauna and sun deck. Return emotionally refreshed, physically fit, and intellectually stimulated. Choose from four itineraries: a sail from Puerto Montt, Chile, to Easter Island via Robinson Crusoe Island; a journey from the remote Easter Islands to Tahiti with stops at many small islands including Pitcairn, settled by descendants of the *Bounty* mutineers; a circle out from Tahiti through the rarely visited Marquesa Islands; or a cruise from Tahiti via Bora Bora and the Cook Islands to Fiji. Those who prefer a longer voyage may link two or more cruises for a single adventure of up to 50 days in length.

February, March, October, November, 16-21 days (from U.S.), $3,490-$11,075 + air. 1986-87 departures in early spring & late fall.

Society Expeditions, 723 Broadway East, Dept. ATA, Seattle, WA 98102. (800) 426-7794 or (206) 324-9400.

TAHITI PITCAIRN

SAILING IN PARADISE

Sail the south Seas paradise of French Polynesia on the 46' ketch *Roscop*, exploring Huahine, Raiatea, Tahaa, and Bora Bora on a 1-week or 2-week cruise. Indulge yourself in a world of opalescent seas, tropical beaches, tranquil lagoons, quiet villages. Enjoy endless hours of relaxing, snorkeling, shelling, and exploring. *Roscop's* sailings are open to individuals and couples to join, April through December. Also available is the 38' sloop *Vanessa*, based in Raiatea and ready to set sail on the dates of your choice to explore Tahiti's outer islands.

Or, depart Papeete for Pitcairn Island, legendary pinpoint of the Pacific where Fletcher Christian and the *Bounty* mutineers stepped ashore in 1790. Their descendants still live on Pitcairn. "You're assured a fascinating sojourn to this windswept island when you join a 5-week expedition on board our large schooner," promises Ocean Voyages. The trip includes two weeks on Pitcairn, round-trip passage between Tahiti and Pitcairn (1,300 miles each way), and round-trip air between Tahiti and Los Angeles.

Roscop: April through December, 8 or 14 days, $950 or $1,595 + air. *Vanessa*: Year round, 7, 14, or more days. $815, $1,500, and up + air. Pitcairn: Jun. 21-Jul. 30, Oct. 19-Nov. 26, $5,955.

Ocean Voyages, Inc., 1709 Bridgeway, Sausalito, CA 94965-1994. (415) 332-4681.

Testing Tahiti's cycling trails—*Off the Deep End Travels, WY.*

TAHITI
POLYNESIA

THE SOUTH SEAS ON TWO WHEELS

Discover paradise by bicycle on this leisurely, 2-week tour of five South Sea Islands. Cruise between islands by schooner and ferry. Relax in first-class plantation-style hotels and tropical bungalows. Take easy day trips, over mostly level roads, as you glide through lush foliage, past dramatic mountain vistas, and rendezvous on serene, idyllic beaches. Loafing is encouraged.

First, circle Tahiti on a coastal route cooled by tradewinds, passing dense, fragrant forests, and deep blue lagoons. Stop at local museums for an overview of Polynesian culture and original Gauguins. Take a swim under a waterfall. On Moorea, you can cycle up to Belvedere Overlook or laze at the shore. Try snorkeling, wind surfing, or an outrigger canoe. On the outlying islands, explore the ancient temples of Raiatea, and savor the best pedaling of all on Huahine, where trees are laden with papaya and exotic blooms, and white beaches sparkle. Finally, return to Tahiti for an optional one-day, 71-mile loop of the island or spend the day shopping.

March-November, 16 days (from U.S.), $1,375 + air. 1986 departures: Mar. 1, Apr. 12, May 3 & 24, Jun. 14, Jul. 5 & 26, Aug. 16, Sep. 13, Oct. 4 & 25.

Off the Deep End Travels, P.O. Box 7511-F, Jackson, WY 83001. (800) 223-6833 or (307) 733-8707.

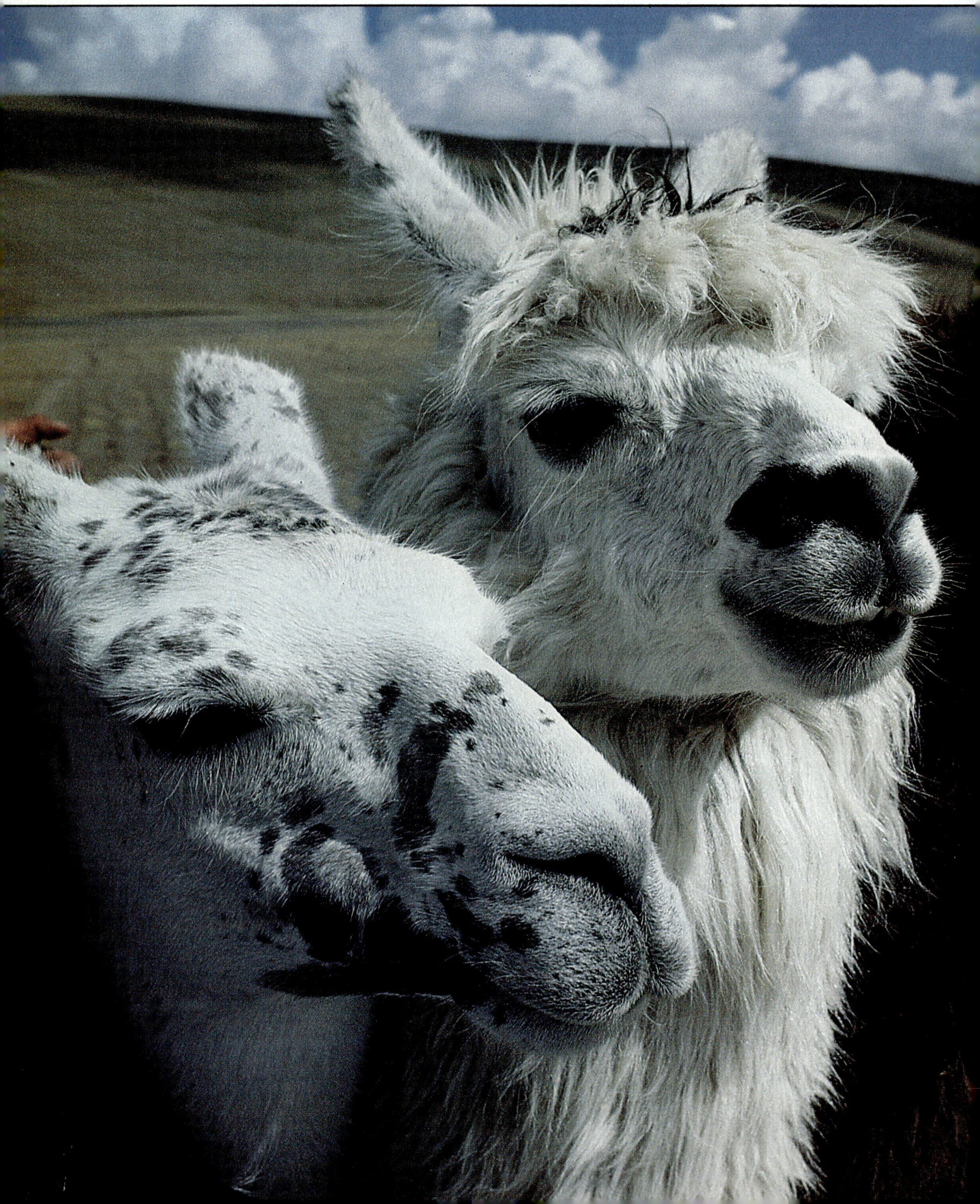

SOUTH & CENTRAL AMERICA

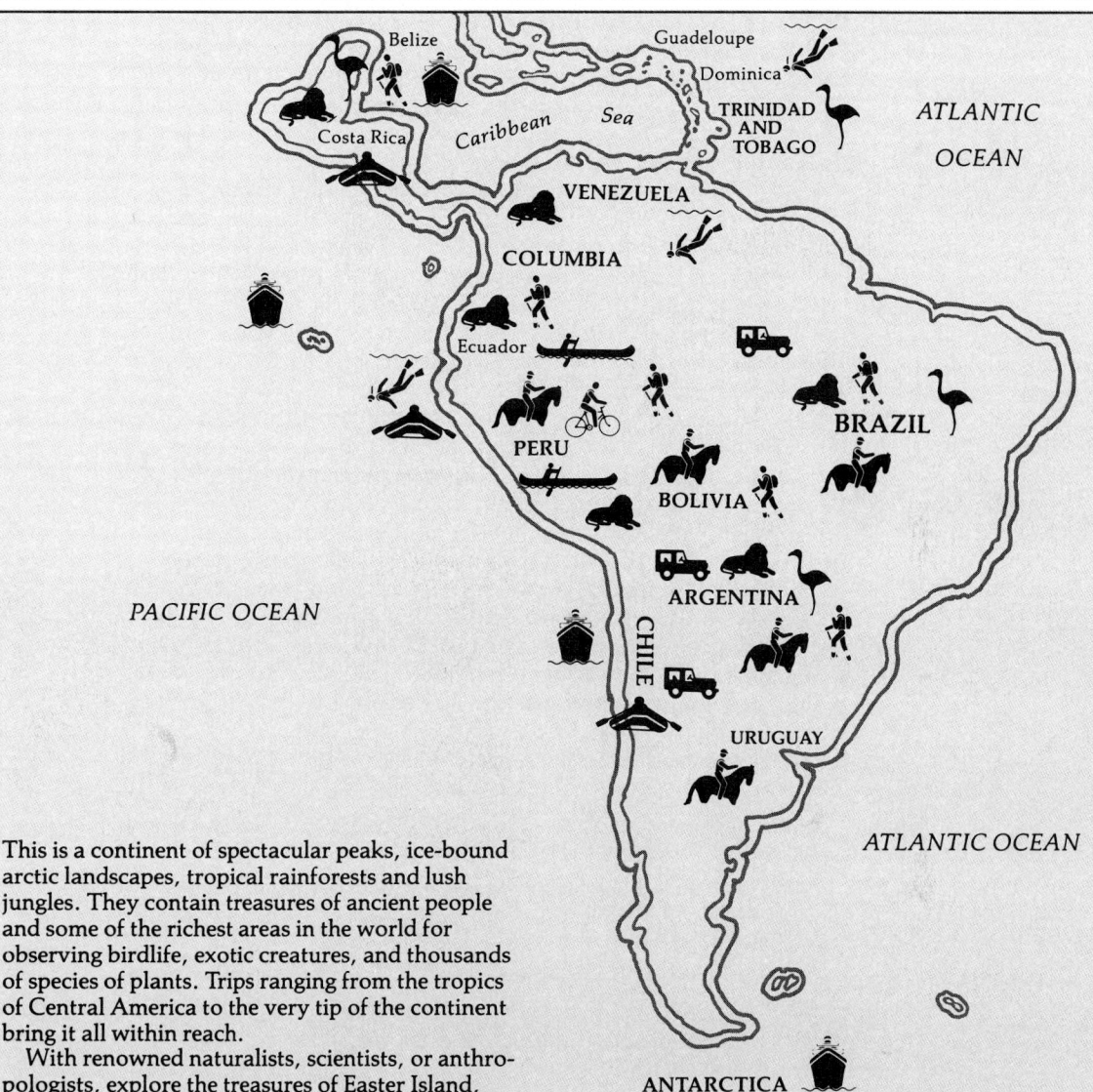

This is a continent of spectacular peaks, ice-bound arctic landscapes, tropical rainforests and lush jungles. They contain treasures of ancient people and some of the richest areas in the world for observing birdlife, exotic creatures, and thousands of species of plants. Trips ranging from the tropics of Central America to the very tip of the continent bring it all within reach.

With renowned naturalists, scientists, or anthropologists, explore the treasures of Easter Island, and view close up the amazing wildlife of the Galapagos. On some trips you examine the ruins of Machu Picchu, the "lost city" of the Incas. On others, venture into the Antarctic, or explore the Amazon Basin, unbelievably rich in its species of birds, exotic plants and butterflies.

Cruise an exquisite jungle river in Belize, learn to boardsail in the warm Caribbean, raft a tropical river in Costa Rica, sail a schooner in the Grenadines, or dive on coral reefs of Guadeloupe.

Llamas carry the gear when you climb peaks in Bolivia. The old Patagonian Express transports you across the Andes. You careen down Chile's Bio Bio on rafts, and ride horseback with the gauchos in Argentina.

Whether by boat or bicycle, raft or canoe, train, expedition vehicle or on your own two feet, these adventures lead to a colorful and wondrous world.

Two highcountry "natives"—*Mark Houston for American Alpine Institute, WA.*

ANTARCTICA

THE LAST MOST GLORIOUS FRONTIER

Voyaging close to the South Pole on a luxurious expedition ship, the *Society Explorer* or the *World Discoverer*, take in the haunting beauty of the ice-bound landscape in the company of other nature enthusiasts led by world renowned naturalists and scientists. Explore the waters along the edge of Antarctica—and perhaps stand where no other human has ever stood—while enjoying such amenities as a wine cellar and fine cuisine, a library, and lectures by leading experts on the region.

Itineraries vary from year to year, but a 22-day voyage, for example, might begin by flying to Santiago, Chile, and on to Puerto Williams, where you board ship. Cruise "Darwin's" Beagle Channel and approach Cape Horn—and land, weather permitting. Then, cross Drake Passage and reach the Antarctic Peninsula. There, a fleet of Cousteau-designed, inflatable boats takes you from ship to shore—to cormorant nesting areas, to rocky beaches where only seals have been before, and to dense penguin rookeries. Witness the "calving" of glaciers and visit scientific research stations. On the tenth day, follow in the footsteps of Sir Ernest Shackleton and land on Elephant Island, then visit Coronation Island in the South Orkneys, site of a huge Adelie penguin colony. Cruise on to the South Georgia Islands to observe colonies of colorful king penguins, wandering albatross, thousands of fur seals, and remains of old whaling stations. Finally, spend two full days in the Falkland Islands, to observe the wildlife—including over 50 breeding species of birds—and visit Port Stanley. On the twentieth day, cruise the Strait of Magellan and disembark at Punta Arenas to fly to Santiago, and on to Miami. Variations on this trip include a shorter, 15-day voyage, and an extensive 35-day trip circumnavigating Antarctica, disembarking at Wellington, New Zealand.

November-January, 15-23 days (from U.S.), $4,750 & up. + air. 1986-87 departures: Nov. 14 & 23, Dec. 3, 14, 17, 27, Jan. 7, 9, 18, 20, 30.

Society Expeditions, 723 Broadway East, Dept. ATA, Seattle, WA 98102. (800) 426-7794 or (206) 324-9400.

ARGENTINA
BRAZIL

CARNIVAL IN RIO CAPERS

Pack your hiking boots, riding boots, and dancing shoes for a trip that combines a pony trek, a riverboat cruise, and foot hikes, topped off by a 3-day carnival.

Arrive in Buenos Aires and get acquainted with the sidewalk cafes and bustling boulevards. Then take a motorboat across the Delta of the Parana River for an overnight with a ranching family in the Pampas, where local gauchos share their traditional songs and games. Hop by plane and jeep into the Potrerillos Valley at the base of Mt. Aconcagua, the Andes' highest peak. At Los Horcones lagoon, mount gentle, sure-footed ponies and follow your arriero (Andes guide) across the Horcones River. Overnights, camp in a valley. On the third day, ascend Aconcagua's major glacier, surrounded by icy walls and roaring avalanches. Leave the Andes heights and enter the Amazon jungle for a 3-day riverboat cruise, where you learn to recognize different species of parrot, macaw, owl, palm trees, and orchids. Finally, return to city life for the Rio Capers carnival and three days of partying and dancing with the locals.

January, 21 days (from L.A.), $5,500 including air. 1986 departure: Jan. 28.

Capers Club 400, P.O. Box 5489, Beverly Hills, CA 90210. (213) 657-0916.

<u>ARGENTINA</u>
<u>CHILE</u>

THE WILDS OF PATAGONIA

Some call this land on the southernmost tip of South America—Patagonia; others call it the "uttermost end of the earth." Find out why on this 21-day journey. It's a land of Alaskan-size fjords, glaciers which fall into the sea, red and yellow Magellan beech trees with parrots nestling above and penguins pacing beneath. There are great lakes and forests, rolling pampas, and the fantastic spires of Fitroy (11,073') and Cerro Torre (10,280').

Travel in an expedition vehicle over rough roads, camping and occasionally staying in simple inns. Start with a quick visit to cosmopolitan Buenos Aires and end in Santiago, Chile's capital. In between, explore Glacier and Paine national parks, take an optional

Patagonia at the southernmost tip of South America—Mountain Travel, Inc., Ca.

overnight backpack trip to Grey Glacier, and enjoy a motor launch ride on the Last Hope Sound.

January, 26 days (from U.S.), $1,890 + air. 1986 departure: Jan. 10. In 1987: Jan. 9.

Mountain Travel, 1398 Solano Ave., Albany, CA 94706. (800) 227-2384 or (415) 527-8100.

ARGENTINA
URUGUAY

RIDE WITH THE GAUCHOS

During two weeks, with most days on horseback, you experience many aspects of these fascinating lands. From the mountains in northwest Argentina, through the pampas in Mesopotamia, to the beaches of Uruguay, staying in private estancias and in fine hotels, you have a taste of proverbial South American hospitality. Outstanding experts accompany your trip.

The trip begins with arrival at the Jujuy airport in Argentina and transfer to Volcano. For two days, ride on sturdy Criollo horses with Gaucho saddles through the Quebrada of Puramarca, a mountainous region of colorful rock formations. Camp out one night and stay at a private estancia another. After flying to Buenos Aires and driving to Entre Rios province, spend four days at a luxurious private estancia and ride to your heart's content, participating in ranch activities if you wish. Fish the Rio Parana one day and attend a gaucho asada. Still to come: By train, hydrofoil, and car to Montevideo and five days of riding along the beaches and through the pampas; a night at an old Spanish fort; a day in Buenos Aires; then home.

Spring & Fall, 14 days, $1,400 + air. 1986 departure: Mar. 30, Apr. 27, Oct. 19, Nov. 16, and other dates.

FITS Equestrian, 2011 Alamo Pintado Rd., Solvang, CA 93463. (805) 688-9494.

BELIZE

FOR THE ACTIVE EXPLORER

Physically fit and ready for true adventure? Get ready to tackle Belize. You trek, climb, and hack through dense tropical forests rich in wildlife. Explore caves once used by the Maya for ceremonial rituals, rediscover ancient pyramids, and take a river trip surrounded by a vast variety of birds, orchids, and butterflies.

Meet your jungle guide in Belize and drive to the base camp, where your group of six settles into the native palapa-style accommodations. Board a boat at Guinea Grass, and cruise an exquisite jungle river to the ancient Maya site of Lamanai. Spend a day preparing for your jungle trip and relaxing in the sun and water. Then put on your pack, and take a short hike to Mountain Cow Cave, using headlights and ropes to squeeze through the small opening to chambers glistening with stalactitic formations. A full day of trekking through lush tropical surroundings to Caracol is next. Continue on to Mountain Pine Ridge to view Victoria Peak and the famous Hidden Valley Falls. Here you explore caves, trek naturalist trails, and swim in the Rio On. Spend another day trekking to a sinkhole where you descend by ropes and ladders to discover a cave opening the size of a stadium. Explore the chambers and return for a refreshing swim in the Caves Branch River. Spend your final days jet-skiing, waterskiing, or windsurfing. Optional 3-night extension to Tikal, the peak of the Maya kingdom, or to the small fishing village of San Pedro on Ambergis Cay for diving, fishing, or beachcombing.

January-May, 8 days $852, 10 days $1,065 + air. 1986 departures: Jan. 10 & 24, Feb. 7 & 21, Mar. 7 & 21, Apr. 4 & 18, May 2 & 16.

Adventure Belize, 5059 Commonwealth Dr., Sarasota, FL 34242, (813) 346-1997. (Also: Box 35, Corozal Town, Belize, Central America. Tel. 04-2187).

BELIZE

A TROPICAL BIRDING ADVENTURE

Belize, with its microcosm of neotropical habitats, is an ideal location to observe many species of tropical birds as well as wintering North American birds. Beginners and veteran birdwatchers join Dr. James Parker, an experienced tropical ornithologist and ecologist, on this 9-day ornithological survey to the rainforests, islands, savannas, and agricultural areas of this small, friendly country.

Your itinerary offers intense birding during daylight hours, including mist-netting. Evenings, you hear seminars and discussions on tropical ecology and ornithology, plus summaries of the days' sightings. Visit various habitats including coastal mangrove swamps, Caribbean cays and rookeries, rainforest marshes, plantations, and orchards. Expect to see about 230 or more bird species including White Hawk, Trogons, Manakins, Toucans, Cotingids, Tanagers, Parrots, Jabiru Stork, and more. Transportation is by truck or bus over sometimes rough Belizean roads. Overnights are spent in hotels and at rainforest and coral reef field stations.

February, April, May, August, 9 days, $795 + air. 1986 departures: Feb. 14, Apr. 18, May 23, Aug. 9.

International Zoological Expeditions, 210 Washington St., Sherborn, MA 01770. (617) 655-1461.

BELIZE

TRACING MAYAN CULTURE

Enjoy a river trip from Guinea Grass to Lamanai, an ancient Mayan cultural center. As you head leisurely downstream, watch for national treasures such as the Keel-billed Toucan and black orchid. There's also plenty of time to swim in the freshwaters of Hill Bank Lagoon, and to amble along pathways lined with 100-ft. tall trees tangled with lianas.

Meet your guide in Belize and drive to the base camp to meet the rest of your group (limited to six) for a buffet dinner. Next day, swim and breakfast before visiting the ceremonial center of Altun Ha (where the famous jade head Kinich Ahau was found), the site of the Nohmul, and the surrounding countryside. The following day your jungle river trip to the Mayan "site of Lamanai" begins. En route, observe overhanging tropical foliage, a variety of exotic birds, huge temples, and massive Olmecan masks. In Corozal, rest and get to know the people, their food, and culture. Continue on, stopping at Guanacaste Park, and the Department of Archaeology with its artifact collections. In Mountain Pine Ridge, you amble naturalistic trails, explore caverns, and sit by cascading waterfalls. On to Hidden Valley Falls, Rio On, Baldy Beacon, and more. Take a boatride to the botanical gardens, then return to base camp at Consejo. Sun, relax, or take an optional 3-day extension to the Mayan kingdom of Tikal or to San Pedro on Ambergis Cay. Custom trips are also available.

January-May, 10 days, $1,065 + air. 1986 departures: Jan. 10 & 24, Feb. 7 & 21, Mar. 7 & 21, Apr. 4 & 18, May 2 & 16.

Adventure Belize, 5059 Commonwealth Dr., Sarasota, FL 34242. (813) 346-1997. (Also: Box 35, Corozal Town, Belize, Central America. Tel. 04-2187)

BOLIVIA

THE CORDILLERA REAL—HIKING AND CLIMBING

Though the Cordillera Real is one of the world's major ranges with some of the most varied alpine climbing, it probably is the least known among comparable mountain groups due to Bolivia's remoteness and lack of traditional tourists. Participants begin

Rope team in Bolivia's Cordillera Real—*Mark Houston for American Alpine Institute, WA.*

acclimatization either with day hikes in the Cuzco-Machu Picchu area or with a 7-day trek through the Inca's sacred Urubamba Range.

This 2-week expedition starts in the capital city, La Paz at nearly 13,000 feet. On several days of acclimatization you explore Lake Titicaca and visit villages, then walk up the gentle valley system of the Condoriri Lake Group with llamas carrying the bulk of the gear. Unnamed minor summits and ridges, rock buttresses, and 16,000- to 18,000-foot peaks tower above the valley with a diversity of routes—some hard, others not difficult—for hiking, scrambling, exploring, and climbing to summits. Following the ascents, trek cross-country, camp by Zongo Lake, then move to high camp to climb Huaynba Potosi (19,996 feet), serious glacier travel but no technical barriers.

May-September, 12 days, $1,080 + air. 1986 departures: May 9, Jun. 6, Jul. 11, Aug. 8, Sep. 5.

American Alpine Institute, 1212 24th -D, Bellingham, WA 98225. (206) 671-1505.

BOLIVIA

BOLIVIA LLAMA TREK

Take this high altitude trek through the Royal Cordilleras, and discover the Altiplano world of pristine glaciers and jewel-like lakes, brightened by the rainbow colors or the local Amayra people's weaving. Llamas carry the camp gear as you cross spectacular passes at 16,000 feet beneath 21,000-ft. peaks, and camp in remote meadows where alpacas graze. Designed for those who are truly physically fit, this 2-week journey brings you close to snowfields, where mountain scrambling, glacier walking, even ice caving are all possibilities.

Begin in La Paz, a city of markets, churches and plazas, then travel to the pre-Inca site at Tiahuanco. A 6-day trek traverses the heart of the Cordilleras, circling the Negurni and Condoriri massifs. You descend to Lake Tuni and rendezvous with your vehicle for return to La Paz.

May-September, 17 days (from U.S.), $1,040 + air. 1986 departures; May 19, Jun. 23, Jul. 28, Sep. 1. In 1987: May 11, Jun. 15, Jul. 20, Aug. 24.

Overseas Adventure Travel, 6 Bigelow St., #102 Cambridge, MA 02139. (800) 221-0814 or (617) 876-0533.

BRAZIL
ARGENTINA

A NATURALIST ADVENTURE

Explore two relatively unknown naturalist paradises—the Pantanal of Brazil and the Valdes Peninsula—in Patagonia.

From Rio de Janeiro—catch a flight to Corumba for the start of your adventure through the Pantanal, a birder's wonderland and the world's largest wetlands located in southwestern Brazil near the Bolivian border. Via boat, canoe, van, or by foot, view a succession of exotic yet accessible scenes—nesting colonies of jabirus, herons, roseate spoonbills, flocks of noisy macaws, and long-snouted alligators sunning themselves just above the water line. After the Pantanal, fly to Iguacu Falls, at two miles wide the most overwhelming falls in South America. Then head off for your 4-day

The Morpho butterfly, a winged wonder of the Amazon—*R. Ryel for International Expeditions, Inc., AL.*

excursion to the Valdes Peninsula, situated in northeastern Patagonia. Highlights include visits to Punta Tombo with its colony of over one million Magellanic Penguins; Punta Loma with its colony of sea lions; Punta Norte, with the largest sea elephant colony in the world on continental land; and witnessing whale mating rites. A day in Buenos Aires ends the journey.

March-November, 17 days (from U.S.), $2,400 + air. 1986 departures: Mar. 14, Apr. 18, Jul. 11, Aug. 15, Sep. 16, Nov. 14.

Turtle Tours, Dept. AG, 251 E. 51st St., New York, NY 10022. (212) 355-1404.

BRAZIL
VENEZUELA
COLOMBIA
ECUADOR

TRANS AMAZON

There is no place like it. Its uniqueness is the intricate interplay of water, plant, and animal in an ecosystem untampered with—until now—since the Ice Age. It's the Amazon—the world's least touched jungle and river. And you see the best of it on this 4-country, 9-week sojourn covering 7,850 miles and proceeding from Rio to Quito via Manaus (or in reverse). Twenty adventurers (under 40) travel in fully-equipped expedition vehicles suitable for rough terrain, carrying everything from shower facilities to mosquito nets. Alternate camping and hotel stays in cities.

The sights and sightseeing are an unforgettable mix. Ruins and relics of ancient cultures. A modern-age gold mine. Astonishing vistas, like the Pantanal, where cattle graze alongside egrets and benign alligators! Mount Roraime, setting of Conan Doyle's *The Lost World*. The bustling river port of Manaus, center of the Amazon's colorful commerce. Venezuela's La Gran Sabana, with its flat-topped mountains, waterfalls, and spectacular views. White sand Caribbean beaches. Native villages. Indian markets. Tour virginal wilderness areas and shop in exotic capitals like Bogota, with its Gold Museum and splendid Inca artifacts.

February, May, December, 63 days (from South America), $1,570 + air & some meals. 1986 departures: Feb. 15, May 17, Dec. 23.

Adventure Center AG, 5540 College Ave., Oakland, CA 94618. (800) 227-8747 or (415) 654-1879.

CARIBBEAN **A WATER LOVER'S DREAM**

Learn to boardsail the easy way—in warm, reef-protected waters, or improve your technique with the guidance of expert instructors. Whether you're a novice or skilled athlete, the Turks and Caicos islands, British Crown Colonies, are an ideal environment for a 6-day active vacation—three nights on a catamaran and three at a plush resort.

The first day, receive dry-land instruction on the principles of boardsailing, with exciting videos. The next day, there's an hour of group instruction and four hours of individual lessons. Snorkel out to the coral reefs for a look at rare plant and animal life. More boardsailing and four more hours of individual instruction. (Also optional diving to the coral reefs on the edge of the continental shelf.) Relax a bit, as you spend a full day sailing aboard a 50-ft. ocean-going catamaran to uninhabited islands. Fish off the deck, snorkel in shallow water, or swim. Spend the last morning testing your newly gained skills at a windsurfing regatta.

January-May, November & December, 6 days, $980 + air. 1986 departures: Jan. 10 & 24, Feb. 7 & 21, Mar. 7 & 21, Apr. 4 & 18, May 2, Nov. 7 & 14, Dec. 6.

Progressive Travels, P.O. Box 775164, Steamboat Springs, CO 80477. (800) 245-2229 or (800) 826-8621 (in CO).

CARIBBEAN **BEACHES AND BICYCLES**

St. Kitts and Nevis offer more than sun, sand, and surf. As volcanic islands, their terrain ranges from sandy beaches to picturesque plantations to gorgeous rainforests. See it all by bicycle as you pedal unhurried along paved roads. The 6-day trip is a wonderful mix of activities. Besides cycling, swim in tropical streams, go sailing or windsurfing, snorkel, spend a lazy day on the beach, and climb the slopes of Mt. Liamuiga to the rim of the crater. Sightsee as you cycle to the fortress of Brimstone Hill, the Gibraltar of the West Indies, and spin past the prehistoric Carib Rock pictographs. Plus, spend a full day of sailing to Nevis on a 75-ft. catamaran.

Stay in tranquil island resorts and a historic plantation. Eat curried lobster, coconut-stuffed lambchops, and other assorted island dishes. The cycling itinerary is flexible to suit novice or expert riders.

March-May, November & December, 7 days, $1,140 + air. 1986 departures: Mar. 2 & 16, Apr. 6 & 20, May 4 & 18, Nov. 2, 16, Dec. 7.

Progressive Travels, P.O. Box 775164, Steamboat Springs, CO 80477. (800) 245-2229 or (800) 826-8621 (in CO).

Tackling the powerful white water of the Bio Bio in Chile—Eve Burton for Nantahala Outdoor Center, NC.

CHILE

RUNNING THE RIO BIO-BIO

The approach to the Bio-Bio is via a day in Santiago and a luxurious overnight ride upriver on a narrow-gauge, steam-powered train. Spend the night at a rustic resort near the natural hot springs of Manzanar before proceeding to the put-in on the Bio-Bio, Chile's largest, wildest and most scenic river. Tumbling down the steep western slope of the Andes through the area known as "The Switzerland of South America", it excels in sheer beauty and powerful world class whitewater. Admire spectacular waterfalls, hot springs, glaciers, and alpine lakes with snow-capped peaks and a smoking volcano looming overhead.

Off the river, spend some time fishing for brown and rainbow trout, hiking up to the flanks of the Volcan Callaqui, splashing in the water, or simply stretching back on soft beaches to marvel at the stars of the southern hemisphere. At trip's end, there's a day in Chillan for a farewell celebration.

December-March, 14 days, $2,075-$2,190 + air. 1986 departures: Dec. 27, Jan. 4 & 18, Feb. 1 & 15, Mar. 1. In 1987: Jan. 10 & 24, Feb. 7 & 21, Mar. 7.

SOBEK Expeditions, Box AG, Angels Camp, CA 95222 (209) 736-4524.

CHILE

PROJECT PATAGONIA AND CHILEAN FJORDS

"Let our eight years of expedition-ship experience take you on a voyage through the Patagonian Channels and Chilean Fjords," urges T.C. Swartz, Director of Society Expeditions. "This spine of the Andes creates a spectacular natural wonderland, with glaciers plunging into the sea. It is one of the world's richest birdlife areas, with incomparable scenic beauty. Come see what Darwin saw, and learn from our team of naturalists on board the *Society Explorer!*"

The 13-day adventure begins with a flight from Miami to Punta Arenas, Chile, the world's southernmost city. The next day, board the luxurious Society Explorer for departure through the Strait of Magellan to Puerto Natales. Here, there's a day excursion to Torres del Paine National Park, whose magnificent landscape is home to many endangered species, such as the otter and the black-necked swan. Cruise on through breathtaking fjords to Puerto Eden—and perhaps trade with the Indians—then make a special stop to look for Andean condors. Proceed to Laguna San Rafael, where glaciers constantly break off, and Puerto Chacabuco, site of Simpson River National Park and beautiful Velo de la Novia waterfall. A land expedition enables you to explore Chiloe Island, one of the world's last virgin frontiers, and the charming villages of Castro and Ancud. Disembark at lovely Puerto Montt. A final excursion into Chile's famous lake region before flying over the snow-capped mountains of the Andes to Santiago to connect with the evening flight to Miami.

February & November, 13 & 20 days (from U.S.), $2,990-$10,750 + air. 1986 departures: Feb. 13, Nov. 23

Society Expeditions, 723 Broadway East, Dept. ATA, Seattle, WA 98102. (800) 426-7794 or (206) 324-9400.

CHILE
ARGENTINA

THE PATAGONIAN EXPRESS

This romantic week aboard the majestic old sleeper train, the *Patagonian Express*, evokes an earlier age of overland travel. Along the way are the Chile and Argentina heartland, a side of South America that few travelers know or take the time to see. "Our access revives the forgotten art of train travel," says SOBEK of its Santiago to Buenos Aires sojourn, truly a train-lover's trip with one 36-hour stretch.

Board the overnight, wood-panelled train for a trip through nectarine orchards and wild hazel-nut forests, past snow-capped volcanoes to the village of Puerto Montt. Drive northeast to the Andean Lake District and navigate the deep fjords of Lago Todos Los Santos to enter one of the Andes' most dramatic corridors.

Cross the Continental Divide and pause for a couple of days at the resort town of Bariloche with its many recreational opportunities. Back on board the train for the last leg of the journey, you descend from the moutains across rivers, over high desert plains, and through wheatfields to Buenos Aires for two final days. An alternate ending lets train-weary travelers skip the last leg and fly direct to Buenos Aires.

Year round, 8 days (from Santiago, return Buenos Aires), $995 + air. 1986 departures: Jan. 5, 12, & 19, Feb. 2 & 16, Mar. 2, 9, 16, 23, & 30, Apr. 6, 13, & 20, May 18, Jun. 22, Jul. 20, Aug. 17, Sep. 21, Oct. 19, Nov. 2 & 9.

SOBEK Expeditions, Inc., Box AG, Angels Camp, CA 95222. (209) 736-4524.

The varied terrain of Patagonia—*Mountain Travel, CA.*

CHILE

"THE NAVEL OF THE WORLD"

Some call it Rapa-Nuit, or the "navel of the world," or more simply, Easter Island. It is one of the most remarkable open-air museums in the world—a storehouse of archaeological treasures, located about 2,350 miles west of Chile.

Our 15-day adventure begins in Santiago, the capital of Chile. Tour the city and its sites, including the Beaux Arts, San Francisco Church, and the famous Santa Lucia and San Cristobal hills. Continue on to Easter Island. Here, you have 8 days for exploration led by Tom Love, a professor of anthropology, and Sergio Rapu, archaeologist and expert on the island's prehistory. Enjoy daily outings to major excavations and other sites of interest: Anakena Bay, where the most recent digs and excavations are taking place… the quarry of Rano Raraku, guarded by an army of 16-ft. statues…

Poike Trench, the site of a major native battle in 1680. Fish for tuna, ride horseback, swim, and enjoy a Polynesian feast. On the island, stay in family hotels with private rooms; in Santiago, spend overnights in first-class hotels.

Year round, 15 days, (from U.S.), $2,290 + air. 1986 departures: Jan. 12, Feb. 9, Jun. 22, Sep. 14, Dec. 21. In 1987: Jan. 11, Feb. 8, Jun. 21, Sep. 13, Dec. 20.

Nature Expeditions International, 474 Willamette, P.O. Box 11496, Dept. AG, Eugene, OR 97440. (503) 484-6529.

COSTA RICA — A NATURALIST'S PARADISE

Wilderness connoisseurs often cite tiny Costa Rica's national park system as the best in the world. It offers a wide spectrum of natural habitats, from coastal beaches and rolling savannas to tropical rainforests and cloudforests. Spend over two weeks with an expert naturalist observing the wonderfully varied wildlife and colorful birdlife.

After arriving in San Jose, fly by small plane to Corcovado Park for spectacular birding in the lowland rainforest. Focus on curassows, hummingbirds, trogons, and more. Look for the endangered manatee and 6-foot gar fish in Tortuguero's waterways, and observe anteater, peccary, ceatimundi, monkeys, and colorful birds in the jungle. Watch out for the resplendent Quetzal, a most beautiful bird, in Monteverde Cloud Forest Reserve, as you pass beneath a canopy of hanging gardens created by orchids and other epiphytes.

March, July & December, 15 days (from U.S.), $1,490 + air. 1986 departures: Mar. 15, Jul. 16, Dec. 17. In 1987: Mar. 14, Jul. 15, Dec. 16.

Wilderness Travel, 1760-AT, Solano Ave., Berkeley, CA 94707. (800) 247-6700 or (415) 524-5111.

COSTA RICA — RAFTING AT ITS BEST

The excitement of paddling Class IV white water on some of the world's finest rivers is all the more memorable when combined with tropical jungles and diverse wildlife. These 9-day adventures start with a flight from Miami to San Jose, with the continuing itinerary adjusted according to season. In the dry season (December to June), you raft the Pacuare and Reventazon rivers, and in the wet season (June-December), the Rio Chirripo. Trips include accommodations in San Jose before and after the rafting adventure, transportation to and from the rivers and to other scenic points, and a farewell banquet the last evening.

Highly experienced guides trained in the U.S. lead the trips—and pride themselves in the preparation of delicious river meals at jungle campsites along the rivers. Kayaks are provided (by arrangement) in addition to Avon rafts. On the Rio Pacuare you progress from moderate rapids at the start to breathtaking, powerful water. Soon your raft is hurtling, twisting, and turning around boulders, then on into peaceful large pools. Days on the river are punctuated with cascading waterfalls and crystal-clear pools...with iridescent blue butterflies and awesome jungle...with hiking, swimming, exploring, and relaxing on white beaches. Continue with a run on the Rio Reventazon (translated "bursting"). It lives up to its name with average drops of 90 feet per mile on a 6-mile run. All-in all, it's a great whitewater experience through colorful, spectacular jungles.

Year round, 9 days (from Miami), $1,295 including air. 1986 departures: Jan. 25, Feb. 1 & 15, Mar. 1 & 15, May 24, Jun. 7, Jul. 19, Aug. 16, Sep. 13, Oct. 18, Nov. 8 & 22.

International Expeditions, Inc., 1776 Independence Crt., Birmingham, AL 35216. (800) 633-4734 or (205) 870-5550.

COSTA RICA

RAFTING AND KAYAKING THE "RICH COAST"

If you have a reliable whitewater roll and a true spirit of adventure, you're ready for this moderately strenuous trip involving camping, rafting, and kayaking the whitewater rivers of Costa Rica. Rafters can travel by paddle raft or oar rig (which requires no previous whitewater experience). The cost covers most lodging and meals, rafts, river gear, guides, and cook. You need only supply your own paddle, spray skirt, helmet, life jacket, paddling jacket, and other paddling gear.

Fly to San Jose, the capital of Costa Rica, where you transfer to your base hotel. The next day, travel to the put-in and outfit your kayak for two days of Class III-IV playing rapids on the Rio General. The Upper and Lower Reventazon are next. The Upper area is a fast Class III-V, big water run, for people in good shape and passionate about whitewater. This is one constant rapid: big waves, big drops, big holes. The Lower area is a scenic Class II-III, with plenty of exciting rapids to test your skill, but with minimal danger. Next, you'll hike to the Rio Pacuare, with your gear following you in an ox cart. The Rio Pacaure (Class III-IV) is one of the few remaining tropical wilderness rivers, which flows through virgin jungle. Eddy-hopping is a challenge on this technical river, where waterfalls tumble out of the lush green jungle and creek hikes lead to natural rock slides. After take-out, return to San Jose for farewell banquet and flight home.

October & November, 10 days, $900 + air. 1986 departure: Oct. 24.

Nantahala Outdoor Center, U.S. 19W Box 41, Bryson City, NC 28713. (704) 488-2175.

COSTA RICA

A TROPICAL TREASURE

Indulge yourself in Costa Rica's tropical paradise full of lush, unspoiled beauty—crystal waterfalls, dry savannas, coral reefs, and mountain cloud forests. Or watch the wildlife—jaguar, monkey, sea turtle, crocodile, and over 850 species of birds—close up, if you dare.

Based at rustic, comfortable lodges, explore the jungles and coast of Corcovado National Park, the cloud forests of Monteverde Nature Preserve, and the active crater of Poas Volcano National Park by boat and by foot. If you like, hike each day, or snorkel the coral

Engulfed in a lush Costa Rican jungle—*Kurt Kutay for Journeys International, MI.*

reef. An overnight jungle camp is also an option. Stay in San Jose for several days of shopping and for a farewell dinner. The trip is 11 days, but seven extensions are offered, including one day of whitewater rafting on Reventazon River, a 7-island cruise aboard a 50-ft. yacht, or a day of horseback riding in the Central Plateau.

December-March, 11 days (from U.S.), $990 + air. 1986 departures: Dec. 21, Jan. 17, Feb. 14, Mar. 5, In 1987: Dec. 20, Jan. 16, Feb. 13, Mar. 4.

Journeys International, Box 7545, Ann Arbor, MI 48107. (313) 665-4407.

ECUADOR

ANDES TO THE GALAPAGOS

Developed by a widely acknowledged specialist in nature tours, this 17-day journey features the vegetation and wildlife of the Ecuadorian Andes and the exotic creatures of the Galapagos Island. Fly from Miami to Guayaquil for seven days of mountain exploration by motor vehicle and on foot, and continue by air to Baltra in the Galapagos for a 10-day cruise. Drop anchor at 12 islands in the archipelago before returning to Guayaquil and home.

Your first field trips by foot take place in the subtropical lowlands of the Andes, a haven for brilliant tropical birds. Drive up the western slope (about 7,000') to Cotopaxi National Park with its dwarf wildflowers, then up the "Avenue of the Volcanoes" for two days in Quito before flying to Baltra. Board the *Santa Cruz* for exploring the Galapagos and viewing sea lions and fur seals, penguins and hawks, blue-footed and masked boobies, flightless cormorants, iguanas, albatross, flamingoes, and other wonderful species. Your tour director is a knowledgeable naturalist.

Year round, 17 days (from U.S.), $2,268 + air. 1986 departures: Jan. 19, Feb. 23, Apr. 13, Jul. 20, Oct. 26, Dec. 14.

Questers Tours & Travel, Inc., 257 Park Ave. South, New York, NY 10010. (212) 673-3120.

ECUADOR

CLIMB TROPICAL VOLCANOES

The experienced mountaineer will find this climb up two high-altitude volcanoes a true challenge. The volcanoes, Cotopaxi (19,347') and Chimborazo (20,561'), are just two of the 30 volcanoes that line the valley nestled between the Andes of Ecuador. Cotopaxi is one of the highest active volcanoes on earth. Chimborazo's summit, on the other hand, is the farthest point in the world from the center of the earth.

Though not technically difficult, the climbs are demanding due to the high altitudes and snow conditions. You should be strong, physically fit, and have experience with the use of ropes, ice axe, and crampons. Your trip begins with a visit to the capital city of Quito and ends with a visit to the Banos hot springs. There's time to visit the great markets at Otavalo and Ambato. Most nights camp out. City nights in hotels.

November, 18 days (from U.S.), $1,590 + air. 1986 departure: Nov. 28.

Mountain Travel, 1398 Solano Ave., Albany, CA 94706. (800) 227-2384 or (415) 527-8100.

ECUADOR

CLIMBING EQUATORIAL PEAKS

After touring Indian markets and hiking for acclimatization in the hills above colonial Quito, you climb three of the world's highest equatorial peaks, led by two guides from the Institute. Those with little or no glacier experience begin with instruction in basic snow and ice climbing technique while based in a hut below beautiful Cayambe (18,997'). At the same time, experienced climbers tackle the summit of the peak. Then the entire group, usually six to eight people, travels through the Avenue of the Volcanoes—so called because here the Andes run in spectacular parallel rows—to a centuries-old hacienda. Rest here, then head to Cotopaxi National Park and prepare to ascend the country's second highest mountain at 19,342 feet.

Following Cotopaxi, climb Chimborazo (20,561'), the world's highest equatorial peak. Between climbs, the group takes a break at

SOUTH/CENTRAL AMERICA

Climbers ascend to base camp in Peru's Cordillera Real—Mark Houston for American Alpine Institute, Wa.

a hot springs at Banos—full of flowering trees and birds—the greatest variety of hummingbirds in the world. Each summit climb is made from a mountain hut (your overnight accommodations) in a single day, so you do not have to transport gear. When not climbing, you sleep in hotels or haciendas. For non-climbers, there's an equatorial hiking adventure. Optional extensions to the Amazon Basin and the Galapagos Islands are also offered.

November-February, 14 days, $1,120 + air. 1986-87 departures: Nov. 7 & 28, Dec. 18, Jan. 9 & 30.

American Alpine Institute, 1212 24th D. Bellingham, WA 98225. (206) 671-1505.

ECUADOR

CRUISING THE GALAPAGOS

Six hundred miles off the coast is a wildlife wonderland, otherwise known as the islands of the Galapagos Archipelago. In a stark, volcanic landscape study the intriguing wildlife—sea birds, land and marine iguanas, fur seals and sea lions, and the endangered Galapagos tortoise.

After a brief visit in Quito, fly to Baltra and begin the two-week cruise aboard a motor yacht. The ship serves as a floating home as you explore the islands. You'll observe green sea turtles on the Island of Santa Cruz, great colonies of birds on Tower Island, land iguanas and lava lizards on South Plaza and Santa Fe, albatross, blue-footed and masked boobies, and other creatures on Hood Island. At Floreana Island you lunch at the home of a native resident, Mrs. Wittmer. On Santa Cruz visit the Darwin Research

Station, and see flamingoes, penguins, and many other birds at Isabela and Punta Espinosa. Swim and snorkel with sea lions and fur seals at James Bay. The fascinating journey ends with a day in Quito and another in Cotopaxi National Park, then a visit to the famous Otavalo Market before flying home.

Year round, 22 days (from U.S.), $2,990 + air. 1986 departures: Apr. 13, Jul. 13, Aug. 10, Nov. 2. In 1987: Jan. 4, Apr. 12, Jun. 7, Jul. 12, Aug. 9, Nov. 8.

Nature Expeditions International, 474 Willamette, P.O. Box 14496, Dept. AG, Eugene, OR 97440. (503) 484-6529.

Setting sail in the Galapagos—*S. Steck for Mountain Travel, CA.*

ECUADOR

TREKKING AND CLIMBING VOLCANOES

The director of Palisade Mountaineering, John Fischer, leads two memorable climbing holidays in the Andes—each for 14 days, beginning and ending in Quito, the ancient capital surrounded by enormous glaciated volcanoes.

On one mountaineering and jeep tour you experience the geographic and cultural variety of this smallest of Andean countries. Travel is moderate except for several long days. Drive to Cotopaxi and trek for four days. Cross wide open Andean highlands, grasslands, and lava flows, and descend ridges and valleys. Drive to Otavalo for a day to relax. Then another four-day trek—over the crest of the Andes at 13,000 feet and down the Rio Oyce Oyccahi valley and tropical rainforest. Drive to the jungle town of Tena, the resort town of Banos, and on to Quito. A more challenging trek requires snow climbing and glacier travel techniques, with overnights in mountain huts .The approach hikes to the huts on Cotopaxi (19,347') and Chimborazo (20,702') are up volcanic scree, and the climbs via crevassed, moderate-angle glaciers. Roped teams move together.

May, June, November, December; 14 days; $985 + air. 1986 departures: Easier trek—May 29, Nov. 19; Challenging trek—Jun. 11, Dec. 3.

Palisade School of Mountaineering, P.O. Box 694A, Bishop, CA 93514. (619) 873-5037.

ECUADOR

HEADWATERS OF THE AMAZON

To venture within the Amazon basin requires an exceptional guide like Randy Borman, who leads these river journeys by dugout canoe. Borman was raised in the Amazon by American missionary parents, playing and hunting with Indian friends. He is an excellent naturalist, skilled at pathfinding, navigating, animal spotting, and survival techniques.

Fly to Quito and during the tour's first week drive to the Otavalo highlands with their Indian markets, and to Cotopaxi Volcano National Park, then to the small jungle village of Dureno to begin a trip by dugout canoe on a tributary of the Rio Aguarico. Here the wildlife is especially impressive—toucans, parrots, macaws, monkeys, tapir, caiman, capybara, giant butterflies, kites, and eagles. Camp in thatched jungle huts, take canoe excursions to lagoons, walk under the forest canopy, and learn much about the rainforest ecosystem before returning to Quito and home.

Year round, 17 days (from U.S.), $1,590 + air. 1986 departures: Feb. 18, Apr. 8, Jul. 15, Oct. 14. In 1987: Feb. 17, Apr. 7, Jul. 14, Oct. 13.

Wilderness Travel, 1760-AT Solano Ave., Berkeley, CA 94707. (800) 247-6700 or (415) 524-5111.

ECUADOR

EXPLORE THE AMAZON, LIVE WITH THE JIVARO INDIANS

Explore a rugged and isolated jungle region which includes over half of Ecuador's land area on this expedition into the Amazon, commonly referred to as the "Oriente." Travel through the vast, barely explored territory, composed of the lower eastern slopes of the Andes and the jungle lowlands of the upper Amazon tributaries, laced with large, fast-moving rivers and packed with animal life and vegetation. Live with the Jivaro Indians, the only tribe to practice headshrinking. Observe their ancient rituals, and share in their music, dancing, food, and activities. After the jungle, venture on horseback into the high country, commonly described as "paramo," with its marsh or bog-like pastureland, deciduous forests, and fresh streams. Here you meet the Canari Indians, noted for their leatherwork and weaving.

"This itinerary is designed for those with a true sense of adventure, who don't mind roughing it, and who enjoy and value the primitive," according to Irma Turtle, head of Turtle Tours. The trip begins and ends in Quito, is limited to five to 10 people, and is accompanied by an English-speaking escort and an Indian guide.

June-November, 10 or 16 days (from U.S.), $1,350 or $1,900 + air. 1986 departures: Jun. 21, Jul. 19, Aug. 9, Nov. 22.

Turtle Tours, Dept. AG, 251 E. 51st St., New York, NY 10022. (212) 355-1404.

ECUADOR

EXPLORING ENCHANTED GALAPAGOS ISLES

600 miles off the coast of Ecuador, the Galapagos Islands remain much the same as when Darwin explored them. Animals and birds have evolved in isolation, so they are unique and unafraid. Sea lions frisk with you in the sea, fur seals bark from a few feet away, marine iguanas eat from you hand, giant tortoises listen patiently to your questions. The bird life is amazing—flocks of flamingoes turn the sky pink in flight, and blue-footed boobies, flightless cormorants, and Darwin finches are bold enough to allow close-up study. 15-day explorations of this fascinating archipelago are led by naturalist guides aboard the sailing vessels carrying four to 10 people. "Visit the Galapagos with us as guests of families who have lived here for many years and know the islands intimately," invites Ocean Voyages. On 22-day expeditions, you can climb the volcanoes and explore the more inaccessible sites.

Ocean Voyages calls attention to the possibility of merging this cruise with one to Cocos, the world's largest uninhabited island off the coast of Costa Rica. The island features 70 species of birds and spectacular underwater life. Twelve-day sailings arranged from Puntarenas.

Galapagos: Year round, 15 days $1,595, 22 days $2,325. Cocos: January-May, 12 days $1,550.

Ocean Voyages, Inc., 1709 Bridgeway, Sausalito, CA 94965-1994. (415) 332-4681.

ECUADOR
PERU

FROM THE GALAPAGOS TO MACHU PICCHU

Looking for an adventurous itinerary that brings together the most impressive wilderness attractions south of the equator? Look no further. Your South American expedition starts with a flight to Quito and the volcanic Galapagos Islands. In these enchanted islands you are dazzled by the striking contrast of the vivid blue ocean, succulent green plants, and rust-red and black lava beaches. You often observe whales and dolphins as you cruise these island waters, and on Santa Cruz you encounter the famous Galapagos tortoise. Anchored at night, listen to the sounds of the sea lions calling to their young. A unique array of fauna and flora has evolved in these "living laboratories" which support 77 endemic birds, 11 endemic reptiles, and numerous plants and invertebrates.

Back to Quito and the magnificent Andes for the next experience. Travel through snow-capped peaks to Machu Picchu, investigate colonial Arequipa, and explore the white dunes of Peru's coastal

Land Iguana of the Galapagos hamming it up—*Ray E. Ashton, Jr., for International Expeditions, Inc., AL.*

desert. Conclude the expedition with a journey down the mighty Amazon—an awesome and spectacular river system.

Year round, 22 days (from Miami), $2,995 including air. 1986 departures: Feb. 18, Mar. 4, May 6, Jun. 24. Jul. 8, Aug. 19, Sep. 9, Oct. 7, Nov. 11, Dec. 9.

International Expeditions, Inc., 1776 Independence Crt, Suite 104, Birmingham, AL 35216. (800) 633-4734 or (205) 870-5550.

ECUADOR PERU

AMAZON WILDS, GALAPAGOS ISLES

The living laboratory of the Galapagos Islands, and a remote wildlife reserve in the Amazon jungle are combined with the highland Inca sites of Cuzco and Machu Picchu in this natural and cultural history tour. After an overnight visit to Lima, begin the journey with a visit to an Amazon jungle lodge—the comfortable Explorer's Inn—in Peru's Tambopata Wildlife Reserve. Cruise on the Tambopata River looking for caymans; accompany the resident naturalist on a four-mile hike to Cocococha Lagoon, observing exotic butterflies and plants and monkeys.

The fifth day, fly from Puerto Maldonado to Cuzco for a free afternoon and overnight, then catch the morning train for two days in Machu Picchu. There's a formal tour, also an open day for personal discovery and contemplation. Return to Cuzco to see Inca and colonial sites, continue on via Lima to Quito for two days of sightseeing, then fly to the Galapagos and transfer to the small comfortable yacht, where you spend the next 8 days. Accompanied by a naturalist guide, observe wildlife first studied by Charles

Darwin; stroll with 200-year-old tortoises; swim with colorful fish in crystal-clear Pacific waters; enjoy photographing the fearless and quite unselfconscious animals and birds. On day 18, return to Quito for overnight before flying home.

January-April, November & December, 19 days (from U.S.), $1,575 + air. 1986 departures: Jan. 29, Mar. 12, Apr. 16, Nov. 5, Dec. 17. In 1987: Similar to 1986.

Overseas Adventure Travel, 6 Bigelow St., #102, Cambridge, MA 02139. (800) 221-0814 or (617) 876-0533.

Scuba diving off Guadeloupe—*Carl Roessler for See & Sea Travel Service, Inc., CA.*

GUADELOUPE
DOMINICA

DIVING AND SAILING

On the 56-foot motor sailer *Cadaques*, four to six divers sail and dive in the beautiful waters and reefs near Guadeloupe and Dominica in the French Caribbean. Little known to American divers, they contain unusual sponges, underwater volcanic hot springs, and some of the Caribbean's tamest fish. Discover also the special French ambience of the hospitable islands. It's a super arrangement for families with children as well as for groups of gung-ho divers, or for two couples chartering the vessel. Cruising and diving are tailored to each group's wishes. Dany and Mimi Guignier, the highly skilled hosts, produce excellent meals and know the best dive sites—many of them Dany's discoveries. Trips start Saturdays with flight arrivals in Guadeloupe.

Year round, 7 days, $850 per person, 2-4 persons. Charter only.

See & Sea Travel Service, Inc., 689 Beach St., #340, San Francisco, CA 94109. (800) 348-9778 or (415) 771-0077.

PERU   **AN ANDEAN ODYSSEY**

To experience Peru's most magnificent sights in a week, fly from Miami to Lima and Cuzco, raft the Urumbamba River for two days, ride the narrow gauge train to Machu Picchu to investigate the ancient ruins, then return to Cuzco, Lima, and home. It's a week of dazzling sights by day and comfortable stays in charming river- and ruin-side inns by night, accompanied the whole way by English-speaking guides who bring insight to your visit.

In Cuzco (11,200 feet in the Andes), capital of the former Incan Empire, explore the venerable, rich stonework palaces and visit the native Sunday markets and archaeological sites—a hillside fortress and water temple. On board a whitewater raft drift through the high Andean Sacred Valley—a cultural and natural oasis where wild plum trees grow and ancient watchtowers command the river. At last, at the majestic complex of Machu Picchu, you have two days to explore the network of terraces and tombs, and the chance to make the one-hour climb to Intipunku, "The Door of the Sun," to view the ruins at daybreak.

Year round, 9 days (from U.S.), $1,099-$1,199 including air. 1986 departures: Most Saturdays.

SOBEK Expeditions, Inc., Box AG, Angels Camp, CA 95222. (209) 736-4524.

PERU   **EXPLORING THE AMAZON**

Once you arrive in the jungle-surrounded city of Iquitos (by air from Miami) you're within striking distance of two great wonders of the New World—the Amazon River and the Amazon interior. Journey 50 miles down the world's mightiest river. From Explorama Lodge in the heart of the Amazon Basin, observe the fascinating jungle life which includes almost one fourth of the world's 8,600 species of birds, 25,000 species of exotic plants, and 4,000 species of butterfly fauna. There's more to see—thatch-roof dwellings and dugout canoes of the river people, the antics of the freshwater porpoises, the iridescent beauty of morpho butterflies, orchid-laden trees—truly a paradise for nature lovers.

Begin the week with a full-day excursion up the Manati River, and relax at the lodge before embarking on a fascinating night canoe trip to savor the vibrant sounds of the jungle. After dark, travel up the Sucusari, search the jungle-lined banks by flashlight for the red eyes of the caimen in hopes of capturing one for inspection. Explore a colony of unique Hoatzins—a primitive, pheasant-sized bird. Then motor across the Lorenzo Cocha, a blackwater lake with Victoria water lilies whose leaves exceed seven feet in diameter. Next, test your jungle legs, exploring the Bushmaster Trail, lined with medicinal herbs, leafcutter ants, and poison arrow frogs. Set out on the Trail of Seven Bridges for a Yagua Indian village. The Yaguas show you the use of a blowgun with poison darts, a technique still used for hunting their daily food. Finish off with a 4-hour cruise up the Amazon to Iquitos, where you catch your flight back to Miami.

Year round, 8 days (from Miami), $1,298 including air; Cuzco-Machu Picchu extension, 6 days, $495. 1986 departures: Jan. 9, Feb. 8 & 15, Mar. 8, 22, & 29, Apr. 12 & 26, May 3 & 24, Jun. 14, Jul. 5, 12, & 19, Aug. 2, & 30, Sep. 20, Oct. 25, Nov. 1, 8, 22, & 29, Dec. 6, 20 & 27.

International Expeditions, Inc., 1776 Independence Crt., #104, Birmingham, AL 35216. (800) 633-4734 or (205) 870-5550.

PERU

BIKING IN THE ANDES

A new-style bicycle has been designed especially for mountain cycling on unpaved roads. Dubbed the *klunker*, it is lightweight but tough with 15 speeds and fat, knobby tires for traction. With this 26-pound wonder you may join other cyclists on a challenging adventure in Peru. Spend nearly a week following trails and roads built by Inca engineers and stonemasons in the 14th century—past steep fields where alpaca and llama graze, around cool lakes, and over 16,000-foot passes.

Starting from Cuzco, you visit the Inca site of Pisac, the Vilcanota Valley, and Ollantaytambo and its massive Inca fortress. Then board the train for two days at Machu Picchu, mysterious deserted mountain city some 2,000 feet above the Urubamba Valley. The trip winds up with an overnight stay in Lima. Lodging is in the best hotels and inns available, and luggage is transported by vehicle each day the group is on the road. Bikers meet in and return to Miami.

May-November, 12 days (from U.S.), $1,485 including air. 1986 departures: May 4, Jul. 13, Aug. 3, Nov. 2 & 14.

Ultimate Escapes, 115 S. 25th St., Colorado Springs, CO 80904. (800) 992-4343 or (303) 578-8383.

PERU

LEARN ABOUT CULTURE IN COMFORT

Combine a cultural and natural history journey, exploring archaeological sites, mountain sights, and wildlife environments on this 15-day tour. Designed for your comfort and relaxation, there's no trekking or camping on this trip and the walks are not strenuous.

Start with a visit to Lima's museums, then drive south to the Pachacamac ruins (circa 500 B.C.). Boat out to Islas Ballestas, islands off the shores of Paracas Wildlife Park with colonies of flamingoes and sea lions. Fly over the famous archaeological site of the Nazca Lines. Then head into the highlands to Arequipa (8,000'), a white stone city built in the colonial era. There's more—a visit to Puno and Takili Island and a train ride across the Andes to Cuzco. Finish off the trip with visits to the Inca sites at Pisac and Ollantaytambo, then to Machu Picchu to spend the night and to explore the vine-covered stone buildings in the "lost city" of the Incas. Optional easy day hikes for those who want to participate. Overnights at inns and hotels.

Year round, 15 days (from U.S.), $1,590 + air. 1986 departures: Jan. 24, Mar. 28, Sep. 19, Nov. 14, Dec. 19. In 1987: Jan. 23, Mar. 27.

Mountain Travel, 1398 Solano Ave., Albany, CA 94706. (800) 227-2384 or (415) 527-8100.

PERU

MOUNTAIN AND JUNGLE CYCLING

"Ready for adventure—the thrill of roughing it in the backcountry where travelers rarely venture? Then join our exclusive 2-week cycling expedition from Cuzco to Rio Madre de Dios, a tributary of the mighty Amazon," urges Frank Lister, director of Bicycle Detours. "We cycle, canoe, and hike our way through a remote piece of paradise."

To join this active two-wheeling group, fly from Miami to ima and on to Cuzco, a Spanish colonial city high in the Andes, built on an older Incan capital. It is near the ruins of Machu Picchu, and a day trip to those famous ruins can be arranged. In Cuzco, you start the cycling journey over lightly used mountain roads on a thick-tired, 15-gear mountain bike, traveling 15 to 50 miles each day. Pedal through ancient, tiny pueblos ringed by 2,000-foot Andean peaks. Wake at dawn for a tough 25-mile ascent (a support truck is available) to Tres Cruces; at more than 14,000 feet it's the highest point you reach. After a 55-mile descent, climb aboard Indian dugouts at Atalaya and explore the Amazon jungle, alive with vegetation, parrots, monkeys, and exotic butterflies. Climb out of the jungle by bike. Then head to Cuzco for a fine dinner and connecting flight home.

May to September, 13 days (from Miami), $1,900 including air. 1986 departure: May 18, Jun. 15, Jul. 13, Aug. 17, Sep. 14.

Bicycle Detours-Peru, P.O. Box 44078-A, Tucson, AZ 85733. (602) 326-1624.

PERU

INCA-LAND BY HORSEBACK

High in the Andes Mountains, the ancient Incas carved a capital city out of stone, and kept an even more amazing city hidden from their conquerors. Today, on horseback, by raft, and on your own two feet, spend 10 days exploring the ruins of Cuzco and Machu Picchu and spectacular surrounding landscapes.

Fly to Lima, then to Cuzco for a 4-day visit of the ancient archaeological sites of Sacsayhuaman and Tambo Machay. Then travel through the Sacred Valley of the Incas by raft to explore the ruins at Pisac and Ollantaytambo. Your 5-day horseback ride begins at the Pincopata Ranch. Pass through picturesque villages under snowcapped peaks, and climb seven steep switchbacks toward Mt.

Solcantay, reaching your highest point at 14,000 feet. The descent is along rivers and around waterfalls surrounded by lush vegetation that creates the perfect backdrop for an afternoon soak in a hot mountain spring. A short train ride to Machu Picchu gives you a chance to visit the hidden ruins and climb Huayna Picchu for an overview of the entire Inca site. Then depart for Lima and the flight back to the U.S. or extend your travels with a one-week Galapagos Island sailing trip.

March-June, 14 days (from U.S.), $1,390 + air. 1986 departures: Mar. 31, Apr. 14, May 14, Jun. 17.

Breakaway Adventure Travel, 38 Newbury St., Boston, MA 02116. (800) 343-7184 or (617) 266-7465.

PERU

HIGHLANDS OF THE INCAS

"It's one of the best all-around Andean adventures you'll find," promises Peter Frost, who leads groups up extraordinary mountain ranges, through impressive Inca ruins, and down thrilling whitewater rivers. Camping and trekking alternate with hotel amenities, a night at a hacienda, and a long soak in a hot spring.

Begin your two weeks in Peru with a flight to Lima and a day of sightseeing in Cuzco. Then ride a fast-moving raft down the

Splendor of ancient Machu Picchu, Peru—*Bill Abbott for Wilderness Travel, CA.*

Urubamba River through the Sacred Valley of the Incas. During a 5-day trek with pack animals along the ancient footpaths of the Vilcabamba Range, you cross a spectacular pass between two glacier-clad peaks, Salcantay (20,574') and Humantay (19,239'), and hike down through a high subtropical forest, home to brilliant-hued parrots and orchids. A train ride takes you back in time to the legendary "Lost City" of Machu Picchu, famed for Inca temples, stonework terraces, and a unique astronomical observatory. Finally, spend an overnight by Ollantaytambo, a living Inca village, then return to Cuzco and Lima for a farewell dinner and the flight home.

May-September, 15 days (from U.S.), $1,250 + air. 1986 departures: May 3, & 31, Jul. 12, Sep. 6.

Wilderness Travel, 1760-AT Solano Ave., Berkeley, CA 94707. (800) 247-6700 or (415) 524-5111.

PERU

FOLLOWING THE INCA TRAIL

Hike along the "Camino Inca," the royal road built more than 500 years ago and carved out of living rock. The 5-day, 20-mile trek (Grade 2), designed for the fit and adventurous, links Machu Picchu, the lost city, with Cuzco, the Inca capital. The route connects the only standing system of Inca architectural ruins from the ancient empire, including Inca steps and an Inca tunnel. Travel through cloud forest environments, terraced farmland, the habitat of the Andean spectacled bear and the Andean condor. Climb high passes and descend into subtropical vegetation.

The trip includes exploration of all major geographical regions of Peru. In addition to five days of trekking and an overnight at Machu Picchu, enjoy rafting on the Urubamba River, stays in Cuzco and Lima, and four days exploring the jungles and native peoples of the Amazon from a jungle lodge base near Pucallpa. While trekking, camp by rivers and ruins. In cities, stay in modest, small-scale hotels. Hiking and camping experience is required.

May, September & October, 16 days (from U.S.), $1,250 + air. 1986 departures: May 22, Sep. 4, Oct. 2.

Journeys International, 1120 Clair Circle, Box 7545, Ann Arbor, MI 48107. (313) 665-4407.

PERU

MACHU PICCHU HIGHLAND TREK

The old Inca empire remains mysterious, tempting travelers from around the world to unravel new clues. On this adventurous trip, the leaders are insiders, long-term guides of the Andes, ready to interpret the ancient ruins, local culture, and surrounding landscapes, as your eyes make their own discoveries. Peter Robertson, an anthropologist, has studied the Quechua highlanders. Tom Hendrickson, a mountaineer, lives in Cuzco. Maarten Van de Guchte, a Dutchman, researches Incan carved rocks, and Roger Valencia, native of Cuzco, has explored the Peruvian jungle.

This team invites you to explore the "finest of the Inca ruins around Cuzco and Machu Picchu, to ponder a long-gone civilization and its mysterious purpose." Also explore the surrounding wilderness, during a 1-day raft trip and seven days of trekking the Vilacabamba Range of the Andes, "where the mountain scenery rivals any on earth."

May-September & December, 18 days (from U.S.), $1,195 + air. 1986 departures: May 1 & 22, Jun. 5 & 26, Jul. 10 & 31, Aug. 14, Sep. 4 & 25, Dec. 11. In 1987: Similar dates.

Overseas Adventure Travel, 6 Bigelow St., #102 Cambridge, MA 02139. (800) 221-0814 or (617) 876-0533.

PERU BOLIVIA

LAND OF THE INCAS AND LA PAZ

If your curiosity spans world-class landscapes, richly varied natural history, New World archaeology and local cultures, this trip brings it all together. Cross a South American desert, cruise Pacific islands, view Andean mountains, and visit the Quechua people.

Begin with two days of sightseeing in Lima, then head overland to Paracas, visiting desert oases and picturesque fishing villages. Board a launch for the Ballestas Islands, where you find sea lion, pelican, terns, boobies, and the rare Humboldt penguins. On to Cuzco for a hike up the hills to Tambo Machay, the sacred spring, and Kenko, a shrine with rock carvings. Dine at night to the music of Andean flutes. There's more to come—a visit to the famous Sunday market at Chinchero, a train ride to La Raya Pass (14,000'), and optional whitewater rafting on the Urubamba River. The trip is

Making music on Taquile Island, Lake Titicaca, Peru—D. Rosen for Overseas Adventure Travel, Ma.

highlighted by spending a night on Taquile Island on Lake Titicaca (12,000') staying in the Quechua islanders' homes. The trip ends with three days of sightseeing and shopping in La Paz before the flight home.

April-September & December, 16 & 23 days (from U.S.), $1,200-$1,595 + air. 1986 departures: May 2, Jun. 6, Jul. 11, Aug. 15, Sep. 26, Dec. 12. In 1987: Apr. 24, May 29, Jul. 3, Aug. 7, Sep. 11, Dec. 18.

Overseas Adventure Travel, 6 Bigelow St., #102, Cambridge, MA 02139. (800) 221-0814 or (617) 876-0533.

SOUTH AMERICA

CONQUISTADOR—ACROSS THE CONTINENT

This unusual trip takes travelers from Quito to Rio, exposing them, during 12 weeks and more than 7,000 miles, to the unforgettable Andean landscape and many areas still not commonly seen by outsiders. Expedition vehicles carry up to 24 travelers between the ages of 18 and 38.

The first 3-week segment begins at historic Quito. Heading south, the highlights include a journey through the beautiful "Avenue of the Volcanoes," several days' exploration by dugout canoe of tributaries of the Amazon River, and investigating remains of the earliest Indian civilizations in the desert border area with Peru.

After a visit to Lima, wind slowly back up into the mountains for the next five weeks. Major destinations are Cuzco, the royal capital of the Incas; the ancient ceremonial city Machu Picchu, reached by a four-day trek along the Inca Trail—or train; and Lake Titicaca and its splendid backdrop of the snow-covered Cordillera Real. Descend to the Chilean coast, and during the last four weeks of the trip, leave the Andes behind, viewing the prolific birdlife at the Gran Chaco of Paraguay, the mighty Iguassu Falls, and as a finale, the bustling twentieth-century chic city of Rio.

February, July, August, September, 12 weeks, $2,190 + air. 1986 departures: From Quito: Apr. 26, Jun. 7, Dec. 6; From Rio: Feb. 15, Jul. 26, Sep. 23.

Adventure Center AG, 5540 College Ave., Oakland, CA 94618. (800) 227-8747 or (415) 654-1879.

TRINIDAD TOBAGO

A WINGED WONDERLAND

Discover the exotic birdlife of Trinidad and Tobago in the company of Stephen Quinn, a distinguished illustrator and birdwatcher on staff at the American Museum of Natural History. Quinn is also a former director of the acclaimed Asa Wright Nature Center in Trinidad, renowned for its abundance of unusual feathered creatures. He takes you there and to several other hidden sanctuaries among the diverse habitats on the two islands.

Depart from Miami for Trinidad. At the Caroni Swamp, drift through mangrove canals to observe birdlife, capped by an incredible spectacle of thousands of Scarlet Ibises settling to roost. In Blanchisseuse find about 25 species of montane forest birds, and in Nariva Swamp observe waders in open water. Visit the Aripo Savanna (a wide variety of bird species) and the Arena Forest with giant tropical trees and the explosive "honk" of the Bearded Bell bird echoing from the canopy. Other highlights; Aripo Range and its Dunston Cave, a breeding site for the rare Oil bird of "Guacharo;" Buccoo Reef's "Birds of the Sea"; and 48 Great Birds-of-Paradise on Little Tobago Island.

April, 10 days (from U.S.), $1,795 + air. 1986 departure: Apr. 11.

Discovery Tours, American Museum of Natural History, Central Park West at 79th St., New York, NY 10024. (800) 462-8687 or (212) 873-1440.

VENEZUELA — JOURNEY TO THE LOST WORLD

Mount Roraima, a solitary, 9,000-foot tabletop mountain, inspired Sir Arthur Conan Doyle to dream up the creatures that populate his classic science fiction novel, *The Lost World*. This 17-day expedition to the vast, mysterious Gran Sabana of southeastern Venezuela may convince you that the real flora and fauna of Roraima are equally amazing.

The journey starts with a flight to Caracas and on to Puerto Ordaz, then driving to EL Dorado and Paraitepui. You cross rolling grasslands and ascend steep, muddy trails to the 25-square-mile summit of Roraima to enter a world of mist, bromeliad bogs, dwarf forests, and bizarre sandstone formations. On the lower slopes are more then 800 species of tropical birds, monkeys, sloths, and rare orchids, including many species endemic to Roraima alone. On the second part of the adventure, travel up the Carrao River by dugout canoe to the base of Angel Falls (3,212'), with two days to explore the lush rainforest and observe exotic tropical birds and butterflies.

September, 17 days (from U.S.), $1,890 + air. 1986 departure: Sep. 13. In 1987: Sep. 12.

Wilderness Travel, 1760-AT, Solano Ave., Berkeley, CA 94707. (800) 247-6700 or (415) 524-5111.

VENEZUELA — SAILING AND DIVING THE UNSPOILED CARIBBEAN

The Grenadines island group, in the southernmost part of the Caribbean, boasts the area's best sailing conditions and its least "touristy" islands. Sail out of St. Vincent on an 8-day or two-week cruise on board a private yacht with a group of friends, or join an Ocean Voyages' group. Swim, snorkel, windsurf, explore shoreside villages, and—if you wish—learn to sail. Expert captains and gourmet cooks accompany each trip, bringing you to the best sail areas and private coves, and providing culinary delights from Caribbean waters.

Also, explore the underwater world of the Caribbean on board the classic schooner *Isla de Ibiza*. Eight-day scuba trips in the British Virgin Islands arranged year round (except summer). Or custom-design your own itinerary in the West Indies, Virgins, or Grenadines.

Grenadines: Year round (except Aug.-Oct.), 8 days $795, 14 days $1,385. *Isla de Ibiza*: Year round (except summer), 8 days $960 including scuba.

Ocean Voyages, Inc., 1709 Bridgeway, Sausalito, CA 94965. (415) 332-4681.

INDEX

Above the Clouds Trekking, 66, 76, 79, 89
Adventure Belize, 197, 198
Adventure Center AG, 34, 35, 96, 115, 153, 170, 174, 183, 201, 221
Africa, 11-41
African Experience (SLA), 12, 16
Algeria, 12-14
Alpine Adventure Trails Tours, 160
American Alpine Institute, 77, 88, 199, 209
American World Travel, 121, 160
American Youth Hostels, 116, 163, 164
Antarctica, 194
Arctic Explorers, 124
Argentina, 194, 195, 196, 199, 203
Art Explorer's Tours, 54
Asia, 43-105
Australia, 170-177
Australian Pacific Tours, 172, 173, 177
Austria, 108-112, 166

Backroads Bicycle Touring, 182
Belgium, 113, 146, 147
Belize, 196-197
Bhutan Travel Service, 44
Bhutan, 44, 45
Bicycle Africa, 29
Bicycle Detours-Peru, 217
Bicycle France, 127, 131
Big Five Tours, 17, 21
Bike Hikes, 116
Bike Tour France, 128
Bike Virginia, 148
Bolivia, 198, 199, 220
Bombard Society, 108, 132, 151, 158
Boojum Expeditions, 52, 56
Born Free Safaris, 12, 24, 28
Borneo, 69
Botswana, 15, 28, 41
Brazil, 194, 199, 200
Breakaway Adventure Travel, 218
British Coastal Trails, 119, 120
Burma, 97
Butterfield & Robinson, 109, 151, 152

Capers Club 400, 64, 93, 99, 195
Caribbean, 201
Central America, 193-222
Chile, 195, 202-204
China Passage, 46, 47, 48, 50, 51, 70, 100
China, 45-55, 101
Classic Bicycle Tours, 142, 144
Colombia, 200
Continental Waterways, 136, 137, 140
Cook Islands, 179
Costa Rica, 205-206
Country Cycling Tours, 129, 149
Cross Cultural Adventures, 31-33, 61, 104

Directions Unlimited, 108, 111, 147
Discovery Tours, 41, 55, 132, 152, 222

East African Travel Consultants, 24, 39
Ecuador, 200, 207-213
Egypt, 16-17, 36
England, 115-122
Equitour/Bitterroot, 20, 131, 164
Europe, 107-167
European Canal Cruises, 141
EUROPEDS, 126, 129, 159

Fantasy Ridge Mountain Guides, 95
Fiji Islands, 177-178, 179
Finland, 123, 124
FITS Equestrian, 110, 157, 196
Floating Through Europe, 138, 147, 165
Folkways Int'l Trekking, 20, 26, 45, 60, 74, 112
Forum Travel Int'l, 30, 38, 142, 159, 161, 165, 174
France, 120, 124-141
French Canal Boat Company, 135
French Polynesia, 179
Frontiers International, 139, 154
Fun Safaris, Inc., 39

Gerhard's Bicycle Oddyseys, 166
Goway Travel, 173, 176
Greece, 142-143, 144
Greenland Cruises, 145
Greenland, 144-145
Guadeloupe Dominica, 214
Guides For All Seasons, 67, 74, 77, 84, 85, 102, 113, 142

Hamish Tear Expeditions, 154
High Adventure Tours, 92, 103
Himalaya Inc., 58, 74, 79, 82, 85
Himalayan Excursions, 75, 79, 83, 87
Himalayan Travel, 80, 87, 91
Holland, 146, 147, 148
Horizon Cruises, 136
Hungary, 148

India, 45, 56-63, 91, 99
Indonesia, 64
Inner Asia, 56, 80, 100
International Bicycle Tours, 147
International Expeditions, 28, 206, 213, 216
International Zoological Expeditions, 197
Ireland, 148, 152
Italy, 149-151
Ivory Coast, 38

Japan, 51, 65-68, 69
Journeys International, 27, 71, 72, 89, 207, 219

Kenya, 17-28
King Bird Tours, 46, 63, 69
Kuo Feng Tours, 45, 50 ,55

La Mer Diving, 171, 172, 178, 180, 188

Lapland, 123, 124
Liberia, 29
Lucullan Travels, 125
Lute Jerstad Adventures Int'l, 57, 91, 92, 99

Madagascar, 30
Malaya, 69
Malaysia, 69
Maldives, 180
Mali, 30
McBride's Earth Ventures, 130, 150
Micronesia, 180
Mongolia, 52, 70
Morocco, 31-33
Mount Cook Line, 184
Mountain Travel, 13, 19, 21, 58, 60, 64, 76, 79, 90, 94, 97, 104, 122, 123, 124, 134, 156, 208, 216, 217

Nantahala Outdoor Center, 86, 119, 139, 206
Nature Expeditions Int'l, 27, 177, 182, 186, 205, 210, 189
Nepal, 70-91, 97, 99, 102
New Zealand, 181-184, 185
North Africa, 167
Norway, 152

Ocean Voyages, 185, 190, 212, 222
Odyssey Tours, 62, 101
Off the Deep End Travel, 67, 68, 148, 165, 191
Open Road Bicycle Tours, 113
Outdoor Bound, 118
Overseas Adventure Travel, 25, 35, 36, 37, 73, 103, 199, 214, 220, 221

Pacific Exploration Company, 175, 184
Pacific, 169-191
Pakistan, 92-95
Palisade School of Mountaineering, 211
Papua New Guinea, 185-187, 188
Peru, 213, 215-220
Philippines, 99
Polynesia, 188
Portugal, 152
Progressive Travels, 126, 135, 201, 202

Quest Cycle Tours, 120
Questers Tours and Travel, 49, 208

Romania, 148
Rwanda, 27-28, 34, 37
Ryder/Walker Alpine Adventures, 157, 159, 161

Safariworld, 22, 26, 37
Samoa, 179
Scandinavia, 115
Scotland, 120-122, 152, 153-154

See & Sea, 17, 95, 99, 171, 181, 187, 215
Seychelles, 37
SLA-African Experience, 12, 16
SOBEK Expeditions, 36, 40, 41, 65, 81, 141, 203, 204, 215
Society Expeditions, 105, 190, 194, 203
South America, 193-222
South Pacific, 185
Spain, 155-156
Special Expeditions, 19, 23, 62
Special Odysseys, 146, 179
Sweden, 157
Swiss Hike, 162
Switzerland, 112, 141, 151, 157-162, 163

Tanzania, 24-28, 35-37
Thailand, 63, 95-99
Tibet, 53-55, 91, 99-102
Tobago, 221

Trek Europa, 114, 122, 167
Trinidad, 221
Tunisia, 38
Turkey, 103, 144
Turtle Tours, 14, 15, 200, 212
Twende Safaris, 18

U.S.S.R., 104
UK Waterway Holidays, 122
Ultimate Escapes, 216
United Arab Emirates, 103
Uruguay, 196

Venezuela, 200, 222
Viking Tours & Yacht Cruises of Greece, 143
Voyages, Inc., 70

Wales, 121, 152, 164
West Germany, 141, 147, 148, 162, 163, 164-165, 166
Western Europe, 166-167

Wilderness Journeys, 68, 133, 162, 180
Wilderness Travel, 15, 30, 60, 82, 97, 144, 150, 185, 187, 205, 211, 219, 222
Wind Over Mountain, 37, 52
World Adventure Travel/Tenzing Treks, 69
World Adventure Travel, 72, 111
World Balloon Tours, 155
World Nature Tours, 48
World on Wheels, 116

Yemen, 104

Zambia, 38-41
Zimbabwe, 15
Zimbabwe, 15, 39, 41